Sound Tracks

MICHAEL JARRETT

sound

IN THE SERIES

Sound Matters

EDITED BY MICHAEL JARRETT

tracks

A Musical ABC

VOLUMES 1–3

TEMPLE UNIVERSITY PRESS   PHILADELPHIA

Temple University Press, Philadelphia 19122
Copyright © 1998 by Temple University
Published 1998
Printed in the United States of America

⊗ The paper used in this publication meets the requirements of the
American National Standard for Information Sciences—Permanence
of Paper for Printed Library Materials, ANSI Z39.48-1984

Text design by Erin Kirk New

Library of Congress Cataloging-in-Publication Data

Jarrett, Michael, 1953–
  Sound tracks : a musical ABC, volumes 1–3 / Michael Jarrett.
    p.   cm. — (Sound matters)
  Includes bibliographical references, discographies, and filmographies.
  ISBN 1-56639-641-7 (cloth : alk. paper)
  1. Popular music—History and criticism. 2. Popular music—
Terminology. I. Series.
ML3470.J38   1998
781.64—dc21   98-3033

For the Boys—

Adam, Nathaniel, and Ian

Contents

Sound Tracks

Introduction

I insist … on being interested only in books left ajar, like doors.
—André Breton, *Nadja*

Casually thumb through these pages and you'll figure out that, as
Nietzsche said of *The Dawn*, "A book such as this is not for reading
straight through or reading aloud but for dipping into" (sec. 454).
Less obvious, perhaps, are my reasons for embracing a form that en-
courages reading this way. Why forsake the sustained argument of traditional scholarship for the fragmentation associated with MTV and
kids with attention deficits? Why three ABCs of short essays, filled
out with supplements? Certainly, I ought to justify the form of this
book. Before doing that, though, I want to account for its existence
and explain why I wrote it.

This book greatly expands an assignment given by Marc Weidenbaum, one of two senior editors at Tower Records' *Pulse!* Marc
asked me in 1993 to take over a newly established column called
"Definition of Sound." I had been writing for the magazine for just
over five years, mostly about jazz and gospel music, and I suspect
Marc saw no future in locating a different amateur lexicographer every month. I quickly committed to the column as a regular gig. After
all, its requirements were pretty straightforward. Excepting the occasional editorial nudge—from Marc, Ned Hammad, or Jackson
Griffith—I was to write 140-word, extended definitions on any musical topics that struck my fancy. My goal was Brechtian (a term Marc
might very well have used when he first described the column): Under the guise of entertainment, I was to aid readers in understanding
some of the terms regularly tossed around by the magazine's writers.
Every once in a while, I could experiment a bit and let whimsy guide
my efforts. Here was a project tailored to my temperament! That temperament—indisputably postmodern—is best illustrated by an anecdote from my childhood. Just about all my friends have heard it. The
story evokes a decisive, formative moment; it describes an experience
that fixed in me an already developing love of popular and, specifi-

cally, African-American music. I'm telling it here because it turns out to be a myth, a tale useful for explaining the origins, aims, and functions of this book.

■

My car radio taught me just about everything I needed to know about the Motown Sound, but my first encounter with what I would later regard as real soul music occurred in a physical-education class in Chattanooga, Tennessee. I was a junior at Brainerd High, a school that, while racially integrated, was still known as the Home of the Fighting Rebels. "Dixie" was our theme song. Our symbol was the Confederate flag—the Stars and Bars. We waved it at football games; it was stamped on class rings. The year was late 1969.

My phys-ed class—forty or so boys—had just finished playing several rounds of everybody's favorite game, battle-ball, a particularly rough variant of dodge-ball. We had returned to the locker room and were changing out of our blue-and-white gym suits, back into school clothes. The room buzzed with conversation.

Then, all of a sudden, a black guy in white cotton briefs—his name was James Sears—squealed "Yeeeeah, Yeah-Yeah!" James leaped onto one of the room's narrow wooden benches and started dancing, gyrating his hips like he was swinging a hula hoop while his feet did a double-time shuffle. He kept grunting and screaming "Popcorn." A few times he shouted "Looka here!" and "Gotta-hava-mutha-for-me!" When he finished this impromptu performance, everybody laughed and shook their heads. A few guys might have clapped.

Now here was a story my parents would enjoy. "Daddy," I'd say at the supper table, "you shoulda seen that black guy! He was wild— totally out of control!" Then, in mock-serious tones, I'd ask, "Mother, do you think he's demon possessed?"

"Michael, don't make fun of the things of the Lord," my Dad would say. To which I'd reply, "Come on, Daddy! You know I'm just kidding."

Mom and Dad were never glib about spiritual matters, and while they undoubtedly spent no time pondering or trying to name the species of bug that had bitten James Sears, they never once doubted where he had contracted that bug. That, after all, was partly why our independent Baptist church sent missionaries to Africa, and it was precisely why my parents prohibited their children from attending dances. "Be not drunk with wine," Mother would say, quoting the Apostle Paul, "but be filled with the Spirit." Then she would amplify, unconsciously repeating Augustine and consciously citing John's first epistle: "Satan wants us to lose control; God wants to control us. 'Love not the world, neither the things that are in the world.'"

I was not a rebellious child. I kept my parents' rules. I never fornicated, drank alcohol, smoked tobacco (or any other substance), took God's name in vain, went to the movies, or attended a high-school dance. I knew lots about being marginalized. And I also knew, beyond a shadow of a doubt, who had possessed James Sears. It wasn't Satan. It was James Brown, Soul Brother No. 1.

Eighteen months before the locker-room experience, my ninth-grade class had taken a trip to Washington, D.C., where we toured all the predictable sites of civic interest: the White House, the Capitol, the Smithsonian Institution, Arlington Cemetery, memorials to Lincoln, Jefferson, and Washington. We also saw buildings burned to the ground; they were still smoldering from the violent wake that followed the assassination of Martin Luther King, Jr. And I was moved— troubled in the most conventional sort of way. James Sears was there, too, but I never asked him how he felt about what we'd seen. Maybe he felt black. I say that because, later, when James did the Popcorn, I felt white: bleached out and terribly pale.

Did James Sears—a boyish reflection of a pop star I hadn't yet seen or heard—make me want to be black? Possibly. I do not doubt that he prompted racial envy. Still, such an assessment diminishes the profound effect James had on me. He became an icon, inseparable in my mind from James Brown. Flannery O'Connor would call him a "means of grace," so thoroughly did he alter my conception of the world and my place in it. Certainly, he spoke of much more than race. The epiphany he brought me cut deeper than skin color. It said: The world is worth knowing; it is worth loving.

Postscript: One night, shortly after Bill Clinton was first elected president, I dreamed my way back to Washington. I was standing beside a stairway in the White House. I looked up and saw the President. "Mr. Clinton," I asked, "do you like James Brown?"

"Mike," said the President, "I have an almost religious affection for James Brown."

■

Even though self-revelation has become de rigueur in cultural studies and critical theory, I'm still convinced that it's generally a good thing. It doesn't hurt readers to picture—and, yes, to hear—the author of the text they're reading. My anecdote, I'm confident, allows that. In a highly compressed form, it pictures a kind of primal scene that tells how I was, in effect, conceived as theorist and journalist. But it is a story. Its information is encoded as narrative. And that means it's woefully inadequate as exposition or analysis. I could, however, retell it—transpose the story into another register that would make manifest its political and psychological dimension. It might sound like this:

> At its most elemental, my story is a Myth of Othering: Confronted by his cultural illiteracy—his exclusion from and inability to read, not just black culture, but electronic culture—a white boy compensates. Projecting his own feelings of exclusion onto a black classmate—who *appears* to be a model of ecstasy under control (an icon of grace, marking an entrance to another world)—the white boy idealizes blackness as a solution to being marginalized, cut off from the world. He falls in love with soul music, specifically, and with popular culture, generally.

Or, if motivated, I could once again rewrite. But let's say this time I didn't scrutinize the ideology that informs and enables my writing. Instead, I just accepted as a given the social and psychological forces that shape me and abandoned the "plain" or "invisible" style of writing employed in my anecdote (and typical of realist narratives). Then, the production of "poetic" or artistic effects might become my primary goal. For example, I could write a "talk poem"—modeled after David Antin's work—that relies on the cadences of my Southern drawl: something like, "Thirteen Ways of Looking at a White Boy Looking at a Black Boy Who Knows Damn Well That He's Being Looked At."

Here's my point. Robert Ray expresses it perfectly in *The Avant-Garde Finds Andy Hardy*: "An author producing a text always finds himself, like someone playing a video game, provided with three knobs, labeled *narrative*, *expository*, *poetic*. At any point during the text's creation, he can adjust the balance (as one would adjust a television's colors), thereby increasing (or reducing) the level of *any* of the three" (200). And that's why I'm attracted to the ABC form. It allows knob twiddling. As Roland Barthes put it, in *A Lover's Discourse: Fragments*, this method of organizing information frees "horizontal discourse" (7). The themes and motifs sounded in an ABC might resonate, generating the equivalent of overtones, but they are not integrated on a higher level (vertically, as a unified work). Instead, they are distributed by means of an unmotivated series—the alphabet. Which is to say that ABCs lend themselves to a variety of approaches; they lend themselves to fancy. And while they imply copiousness—what can't find its way into this form?—they aren't encyclopedias. Rather, we might regard them as *potential* encyclopedias. Topics in ABCs suggest a reservoir of cultural history. They skim surfaces, suggesting unplumbed depths.

Perhaps because they're more evocative than fully descriptive, ABCs have historically been associated with children's literature. The avant-garde has favored them, too. But the popular music press—with its penchant for annotated lists and catalogs of reviews—has been especially adept at exploiting the fast shuttle between anecdotal, analytical, and metaphorical discourses enabled by alphabetical organization. In fact, books and columns written by Robert Christgau, Lester Bangs, Greil Marcus, Ellen Willis, Simon Frith, Anthony De Curtis, Greg Tate, Ira Robbins, Ann Powers, and Simon Reynolds have wrapped cultural insight in formal daring more tightly than any number of treatises published by academics. They've alerted me to new sounds, told me about new worlds. They've served a function similar to the one James Sears once played in my life. They're paradigms of invention.

Over and over, the vanguard of music writers has suggested new modes of writing for an electronic age. Not only has it shown that contemporary sounds—of whatever stripe—are worth thinking about, it has also repeatedly demonstrated that sounds form a vehicle suitable for thinking. Many of us think *with* music. Music doesn't reflect our individual lives or the greater culture, because it isn't outside our lives or our culture. Music isn't a way to get at the weightier topics of cultural studies, though that's how it's often used. Rather, it's an apparatus; it's an important part of our culture. Writing about music is a way to do cultural studies, and the critics I've mentioned understand this. Their importance, however, does not derive from their orientation to music, the object of study. Rather, it derives from their orientation to readers, the so-called mass audience. Like the music and musicians they describe, these writers have turned "popularity" into a research problem. They've benefited from precisely the same tensions that drive popular music: How can I say something meaningful—perhaps unique—and still get lots of people to listen?

It's time for cultural studies to ask the same question. First, it's the socially responsible thing to do. Academics need to communicate more effectively with students and an interested public. Second, and more selfishly, such communication could transform scholarship in unpredictable ways. Granted, that's a bit melodramatic. Better to say that academics need to take up the problem of popularity more routinely, and hasten to add that plenty of academics are already doing this. Witness recent books by Simon Frith, Andrew Goodwin, John Corbett, Robert Ray, Krin Gabbard, Robert Walser, and Susan McClary. To this list, I'd like to add the book you're holding.

I suppose this book really wants to be a box of pop-music singles—or at least it should be regarded as critical theory and cultural studies at 45 rpm. Very few of the book's topics receive anything resembling symphonic development. They rarely strive to spiral like Coltrane's improvisations. Instead, this book is intentionally incomplete. (Then again, how could it be otherwise?) The number of entries is limited to three fairly idiosyncratic passes through the alphabet. The supplements that fill out these entries are—and again I'm quoting Barthes—"not authoritative but amical: I am not invoking guarantees, merely recalling, by a kind of salute given in passing, what has seduced, convinced, or what has momentarily given the delight of understanding (of being understood?)" (*Lover's Discourse*, 9). Most of all, I'm trying my best to get readers to dance. The goal is a book that's as infectious as James Sears doing the Popcorn.

■

Many people made this book possible. I'm especially indebted to the staff at *Pulse!*: Marc Weidenbaum (who's moved on but still shouts encouragements), Jackson Griffith, Ned Hammad, Jason Verlinde,

Peter Melton, Mike Farrace, Suzanne Mikesell, Mara Wildfeuer, and Babs Baker. A large chunk of what appears here first appeared in *Pulse!* Thanks for the writing assignments and for permission to reprint. Other portions of this ABC also appeared in *South Atlantic Quarterly*; *Jazziz*; *Black Sacred Music*; *Cadence*; *Integrating Visual and Verbal Literacies*, edited by W. F. Garrett-Petts and Donald Lawrence (Inkshed Publications, 1996); and liner notes to James Blood Ulmer's *Harmolodic Guitar with Strings* (DIW/Sony Music, 1993). Here again, I'm grateful for permission to reprint. Thank you Michael and Lori Fagien, Anthony DeCurtis, Will Garrett-Petts, Jon Michael Spencer, Bob Rusch, Arthur Levy, and Kazunori Sugiyama. I'm most appreciative to the many musicians, publicists, producers, critics, and cognoscenti who made possible the interviews that fill out my short essays. Will Kinnally, Terri Hinte, Don Lucoff, Roy Parkhurst, Rob Gibson, David Sanjek, and David Dorn deserve special mention. Paul Hamilton, David SanSoucie, Bob Buckingham, John Dawson, Mike Flannelly, Carter Harris, Cecilia Heydl-Cortinez, Eric Whiteside, Jay Jackson, Byron Borger, Susan Hengel supplied me with information and ideas. My friends and colleagues have been consistently supportive—always ready to take an interest in my obsessions. I want to single out and acknowledge Robert Ray, Gregory Ulmer, Krin Gabbard, Gary Collison, Chris Keathley, Meredith Rousseau, and Nkanyiso Mpofu. Thanks for reading and commenting on my work. Financial support, especially from the Advisory Board at Penn State York and Penn State's College of Liberal Arts, lightened my teaching load and afforded me time to write. I'm blessed with administrators who care about scholarship (and know a good tune when they hear one): Don Gogniat, John Madden, and Tom Getz. Linda Kline helped me transcribe several of the interviews. Carole Wagner routed the steady stream of promotional materials that continues to come my way. Thanks for your diligence. And then there's Pam, my wife. She's an EOM (you can look it up), but she loves me, which is both confusing and amazing. I want to thank her and our sons publically. Their care sustains me. Thanks to David Updike for copyediting and to Erin Kirk New for designing the text. Finally, I'm grateful to Janet Francendese, Charles Ault, and Ann-Marie Anderson at Temple University Press. Janet believed in this project from the git-go.

volume
one

ambient music—Sound used functionally to simulate or enhance an environment. [From the Latin verb *ambire*, "to go around."]

Before French composer Erik Satie (1866–1925), the term "ambient music" would have qualified as an oxymoron. Musicians, whether playing in cafe or concert hall, strove against noise. Satie, however, imagined a utilitarian music, capable of conspiring with ambient sounds to produce a more livable environment. He dubbed it *musique d'ameublement* (furniture or furnishing music). Beginning in 1940, Muzak capitalized on this concept. American composer John Cage (1912–1992) employed it as a principle of invention, reframing music to include the sounds of one's environment. Art rocker and conceptualist Brian Eno (1948–) settled on "ambient music" as a label for decorative sounds that exist on "the cusp between melody and texture."

New age music conventionalized Eno's innovations; electronica extended them.

■

Readings

John Cage. 1961. *Silence*. Middletown, Conn.: Wesleyan University Press.

Brian Eno. 1996. *A Year with Swollen Appendices: Brian Eno's Diary*. Boston: Faber and Faber.

Kyle Gann. 1996. "Ambient Lives!/Stinks!" *Village Voice*, 1 October, 52.

Richard Kostelanetz, ed. 1987. *Conversing with Cage*. New York: Limelight.

Joseph Lanza. 1994. *Elevator Music: A Surreal History of Muzak, Easy-Listening, and Other Moodsong*. New York: St. Martin's.

Bill Milkowski. 1983. "Eno." *Down Beat*, June, 14–17, 57.

Erik Satie. 1996. *A Mammal's Notebook: Collected Writings of Erik Satie*. Ed. Ornella Volta. Trans. Anthony Melville. London: Atlas.

Roger Shattuck. 1955. *The Banquet Years: The Origins of the Avant Garde in France, 1885 to World War I*. New York: Vintage.

Robert Smithson. 1979. *The Writings of Robert Smithson*. Ed. Nancy Holt. New York: New York University Press.

Eric Tamm. 1989. *Brian Eno: His Music and the Vertical Color of Sound*. Boston: Faber and Faber.

David Toop. 1995. *Ocean of Sound: Aether Talk, Ambient Sound and Imaginary Worlds*. New York: Serpent's Tail.

William Carlos Williams. 1992. *Paterson*. Rev. ed. New York: New Directions.

Jack Womack. 1987. *Ambient*. New York: Grove.

Recordings

Aphex Twin, *Selected Ambient Works Vol. II* (Sire/Warner Bros.).

Carla Bley, *Dinner Music* (Watt/ECM).

Harold Budd, *The Pavilion of Dreams* (Editions EG).

John Cage, *In a Landscape* (Catalyst).

Ry Cooder, *Music by Ry Cooder* (Warner Bros.).

Miles Davis, *In a Silent Way* (Columbia/Legacy).

Herbert Distel, *Die Reise* (hat ART).

Brian Eno, *Another Green World* (Editions EG).

———, *Brian Eno/Instrumental* (Virgin).

Brian Eno and Harold Budd, *Ambient 2/The Plateaux of Mirror* (Editions EG).

Wayne Horvitz/Butch Morris/Bobby Previte, *Nine Below Zero* (Sound Aspects).

The KLF, *Chill Out* (Wax Trax!).

Pauline Oliveros, Stuart Dempster, and Panaiotis, *Deep Listening* (New Albion).

The Orb, *U.F.Orb* (Big Life/Mercury).

Various, *Austral Voices: For Telegraph Wires, Tuning Forks, Computer-Driven Piano, Psaltery, Whirly, Cello, Synthesizer and Ruined Piano* (New Albion).

Various, *In Memoriam: Gilles Deleuze* (Mille Plateaux).

Various (David Toop, prod.), *Ocean of Sound* (Virgin).

Vienna Art Orchestra, *The Minimalism of Erik Satie* (hat ART).

LaMonte Young, *The Well-Tuned Piano* (Gramavision).

Videos—The movies that prompt the ardor of cinéphiles are, most often, arresting for their images. The following movies, however, honor ears as much as eyes. They're pleasurable, not because of their "sound" tracks, but for their audio tracks, which artfully combine, music, noise, and voice. A few, in all honesty, are better heard than seen.

Michelangelo Antonioni/Giovanni Fusco and Vittorio Gelmetti. 1964. *Red Desert*.

Jean-Jacques Beineix/Vladimir Cosma. 1981. *Diva*.

Francis Ford Coppola/Walter Murch and Carmine Coppola. 1979. *Apocalypse Now*.

Brian Eno. 1988. *Thursday Afternoon*.

Federico Fellini/Nino Rota. 1963. *8 ½*.

Jim Jarmusch/Neil Young. 1996. *Dead Man*.

Sergio Leone/Ennio Morricone. 1968. *Once Upon a Time in the West*.

Terrence Malick/George Tipton. 1973. *Badlands*.

Chris Marker/Trevor Duncan. 1965. *La Jetée*.

Michael Mann/Elliot Goldenthal. 1996. *Heat*.

Ridley Scott/Vangelis. 1982. *Blade Runner*.

Andrei Tarkovsky/Eduard Artemev. 1979. *Stalker*.

Interview—Carla Bley and Steve Swallow talk about Erik Satie (April 1995)

CARLA BLEY: When I was 12 or 13, I had a wire recorder. It worked for 15 minutes. I had taped something that was on the radio, and 15 minutes later its ability to record died. All I had taped was "Parade" by Erik Satie. I listened to only that piece for as long as my interest in wire recorders lasted. Of course, anyone who can't play the piano plays Satie, plays the "Gymnopedies" or the "Gnossiennes." My daughter plays them now. Aside from that, I read a book. Steve and I were talking about it yesterday. It's so weird how these things cycle back. It was about four French artists: one was a painter . . .

Oh, The Banquet Years, *by Roger Shattuck. That's a fine book.*

BLEY: Alfred Jarry, Apollinaire, Satie, and Henri Rousseau. When I read the Satie chapter—this is what we were trying to decide yesterday—did he make me become like him?

STEVE SWALLOW: Which is the cart and which is the horse?

BLEY: Was I already having the cup of coffee at 8:19, or when I read the book, did I start having it at 8:19?

SWALLOW: In the book there's that wonderful schedule of Satie's day, precise to the moment.

BLEY: That's what my day is like.

SWALLOW: It's not an exaggeration. I think reading that book gave you the license. . . .

BLEY: It was okay to be like that.

I've considered Satie as someone who might grant your listeners insight into things that you've done.

BLEY: Wit and simplicity. The irreverence of furniture music.

SWALLOW: There's the classicism of it, and that's true of Carla's music as well. It definitely Apollonian as opposed to Dionysian. It's very strict. Even at its funniest, it's very severe.

bolton—To envy the possessions or qualities of
another (typically, the artistic creations of a racial group
perceived as particularly "genuine" or "authentic") to such
an extent that identity is lost or becomes (comically or
tragically) parodic. [After *Michael Bolton*.]

A serious emotional disorder, boltonism frequently manifests itself
within the realm of aesthetics. It is especially common to soul music,
where it has been dubbed the "blue-eyed affliction." In chronic cases,
white singers, filled with self-loathing (guilt induced by feeling inauthentic and privileged) and an insatiable lust for fame (desire for the
power that comes only with privilege), seek resolution to their conflicts by displaying a variety of behaviors known as "boltoning." Most
often, this involves simply "boltoning up" a song (hyper-emoting that
evokes both pity and scorn from listeners). But it may also take ex-

treme forms: writing already written r&b tunes, claiming to be Sam Cooke's love child, sitting on the dock of the bay, etc.

■

Commentary and Expansion

Defining "bolton" wasn't my idea. Marc Weidenbaum, one of the senior editors at Pulse!, assigned it to me right after the Isley Brothers sued Michael Bolton for copyright violation—and won.

Five minutes' reflection on this case prompted me to recall similar cases involving Kris Kristofferson and Leonard Cohen, the Chiffons and George Harrison. I also remembered plagiarism charges leveled against Joseph Biden, Jacques Attali, and Martin Luther King, Jr. And I wondered, isn't copyright a political means of controlling technologies of writing, limiting the conceivable effects of mechanical reproduction? In our culture, composers can claim melodies as their property—but not rhythms, chord changes, or, for that matter, song titles. Finally, I reflected on the work of two cultural theorists: Theodor Adorno, who declared that all pop songs were assembled from interchangeable parts, and Jacques Derrida, who treated "citation" not as a stable concept, but as a slippery term referring to a host of vexed questions.

As it turned out, Michael Bolton's practice—whatever one called it—seemed less and less exceptional to me. I realized that I cared absolutely nothing about the relationship between the song he claimed he had written and one the Isley Brothers claimed they had written years earlier. Declaring Bolton a plagiarist was not only problematic, it was boring. It got me nowhere, and it certainly wasn't what made him notorious. What fascinated me was my own intense disdain for Bolton. Why did I find it necessary to loathe everything about him? My answer came by playing through the assignment Marc had given me. First, it forced me to treat the proper name "Bolton" as nothing but a nominalization, a noun that had once been a verb. Then, it required me to describe this imaginary, originary verb. In doing so, I discovered what I had both feared and suspected: Boltoning was central to my own experience of pop music. That revelation gave me cause to extend my mock definition.

Boltonism has no known cure, but acute episodes and mild cases—if detected early—are treatable. Traditionally, clients are encouraged to sublimate. For example, shopping for tunes is routinely prescribed as a socially acceptable alternative to boltoning (though all competent therapists caution against singing along with one's purchases). But therapeutic shopping is not without its critics. Some professionals argue that the vicarious pleasures normally obtained through buying and listening to records inevitably fail to alleviate the pain experienced by those suffering from boltonism. "These guys want to get busy," said one prominent caregiver, "and nothing less than a top position at a major record label will keep them from trying to land a gig at Carnegie Hall. Recently, a patient of mine—whose boltonism is now thankfully in remission—told me, 'Jim, do you know what most therapists forget? Even garden-variety boltons possess egos and talents that your typical record-rack-riffling, swill-slurping schmucks only dream of. If we can't find jobs in areas such as production or A&R, we use our talents in more visible and audible ways: as weapons—to cause pain, pity, love, whatever. And that's *scary*.'"

Indeed it is, say a majority of left-leaning professionals. They regard boltonism as a symptom of late capitalism. "Wasn't it Theodor Adorno who identified self-loathing as the central experience of the fan?" asks Otto Franz, professor of cultural studies at the University of Massachusetts. Franz declares:

> The more ardent the fan, the more he hates who, what, and where he is. He feels—Wasn't it Rimbaud who noticed this?—he feels that real life is always happening somewhere else. Capitalism situates itself as the fan's only hope of redemption, and the marketplace becomes a sanctuary, promising solace through acquisition. But capitalism is a cruel master—or perhaps, mistress. It always reneges on its promises. It says, "What you bought yesterday is not sufficient for today; what you buy tomorrow might bring peace." In short, this is how the emptiness of fans *motorvates*—that's Chuck Berry's term—the "free" market.

It is precisely over this point that left-leaning authorities on boltonism part ways with their more centrist colleagues. Centrists argue that consumption isn't maladaptive unless taken to the extremes of boltonism and other consumer neuroses. Leftists take another tack; they argue that consumption, used as a coping mechanism, is analogous to gluttony. Ultimately, it kills. And it makes no one happy—except farmers and grocers. Boltoners, then, at least to some, are mildly (or aberrantly) afflicted capitalist consumers. Why? Because they'd rather make a record than buy one. They are incapable of living vicariously and thus frequently become targets of ridicule. Once again, Franz explains:

> Even though there are lots of reasons to make music or any sort of art, boltoners create as a *sincere* response to self-hatred. They are never ever cynical. Some people find this appalling. They see boltoners not only as mawkish parodies of things held "authentic," but as grim reminders— reminders of what they fear they could become or—*gasp*—already have become. This is why so many music journalists take refuge in cynicism and satire. They find the prospect of boltoning more scary than ridiculous. Especially white guys. By positing one thing—usually the racial Other—as genuine, they self-reflexively declare themselves counterfeit. Not to worry, there's always a really convenient, egregious boltoner onto which they can transfer their negative feelings.

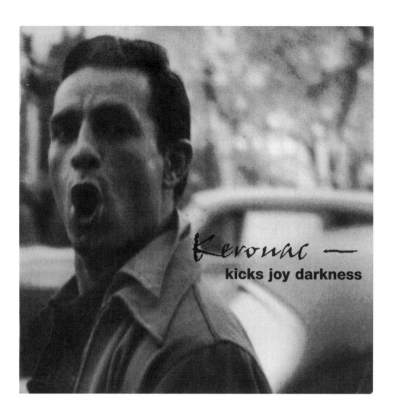

Kerouac —
kicks joy darkness

cool—1. Approbation directed toward a perceived
lack or blunting of requisite emotion in another. 2. Good
(in the Platonic sense).

Cool, the attitude-as-aesthetic that most profoundly affects jazz and
rock, takes two distinct forms. Prophetic cool—which finds its archetype in Jesus zip-lipped before Pontius Pilate—is characterized by
barely harnessed rage. It's evident in the demeanor of Miles Davis,
Billie Holiday, the young Bob Dylan, Bob Marley, and Ice-T. Philosophical cool—whose archetype is Heraclitus quipping "No hep-cat
can step in the same river twice"—belies the existential void lurking
behind a persona. It's epitomized by the sweet seductiveness of Bix
Beiderbecke, Lester Young, Chet Baker, Anita O'Day, Frank Sinatra,
Serge Gainsberg, Elvis Presley, Keith Richards, Nico, Snoop Doggy
Dogg, Liam Gallagher, and the old Bob Dylan.

Readings

James Baldwin. 1990. "Sonny's Blues." In *From Blues to Bop: A Collection of Jazz Fiction*, ed. Richard N. Albert. Baton Rouge: Louisiana State University Press.

Jean Baudrillard. 1990. *Cool Memories, 1980–1985*. London: Verso.

Howard Becker. 1963. *The Outsiders: Studies in the Sociology of Deviance*. New York: Free Press.

Roy Carr, Brian Case, and Fred Dellar. 1986. *The Hip: Hipsters, Jazz and the Beat Generation*. London: Faber and Faber.

Ann Charters. 1992. *The Portable Beat Reader*. New York: Viking.

Julio Cortázar. 1966. *Hopscotch*. Trans. Gregory Rabassa. New York: Pantheon.

Marcel Danesi. 1994. *Cool: The Signs and Meanings of Adolescence*. Toronto: University of Toronto Press.

Ralph Ellison. 1947. *Invisible Man*. New York: New American Library.

Graham Greene. 1938. *Brighton Rock*. New York: Penguin.

J. K. Huysmans. 1931/1969. *Against the Grain (A Rebours)*. New York: Dover.

Jack Kerouac. 1955. *On the Road*. New York: New American Library.

Gary Lindberg. 1982. *The Confidence Man in American Literature*. New York: Oxford University Press.

Richard Majors. 1992. *Cool Pose: The Dilemmas of Black Manhood in America*. New York: Lexington/Maxwell Macmillan.

Milton Mezzrow with Bernard Wolfe. 1946. *Really the Blues*. New York: Citadel.

Richard Miller. 1977. *Bohemia: The Protoculture Then and Now*. Chicago: Nelson-Hall.

John Osborne. 1957. *Look Back in Anger*. New York: Penguin.

Thomas Parkinson, ed. 1961. *A Casebook on the Beat*. New York: Crowell.

Ishmael Reed. 1969. *Yellow Back Radio Broke-Down*. Garden City, N.Y.: Doubleday.

Jean-Paul Sartre. 1964. *Nausea*. Trans. Lloyd Alexander. New York: New Directions.

Gene Sculatti, ed. 1982. *The Catalog of Cool*. New York: Warner Books.

———. 1993. *Too Cool*. New York: St. Martin's.

Peter N. Stearns. 1994. *American Cool*. New York: New York University Press.

Cool Game—Smoke

First, let's go over the rules:

The name of this game is *Smoke*. It's designed to turn upstanding citizens into Beat poets. To play, all you need is one or more friends, a few sheets of unlined paper, and a couple of pencils (abusable substances are optional). Follow these simple instructions, and in the time it takes to make an alto sax squeak you'll be blowing righteous riffs like the pros: Jack Kerouac, Allen Ginsberg, Lawrence Ferlinghetti, Kenneth Rexroth, Gregory Corso, and Zippy the Pinhead.

STEP ONE
Player One, think of (1) someone *famous* or (2) someone *common*—known to both you and your friend(s). Smile enigmatically (like Buddha, Charlie Parker) when you come up with a name. Nod your head knowingly as you picture this person. Groove on his or her essence. For the moment, say nothing.

STEP TWO
Player Two, ask Player One the following question: "If the person you're imagining were smoke, what kind of smoke would he or she be?" Write down Player One's response. Encourage him to invent a metaphor, but prohibit him from using a metonym—that is, from naming something *actually* associated with the mystery person. 'Cause as every hip rhetorician knows: metaphors are Beat; metonyms are square.

STEP THREE
Ask Player One lots more silly questions as you attempt to guess the identity of the mystery person. But in place of "smoke" substitute other common nouns. For example, say, "If this person were cheese, what kind of cheese would he or she be?" Or try brands of soap, makes of cars, names of cities or towns, items of clothing, musical instruments, weather, and food. Get loose! Dig this gig! But remember to record all answers.

STEP FOUR

After somebody—the winner—nails the mystery person's name, arrange your laundry list of real-gone images so that it looks poetic. Kerouac recommends that you avoid periods, "false colons and timid usually needless commas" in favor of vigorous "space dashes" (modeled on the "jazz musician drawing breath between outblown phrases"). Next, spin some cool sides. Bill Evans and Thelonious Monk work best, but Bud Powell at low volume is also good. The winner reads the smoke-poem aloud, then he or she thinks up a new mystery person. Repeat the above steps until early morning—or until most players have abandoned consciousness.

Now let's give the game a test run:

Let's say Player One is thinking of Tom Waits. We ask, "If the person you're imagining were smoke, what kind of smoke would he or she be?"

Player One: "Smoke oozing from under a flophouse door."

"Well, what if this person were an animal?"

"A barking frog, a braying ass. No, I've got it. He's the raven in that poem by Edgar Allan Poe."

"Oh, he's a guy. Here's a tough one. What if he were a Greek rhetorician?"

"Easy. Demosthenes, who practiced declamation while his mouth was full of pebbles. Gotcha on that one, didn't I?"

"Food?"

"Oatmeal cooked up with pea gravel, topped with taco sauce."

"A Dickens character?"

"Jesse Hexam's son in *Our Mutual Friend*. I quote: 'There was a curious mixture in the boy of uncompleted savagery and uncompleted civilization. His voice was hoarse and coarse, and his face was coarse, and his stunted figure was coarse; but he was cleaner than other boys of his type.'"

"Had that one on the tip of your tongue, did you? How about a woman? What if this dude were a bird?"

"Marianne Faithfull after a rough night; the Sibyl in Eliot's *Waste Land*. And he's cordovan shoe polish, a bent bottle cap, a stuck valve on a cornet."

"OK, OK. How about a street?"

"The Trans-Siberian Railroad."

"A novel?"

"*The Satyricon*, *Gravity's Rainbow*, or maybe *Gargantua and Pantagruel*."

"A time?"

"Berlin, between the wars."

"Is it Louis Armstrong? William Burroughs? Keith Richards? That African singer—Mahlathini—who sounds like a goat? God, it's Tom Waits! A physician friend of mine, named Jay, claims that the man's pipes are 'too tightly approximated' . . . 'edema of the vocal chords,' 'spasmodic dysphonia,' something like that. And while that diagnosis may be accurate, Waits is probably best pictured, not described. He's Baudelaire in a fifty-dollar suit, a Harry Partch gig on Cannery Row, gospel singer Blind Willie Johnson after a wrestling match with Jesus, Foghorn Leghorn pissed speechless."

Now, coin a few images of your own; shape them into breath units (what square poets call lines). Reach deep into the bowels of your soul; shut off the scrutinizer valve; rear back on your heels and let fly. Burn! Recite what you've written, while madly waving your arms. Now you're making "bop prosody"—Beat poetry: surrealism with a real gone rhythm.

cool jazz—A relaxed, contrapuntal style of bebop, developed during the early Cold War period, closely identified with the vibratoless trumpet of Miles Davis, the pianoless quartet of Gerry Mulligan with Chet Baker, and the orchestrations of Gil Evans and Shorty Rogers.

To admirers and detractors alike, a network of adjectives predicates cool jazz, granting it a cultural context. It's modern music: cerebral, composed, and arranged. It favors muted, pastel tones. It's racially coded as "white" (as soul inverted), and on geometaphorical maps of American music, it's located squarely on the West Coast. Cast in structuralist terms, however, cool jazz has meaning because of its relational difference to other jazz styles. It is determined—made to signify—by the predicates it excludes: blues-based, improvised, hot jazz (swing or bop) whose pleasures, far from pacific, are direct and corporeal.

Readings

William Claxton. 1992. *Jazz West Coast: Artwork of Pacific Jazz Records*. Tokyo: Bijutsu Shuppan-Sha.

Gary Giddins, ed. 1996. "What Was Cool Jazz?" *1996 Jazz Supplement* to *Village Voice*, 25 June, 1–20.

Ted Gioia. 1992. *West Coast Jazz: Modern Jazz in California, 1945–1960*. New York: Oxford University Press.

Donald L. Maggin. 1996. *Stan Getz: A Life in Jazz*. New York: William Morrow.

Lewis Porter, ed. 1991. *A Lester Young Reader*. Washington, D.C.: Smithsonian Institution Press.

Thomas Pynchon. 1984. "Entropy." In *Slow Learner: Early Stories*. Boston: Little, Brown.

Recordings

1. Gerry Mulligan, *The Complete Pacific Jazz Recordings of the Gerry Mulligan Quartet with Chet Baker* (Pacific Jazz).
2. Miles Davis, *Birth of the Cool* (Capitol).
3. Jimmy Giuffre, *The Complete Capitol and Atlantic Recordings of Jimmy Giuffre* (Mosaic).
4. Lennie Tristano, *Lennie Tristano/The New Tristano* (Rhino/Atlantic).
5. Jim Hall, *Concierto* (Epic/Associated/Legacy).
6. Chet Baker, *Let's Get Lost: The Best of Chet Baker Sings* (Pacific Jazz).
7. Shorty Rogers, *Short Stops* (Bluebird).
8. The Gil Evans Orchestra, *Out of the Cool* (Impulse!).
9. Hal McKusick, *Now's the Time (1957–58)* (GRP/Decca).
10. Franz Koglmann, *A White Line* (hat ART).

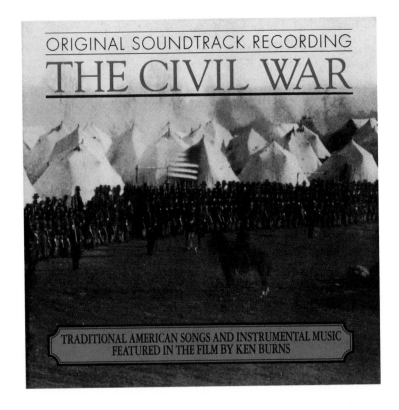

ORIGINAL SOUNDTRACK RECORDING

THE CIVIL WAR

TRADITIONAL AMERICAN SONGS AND INSTRUMENTAL MUSIC
FEATURED IN THE FILM BY KEN BURNS

"Dixie"—A nineteenth-century hit fraught with symbolic weight.

Probably, there is no song in the history of America with a more checkered past than "Dixie." In Congress, before the Civil War, it elicited ovations from both abolitionist Republicans and proslavery Democrats. After the Southern states seceded from the Union, the Confederacy adopted the song as its national anthem. A brass band played "I Wish I Was in Dixie's Land" at Jefferson Davis's inauguration. But Abraham Lincoln also loved the tune and had it played at his second inauguration.

"Dixie" was introduced on a Broadway stage on April 4, 1859, by Daniel Decatur Emmett, an itinerant musician who was both Union partisan and founder of the first professional blackface minstrel troupe. Almost immediately, the song became popular. Its vast appeal, however, did not indicate consensus. Rather, the popularity of "Dixie" resulted from the song's basic slipperiness. It seemed eager to serve all sorts of agendas and capable of insinuating itself into a variety of contexts.

In a sense, this situation continues today. "Dixie" is far more redolent of meaning than it is explicitly meaningful. It functions as a poetic image. Generations of Americans, nostalgically drawn to the idyllic scene it calls them to conjure, have revered it. And generations, enraged and offended by the antebellum stereotypes it asks them to celebrate, have reviled it. A small community in central Ohio, however, suggests an alternative response to the song. It claims "Dixie" as an authentic product of its African-American tradition. Mount Vernon, Ohio—home of Dan Emmett—sits at the crossroads of popular understanding about "Dixie." Here, explain anthropologists Howard and Judith Sacks, "minstrel hit, proud anthem of the South, [and] hated symbol of racism" meet (16). By revealing repressed information about "Dixie," the town provides a means of hearing this ambiguous symbol anew. Here's how.

In 1976, members of Mount Vernon's black American Legion erected a gravestone with an inscription that expressed "the understanding of four generations of local African Americans" (3). It commemorates Ben and Lew Snowden, celebrated musicians and the children of freed slaves. The gravestone reads: "They taught 'Dixie' to Dan Emmett." The Snowdens are honored as people who shared their musical knowledge.

The epitaph on Emmett's grave—funded in part by traveling minstrels in the 1920s—articulates a completely different sentiment. It calls "Dixie Land" Emmett's song and, thus, casts the musician as owner and inventor.

Emmett's grave is three miles south of the Snowdens', a far cry closer than the sizable divide that separated black and white musicians during the nineteenth century. For example, the Sackses maintain that Ben and Lew Snowden (both of whom could read and write) would have regarded musical authorship as an "irrelevant concept," a misunderstanding of how musical information is exchanged (161–62). Emmett, they note, obviously would have disagreed. He operated from a completely different perspective. Chances are, when he sold

"Dixie" to a publisher, he didn't blink an eye. Asking the question—Who wrote "Dixie"?—is a valuable exercise, not because it's finally resolvable, but because it raises a fascinating array of issues and opens up possibilities long dormant in the song.

Most remarkable is a hypothesis offered by the Sackses. They take issue with the standard interpretation of "Dixie," which maintains that Dan Emmett built the song out of basic minstrel-show materials. They boldly suggest that the song's earliest lyric parallels the biography of Ellen Cooper Snowden—an ex-slave from the tidewater region of Maryland and the mother of the men who taught Dan Emmett "Dixie." Could she be, not the "author," but a central player or vector in the song's creation?

Maybe it's time to hear "Dixie" anew. How about *straight*, as a song of exile? Heard this way, it echoes psalms of captivity found in the Old Testament and anticipates the lamentations that abound in blues and, especially, reggae. Or how about *ironically*, as a signifying song? "Oh, I wish I was in the land of cotton. Yeah, like hell I do!" The point is, Ellen Snowden might just be the First Lady of Jazz. She stands for the person who realizes that songs mean what we make them mean. More pointedly, if "Dixie," when it's sung nowadays, denotes only the Old South, then it is because we have forgotten Ellen Snowden. We have forgotten a basic lesson of jazz: Pleasure lies in plurality—in multiplicity. Instead of banishing "Dixie" from our consciousness, we ought to blow it full of possibilities.

■

Readings

Richard Jackson. 1976. *Popular Songs of Nineteenth-Century America*. New York: Dover.

Hans Nathan. 1962. *Dan Emmett and the Rise of Early Negro Minstrelsy*. Norman: University of Oklahoma Press.

Howard L. Sacks and Judith Rose Sacks. 1993. *Way up North in Dixie: A Black Family's Claim to the Confederate Anthem*. Washington, D.C.: Smithsonian Institution Press.

Recordings

Red Allen, "Dixie Medley," on *Swing Trumpet Kings* (Verve).

Randy Edelman (arrangement), on *Gettysburg: Music from the Original Motion Picture Soundtrack* (Milan).

Lee Greenwood, *American Patriot* (Liberty).

Robin Holcomb, *Rockabye* (Elektra Nonesuch).

Bobby Horton (guitar), on *The Civil War: Original Soundtrack Recording* (Elektra Nonesuch).

Lynyrd Skynyrd, *Southern by the Grace of God—Tribute Tour 1987* (MCA).

United States Military Academy Band, on *Songs of the Civil War* (Columbia).

Anecdote

In the fall of 1969, toward the beginning of my junior year in high school, I sewed a small Confederate flag on a ragged fedora and wore it to school. My purpose was to demonstrate solidarity with my fellow white students. We were opposing the black minority's desire to alter our school's identity. For reasons we refused to understand, they had begun to regard our alma mater—sung to the tune of "Tara," the theme song to *Gone with the Wind*—as offensive and anachronistic. They objected when our marching band revved up a spirited version of "Dixie" at pep rallies and football games. They found little-to-no pride in being called "Fighting Rebels." We white kids confronted this black protest by making the Stars and Bars ubiquitous. We plastered it everywhere: on walls, notebooks, cars, and clothes. I must admit, however, that I was a little embarrassed when Walter drew Kellogg's attention to my hat. We were standing in the hallway, pulling books and bagged lunches out of our lockers, when Walter yelled, "Hey Jarrett, why don't you show Kellogg your hat?" Actually, I shouldn't say I was embarrassed. Terrified is the word. Rumor had it that Kellogg—a budding black radical with a fixation on Mohammad Ali—always carried a knife to school. Since junior high school, he had joked about beating or carving "my white ass," and for just as many years, I had countered his threats with jokes—a strategy typical of endomorphs. "Yeah, let's see what you brought me," Kellogg said.

I pulled the hat out of my locker, held it out to him, and said, "Well, here it is," in the best aw-shucks voice I could muster. But I don't think he even glanced at my handiwork. Instead, he glared at me and whispered, "Mo' power to ya, muthafucka." I believed then, as I believe now, that I had just been rebuked by Jesus Christ.

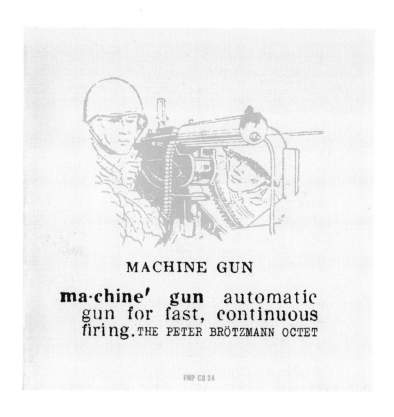

MACHINE GUN

ma·chine′ gun automatic gun for fast, continuous firing. THE PETER BRÖTZMANN OCTET

FMP CD 24

EOM—Abbreviation for "Enemy Of Music"; a person afflicted with audio immune syndrome.

Critics—culturally sanctioned gatekeepers—judge the music a society hears. They're aesthetic regulators. EOMs—self-appointed legislators—judge society by what (and how) it hears. Their *cri de guerre*—"Turn it down! Turn it off! How can anyone stand that noise?"—announces a desire to govern people through the appropriation and control of music (sonic space in homes, at work, on the streets). Accused of disliking music, EOMs demur: "Our so-called 'demands' are only reasonable. We enjoy lots of music." "Music?" bristle EOM antagonists (EOMAs). "Product is more like it. You guys turned 'soft' into a term of approbation! No wonder the 'music industry' accommodates your desires. You make them billions." Indeed. But isn't it equally certain that EOMs and EOMAs comprise a dyad—

mutually determining, opposed terms in a system? They define each other. Understood synchronically (in space), the fans of Celine Dion unwittingly create noizemongers—and vice versa. Understood diachronically (in time), the EOM/EOMA dyad narrates the unfolding story of modern music.

■

Topics for Further Research

It turns out that EOMs have their own saint. His name is Eddie Owens Martin, and he's self-canonized. Biographical material at the American Visionary Art Museum in Baltimore describes him thus:

> Eddie Owens Martin was born July 4, 1908, to a sharecropper family in Buena Vista, Georgia. At age 14 he ran away to New York City, where he lived on the streets, panhandling and hustling. After a 1935 revelation, he invented his own religion, Pasaquoyanism, and anointed himself St. EOM. He believed hair was a spiritual antenna and tried to grow his straight up. He also believed humans could levitate with a special suit he devised. After his parents died he returned to Georgia, transforming the farm house into a spiritual haven and visionary environment, the land of Pasaquan. Martin died on April 16, 1986.

Are EOMs insensitive to good music played loudly, or are they hypersensitive to the sound spectrum? A study of St. EOM's theories could provide an entry point (or, at least, a hook) for opening up these questions.

funk—1. In popular music, especially jazz and soul, the effect of low-down earthiness. 2. A heavily syncopated music—invented by James Brown, extrapolated by Sly Stone, mythologized by George Clinton—built on the One, the first beat of common meter.

In the discourse of music, examples of synesthesia abound. For example, aural sensations are routinely conceptualized through vocabulary associated with taste. "Funk," however, represents a rare instance of smell evoking sound (and odor evoking ardor). The obsolete Flemish *fonck* means "agitation" and is etymologically linked with *funqier* (Old French, "to give off smoke"). It suggests nothing but the blues—panic clouded by depression—and it contrasts sharply with the African concept of *lu-fuki* (literally "bad body odor"). In the Kongo, writes Robert Farris Thompson, body odor signifies exertion and connotes the positive energy of a person—in a word, fecundity. Thus it came to be that one whiff of "the hardest-working man in show business" brings good luck.

■

Readings

Lloyd Bradley. 1996. "The Brother from Another Planet." *Mojo*, September, 78–89.

James Brown. 1986. *The Godfather of Soul*. New York: Macmillan.

Robert Christgau. 1991. "Ulysses No. 1." *Village Voice Rock & Roll Quarterly*, July, 26–27.

John Corbett. 1994. *Extended Play: Sounding Off from John Cage to Dr. Funkenstein*. Durham, N.C.: Duke University Press.

Phillip Brian Harper. 1989. "Synesthesia, 'Crossover' and Blacks in Popular Music." *Social Text*, Fall, 102–21.

Cliff Jones. 1994. "Sly Stone Chose the Dark Side. He Became Darth Vader." *Mojo*, August, 48–56.

Joe McEwen. 1992. "Funk." In *The Rolling Stone Illustrated History of Rock & Roll*, ed. Anthony DeCurtis and James Henke, pp. 521–25. New York: Random House.

Jim Payne and Harry Weinger, eds. 1997. *Give the Drummers Some! The Great Drummers of R&B, Funk and Soul*. Katonah, N.Y.: Face the Music. [Check out Earl Palmer's anecdote on p. 6.]

Vernon Reid. 1993. "Brother from Another Planet." *Vibe*, November, 45–49.

Cynthia Rose. 1990. *Living in America: The Soul Saga of James Brown*. London: Serpent's Tail.

Allan Slutsky and Chuck Silverman. 1996. *The Funkmasters—The Great James Brown Rhythm Sections, 1960–1973*. New York: Warner Bros.

Greg Tate. 1992. "The Atomic Dog: George Clinton Interview by Greg Tate and Bob Wisdom," and "Beyond the Zone of the Zero Funkativity." In *Flyboy in the Buttermilk: Essays on Contemporary America*. New York: Simon and Schuster.

Robert Farris Thompson. 1983. *Flash of the Spirit: African and Afro-American Art and Philosophy*. New York: Vintage.

Rickey Vincent. 1996. *Funk: The Music, the People, and the Rhythm of the One*. New York: St. Martin's.

Recordings—90 Minutes of Maximum Funk

Question to the Beastie Boys (March 1994)

Roland Barthes, a theorist I really care about, once said that people have manna words—words that are magic to them, even the sound of them. Do you have such words?

MCA: "Fluid."

ADROCK: There's words that I use a lot. I don't know if they have significance to me.

MCA: To me, "fluid" is just a focus word. It's about everything, about snowboarding or playing basketball or about rhyming or whatever.

MIKE D: This next thing might be a bad example, and it might get me in trouble. But I would say the word "funk." When you really hear the funk, and it's really on, then that's everything. The problem is, the word is so misused, misapplied right now in terms of music, that it's almost hard to keep the meaning. It's kind of like Adam [Horovitz] was saying to me yesterday. He was talking to this guy about the song "The Payback" by James Brown. And the guy was trying to say that the guitar was playing *nothing*. But see, I figure, well, if the guitar is nothing, then that means the entire band is playing nothing. But, then, that's the best playing ever on like any song. And they're all playing nothing. That's the best shit. To be able to do that, that's the funk. Unfortunately, people confuse the funk with a lot more superfluous musical activity.

ADROCK: I like the word "knickerbocker," as in the New York Knicks.

MIKE D: I like that—love that. You know what I realize, actually, what my word is? I don't want to offend anyone at the table, but "doo-doo."

ADROCK: I was about to say "shit." For some reason, I use that word all the time.

MIKE D: Doo-doo, though. Doo-doo!

Genesis 11:1-9—The Tower of Babel story.

It's compelling when it speaks of technology. It's prophetic when it speaks of CDs and the digital revolution. The Tower of Babel story explains why everything ever recorded is seemingly available—or scheduled (like Jesus) for imminent return. More importantly, it tells why unlimited access to the past is a mixed blessing. To unpack its riches, we need to examine this passage verse by verse. Before we take up that task, however, let's key in on the basic themes of this remarkable story.

1. Genesis 11:1–9 is, first and foremost, a creation narrative. In a nutshell, it's the story of civilization: The deliberations of mankind lead, first, to technological innovation (the invention of brick or, by analogy, binary code), then to institutionalization (the construction of a corporate tower or an enormous database), and, finally, to fragmentation (ambivalence about this brave new world).

2. Two motives—a fear of being "scattered" and an urge to "reach unto heaven"—arouse mankind's desire to erect the tower. They also explain what we might call "digital logic": the drive to gather all recorded music into an easily retrievable form and the drive to create perfect recordings (which may or may not mean "hi-fi").

3. Even more than related tales—the stories of Frankenstein and Pinocchio—the Tower story focuses on the unintended (positive and negative) consequences of the innovations that arise from our aspirations. Which is another way of saying that if today's record stores resemble Babel, in the staggering number of musical dialects they offer, then that's both curse and blessing.

Prophetically, then, the tower of Babel points to the appearance of (a) compact discs (vv. 1–4), (b) a collective dream in which all recordings are envisioned as always available (vv. 5–7), and (c) a new species of listener (vv. 8–9). We now turn to a close reading of the biblical narrative. Hear it speak to our present condition.

[1]And the whole earth was of one language, and of one speech.

Like any story with mythic power, this one takes our current situation and projects it as history, granting it both an origin and an explanation. For example, picture the musical universe of twenty or thirty years ago. What were its features? Ask a boomer. He'll tell you, "Back in the day, a better-than-adequate but general knowledge of popular music could be earned in night school—by cocking one's ears toward a radio—or in a summer session—by toiling in a reasonably stocked record store. The universe of old was manageable; it was written on the charts. Nobody needed critics—Elvis specialists, Madonna scholars, authorities on punk rock. The *lingua franca* spoken at Stax Studio was also spoken at Abbey Road, Chess, Motown, and Electric Lady. And nobody (neither mad dogs nor Englishmen) questioned pop's canon. In fact, no one dreamed that a canon was forming. Popular music was a thing of and for the moment. It was existential; it had no past."

Cut to the present. Musicians suffer from anxiety of influence; the wisdom of elders weighs upon them. Record stores function as museums. (Who needs Cleveland?) And alphabetized under "C," even the most modest collection boasts retrospectives by Can, Captain Beefheart, Hoagy Carmichael, James Carr, all the Carters (Benny, Betty, Carlene, and Mother Maybelle), Johnny and Rosanne Cash, Ray Charles, Clifton Chenier, Don and Neneh Cherry, Chic, Alex Chilton, Charlie Christian, Eric Clapton, the Clash, Buck Clayton . . . well, you get the picture. Between "then" and "now," everything always changes. Perhaps, long ago, the whole pop universe really spoke one language. Perhaps not. But certainly, during the digital age, our minds have undergone a Copernican revolution. We've not only developed a historical consciousness, but chronic self-consciousness of our self-consciousness. We feel distanced from a beatific, mythic past—one that we may have recently created specifically to distinguish "now" from "then."

> [2]And it came to pass, as they journeyed from the east, that they found
> a plain in the land of Shinar; and they dwelt there.

In a story notable for its lack of particulars, the specificity of this verse is arresting. Does the land of Shinar lead us to an ancient bauxite mine or, even more fantastically, to the smooth surface of compact discs, microscopically pitted with binary information? Is Shinar's plain, as more progressive archeologists speculate, actually a plane? Did Bedouins stumble upon an alien landing strip, an outpost or receiving station? The truth is out there waiting for Mulder, Scully, and Roky Erikson to investigate.

> [3]And they said one to another, Go to, let us make brick, and
> burn them throughly. And they had brick for stone, and slime had
> they for mortar.

God's decision—"Let us make man in our own image" (Gen. 1:26)—is echoed by mankind's unified call, "Let us make brick." For what is Adam, who was fashioned out of clay, but a soft, walking brick? The lesson here is simple and profound: Just as the appearance of human beings signifies a concentration of divine spirit, the appearance of brick signifies a massive convergence of diverse technologies (hardware, software and wetware). Three crucial points, which articulate our *perceptions* of technology, arise from this observation:

1. Technologies emerge in response to human will, but they operate with a will of their own.

2. Innovative technologies are manifestations of an often complex, always profit-oriented apparatus. Music, like bricks, is a product of institutions and industries.

3. Technologies are conceptualized as nature perfected. Bricks simulate and perfect stone. CDs record audio events with fidelity, and they're indestructible (or so we were told).

Or at least that's the theory. Read quickly, this verse suggests that inventions catch on when they anticipate the collective desire of the masses. Pushed harder, the verse hints at a much more radical point: We can't always get what we need, but we always get what we want. For example, have you ever noticed that the out-of-print record you're pining for often comes to hand in an almost miraculous fashion? You awaken one morning and think, "Boy, I'd love to snag a copy of Mary Margaret O'Hara's *Miss America*, Pere Ubu's *Modern Dance*, and Ornette Coleman's *Body Meta*. If only they were on disc." Boom! Like an answered prayer, six months later every title is available for purchase. The Tower story declares, "That's not prescience. Your wish list indicates sensitivity to market forces. The market wants records for you before you want them for yourself." Or, stated differently, declaring that such-and-such a record will never be reissued practically assures that it will be reissued—probably soon. The conditions that prompt longing in one consumer impinge on others, too. The record denied resurrection—consigned to oblivion—is the one nobody ever thinks to think about.

> [4] And they said, Go to, let us build us a city and a tower, whose top
> *may reach* unto heaven; and let us make us a name, lest we be
> scattered abroad upon the face of the whole earth.

Much has been made of mankind's pride—his totalizing urge to knowledge and mastery. It leads him to erect the tower—Freud, are you chuckling?—and it leads to God's judgment. Indeed, mankind's desire to have everything at the tips of his digits—to unify all information—not only motivates today's massive retrospective and reissue programs, it informs the slice-'n'-dice aesthetics of hip-hoppers and remixologists. Too little, however, has been made of the twin anxieties that pride belies. These anxieties make the digital age seem goal directed; they give it a shape, a teleology. First, there's a yearning for perfection, a longing to "reach unto heaven." It characterizes the pursuit of better and better sound: the dream of ultimately and finally closing the gap between recordings and things recorded. Then, there's the yearning to make a name (a history or an identity) and, thereby, avoid being scattered. This latter anxiety is, in turn, expressed in two ways: the will to omniscience (which leads to punditry) and the will to omnipotence (which leads to spin doctoring). Omniscience, the will to know everything there is to know about the pop universe, is the bane of critics. Omnipotence, the will to master everything in the pop universe, is the bane of hip-hoppers.

> [5]And the LORD came down to see the city and the tower, which the children of men builded.

To inspect the tower—a combination database, transmitter, and superstore—whose top floor reaches heaven, the Lord must come down. Get the joke? Far less obvious but equally ironic is the inescapable conclusion that this Lord is himself a creation of the tower builders. He's the man upstairs, a wee bit surly and, apparently, not omniscient. The digital age projects another sort of God. He's the guy (the theoretical construct) whose record collection lacks no good thing but all things worthless. He's plugged all gaps, covered all bases. The complete Bear Family and Mosaic catalogs sit on his shelves. God hipped you and your friends to Kathy McCarty, Wagon Christ, and Gavin Bryars. To him, "out of print" is a meaningless phrase. That ? and the Mysterians disc you've been looking for, the one tied up in litigation? God owns two copies—and lots of imports too. More importantly, he boasts absolute knowledge of his immense collection. God's smarter than Brian Eno. He can distinguish techno from house music, jungle from drum 'n' bass. He understands the appeal of acid jazz and country music videos. And he's got the time to appreciate what he's acquired!

> [6]And the LORD said, Behold, the people is one, and they have all one language; and this they begin to do: and now nothing will be restrained from them, which they have imagined to do.

Reissues have been around for a long time. In the early 1930s, Milt Gabler—a pioneering record producer for Decca—began leasing masters and reissuing already classic "sides" on his Commodore record label, arguably the first indie. Spotting a good idea, the majors soon followed suit. John Hammond, for example, piloted a reissue program at Columbia, and when major labels lost interest in their back catalogs, indies moved back in. Riverside Records began business as a reissue label in the early 1950s, leasing material from the Chicago-based Paramount label. Once the fledgling company got on its feet, its founders, Orrin Keepnews and Bill Grauer, signed and recorded Thelonious Monk, Bill Evans, Wes Montgomery, and Cannonball Adderley. Then Riverside went under, only to be resurrected two decades later by the combined power of rock 'n' roll and corporate expansion. In short, here's what happened. The phenomenal success of Creedence Clearwater Revival allowed Fantasy, the band's record label, to purchase the catalogs of Riverside, Prestige, and Milestone Records. Fantasy's president, Ralph Kaffel, promptly initiated a reissue program. At first, he assembled and released "twofers," double albums whose gatefold sleeves featured informative essays on the history and significance of jazz. Later, in the 1980s, as Fantasy continued to record its own artists and acquire more record labels (e.g., Contemporary, Pablo, and Specialty) the label began to transfer its enormous catalog to compact disc. This scenario was enacted repeatedly as companies scrambled to tap their inventories. Consequently, in the 1990s, the past is present.

Just about nothing is restrained from us, and that's both good and bad. On the upside, we can now build a music collection that rivals God's. His Coltrane holdings are no better than ours, thanks to Fantasy/Prestige, Rhino/Atlantic, Bear Family, Razor & Tie, and GRP/Impulse! reissues. He's not the only guy on the block with rare recordings by Howard Tate, Emmett Miller, the Flatlanders, Wire, John Fahey, the Swan Silvertones, the Slits, Webb Pierce, the Louvin Brothers, and Sun Ra. And he no longer has exclusive rights to enter the vaults of Westbound, Folkways, Verve, Ardent, Takoma, Nashboro, Cobra, Duke/Peacock, Savoy, Jewel/Paula, Fury, Delmark, and other record companies.

[7]Go to, let us go down, and there confound their language, that they may not understand one another's speech.

But virtually unlimited access to all music, past and present, has a downside. The tower exacts revenge.

1. While reissues make us omniscient in theory, enabling us to hear anything and everything we want to hear, they make us ignorant in practice. Never before have we felt so finite or heard less of what's available. Never before have we been deluged with so much indistinguishable product. The tower—a corporate apparatus that educates—routinely reminds us that we're growing more knowledgeable about what we don't know. Our attempts to "reach heaven" double back, making us feel more human. To cope—to avoid penury and maintain sanity—we specialize as the pop universe buckles, then explodes. We take up trainspotting in any one of pop's numerous parallel universes and make occasional forays into alien territories.

2. Consequently, we speak mutually unintelligible languages, or we hear exactly the same language differently. (Note: Pentecost is the vision of Babel reversed—absolute entropy coexistent with absolute redundancy). It's possible for two music lovers—who dote on their CD collections to be foiled in all attempts to communicate, to have nothing in common. Elvis is a hero to one; to the other he don't mean shit.

Rule #1: Somebody out there's dying to snap up precisely what you'd most like to avoid or unload.

Rule #2: At least three thousand people are willing to buy anything; there's a market for everything.

It's also possible—and more common—for two people to like the same kind of music for entirely different reasons. What's cool to one is kitsch to the other. For example, How do you understand the pleasures of Esquerita, Esquivel, or, for that matter, Billy Eckstine and Steve Earle? Music, it turns out, isn't Esperanto. In the digital age all of music's potential meanings are liberated; they're up for grabs. Judgment—separating what's good from what's bad—becomes a function of taste. We simultaneously admire and distrust critics presumptive enough to tell us what we can and cannot ignore. Consensus becomes just another name that nostalgia gives the past.

3. When pop's entire past is simultaneously available, history—as a linear succession of ever-evolving, upwardly spiraling styles—is

annulled. All styles become equally contemporary, existing more in space than time, and histories—the narratives that seek to emplot the past—compete with one another for attention and truth status. This allows contemporary musicians (and listeners) three basic responses. They can repress the past and create a new musical language. But, then, who's doing that? They can practice a dialect of their choice: witness Teenage Fanclub (power pop), the Squirrel Nut Zippers (hot jazz), Wayne Hancock (honky tonk), Man . . . or Astro-Man? (surf), Sam Phillips (*Revolver*-era Beatles), and Jewel (Joni Mitchell). Or they can babble like a polyglot—like a John Zorn, Public Enemy, Pooh Stick, Aphex Twin, Goldie, or Beck.

> [8]So the LORD scattered them abroad from thence upon the face of all the earth: and they left off to build the city.

> [9]Therefore is the name of it called Babel; because the LORD did there confound the language of all the earth: and from thence did the LORD scatter them abroad upon the face of all the earth.

The scattering that first appears as judgment transforms itself into an agent of grace as the inhabitants of the pop world learn to live like tourists, forsaking nostalgic dreams of lost homogeny. When we give ourselves over to whimsy, the random drift fostered by the CD's shuffle logic, pop music Babelizes. It fractures into a multitude of tiny enclaves, niches well worth exploring. Surprise waits around every corner.

■

Readings

Gretchen Bender and Timothy Druckrey, eds. 1994. *Culture on the Brink: Ideologies of Technology*. Seattle: Bay Press.

Jacques Ellul. 1990. *The Technological Bluff*. Trans. Geoffrey W. Bromiley. Grand Rapids, Mich: New York: Wm. B. Eerdmans.

———. 1964. *The Technological Society*. Trans. John Wilkinson. New York: Vintage.

Jürgen Habermas. 1989. *Jürgen Habermas on Society and Politics: A Reader*. Boston: Beacon.

Thomas Pynchon. 1966. *The Crying of Lot 49*. New York: Bantam.

Egbert Schuurman. 1995. *Perspectives on Technology and Culture*. Sioux City, Iowa: Dordt College.

Patti Smith. 1978. *Babel*. New York: Putnam.

Manfred Stanley. 1978. *The Technological Conscience: Survival and Dignity in an Age of Expertise*. Chicago: University of Chicago Press.

Greg Ulmer. 1989. *Teletheory: Grammatology in the Age of Video*. New York: Routledge.

John Zerzan and Alice Carnes, eds. 1991. *Questioning Technology: Tool, Toy or Tyrant?* Philadelphia: New Society Publishers.

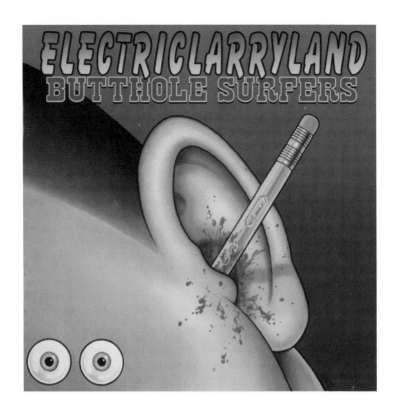

hyperacusis—An abnormal or pathological
sensitivity to auditory stimuli; a variety of hyperesthesia.

Every technology exacts a cost upon its beneficiaries. This is not to say that audio technologies created the symptoms associated with hyperacusis. Rather, they made these symptoms coalesce as a pathology (in much the same way that technologies of writing created or, at the very least, revealed dyslexia). Research suggests that hyperacusis might be linked to a chemical deficiency, causing a malfunction of those parts of the brain concerned with processing information (filtering electrical signals) transmitted from the ears. But the condition also reasserts the more philosophical problem of perception: By what means does the brain determine what to hear—what to focus on; what to ignore—even as it is in the process of hearing?

Reading

David Bowman. 1992. *Let the Dog Drive*. New York: Penguin.

Interview—Charlie Haden on hearing too much (February 1995)

Tinnitus is a ringing in the ears that develops in people genetically. It also develops as a result of accidents, wars—hearing gunfire—and in rock concerts. Mine developed standing next to cymbals, and having very sensitive ears. I developed the condition at a very young age, and it got worse as I kept playing and didn't protect my ears. Then I started wearing earplugs. All along I had another condition which I didn't know but found out about ten years ago, called hyperacusis, which is extreme sensitivity to loud sound. As I understand it, there's something in the inner or middle ear—I don't know what it's called—that stops down to protect you from loud noise. It doesn't work in me. It's like the volume is turned up in my head. A lot of people—when they have tinnitus—they lose their hearing. With me, my hearing has become more and more acute. Every time I take a hearing test, I go off the scale. I hear too much.

Is that a mixed blessing or just a curse?

It's a curse. Right now, as I'm talking to you, I've got an earplug in my left ear. The speaker in a telephone receiver is right next to your eardrum. And it's the same way with headphones. When I play a concert, I have plexiglass around the drums, around Ernie Watts in my Quartet West. I actually have to play on a big stage to distance myself from the drums. It's a real strain on me emotionally, physically, and creatively. Sometimes, even though I can hear everything, it's at a delay because I'm so far away from everything.

You're an exceptionally melodic bass player. I wonder if your condition actually contributed to that?

No. If I had a wish in my life it would be that I didn't have these conditions. If you heard the ringing that I have in my head, you'd run down the street screaming. I've gotten accustomed to it now. I just accept it as part of my being. But if I stop and think about it, it can really drive me nuts.

implied grunge—Singer and bassist Mark Sandman's term for describing the sound of his band, Morphine.

"With grunge, you feedback a guitar, and it fills up a huge area sonically," says Mark Sandman. "And though it's a beautiful sound—don't get me wrong—it has almost become a given, sort of there all the time from beginning to end." Morphine has no guitarist. It's a trio: bass, drums, and saxophone. But it demonstrates that *what's not* structures *what is*. Absence turns out to be a variety of presence. "Nobody," Sandman pronounces, "seems to mind that we don't have guitars. It just seems like the guitars are there. They're imaginary."

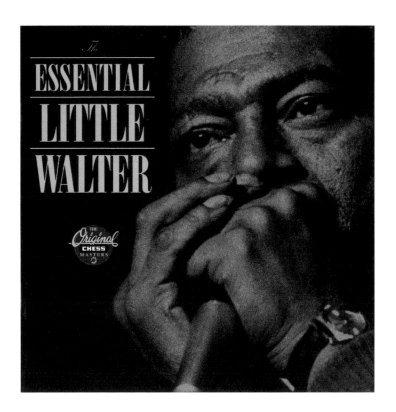

jukebox—A multiselection music machine, coin-operated and equipped with push buttons for the selection of records.

In 1877, Edison invented the phonograph. In 1889, at San Francisco's Palais Royal Saloon, it was equipped with a coin slot. In 1906, Gabel Automatic marketed the first multiselection phonograph, and in 1927, Automated Musical Instruments added a new feature—electronic amplification—to this random-access music machine. But no one had yet heard a jukebox. Its development depended on political, as much as technological, change. The 1933 repeal of Prohibition created a new "narrowcast" market for companies such as Wurlitzer, AMI, and Seeburg. They were able to place hardware in thousands of (now-legal) bars or "juke joints": roadside drinking establishments whose name derived from *juke* or *jook*, the Gullah word for "disorderly and bad," and thus, probably, from *dzugu*, West African for "wicked."

■

Readings

Eric Boehlert. 1994. "Put Another Nickel In." *Billboard, 100th Anniversary Issue*, 1 November, 93–98.

William Bunch. 1994. *Jukebox America: Down Back Streets and Blue Highways in Search of the Country's Greatest Jukebox*. New York: St. Martin's.

Frank W. Hoffman. 1983. *The Cash Box Singles Charts, 1950–1981*. Metuchen, N.J.: Scarecrow.

Birney Imes. 1990. *Juke Joint*. Oxford: University Press of Mississippi.

Vincent Lynch. 1981. *Jukebox: The Golden Age*. Berkeley, Calif.: Lancaster-Miller.

Bubblegum Classics
volume two
the ultimate collection
of pure pop music

Kasenetz & Katz—Jerry Kasenetz and Jeff Katz (collectively, Super K Productions), Buddah Records producers synonymous with bubblegum music.

In the late 1960s, popular music began to pose a question that opened new sonic territories. It went something like this: "What sounds correspond to a hallucinogenic experience?" All acceptable answers were filed under the rubric "psychedelic." Bubblegum, whose *annus mirabilis* was 1968, the year Kasenetz & Katz produced "Simon Says" by the 1910 Fruitgum Company and "Yummy, Yummy, Yummy" by the Ohio Express, translated the sounds of psychedelia into a musical language that kids in their early teens could comprehend—i.e., enjoy and find titillating. (You might say Super K Productions converted acid-laced aural sugar cubes into chewier confections.) Once amplified, the melodic song-craft of bubblegum was transformed into power pop. And that explains how to connect the dots between the Beatles, the Box Tops, and Big Star.

■

Readings

Lester Bangs. 1992. "Bubblegum." In *The Rolling Stone Illustrated History of Rock & Roll*, ed. Anthony DeCurtis and James Henke, pp. 452–54. New York: Random House.

Carl Cafarelli. 1997. "An Informal History of Bubblegum Music." *Goldmine*, 25 April, 16–19+.

Chuck Eddy. 1997. "The Bubblegum/Disco Connection." In *The Accidental Evolution of Rock 'n' Roll: A Misguided Tour through Popular Music*, pp. 109–10. New York: Da Capo.

Recordings—Bubblegum's Best

1. Various, *Bubblegum Classics, Volumes 1–3* (Varèse Sarabande).
2. Jackson 5, *Greatest Hits* (Motown).
3. Archies, *Sugar, Sugar* (Classic Sound).
4. The Ramones, *All the Stuff and More—Vol. 1* (Sire/Warner Bros.).
5. The Pooh Sticks, *Million Seller* (Zoo/BMG).
6. Box Tops, *The Ultimate Box Tops* (Warner Special Products).
7. Tommy Boyce and Bobby Hart, *The Songs of Tommy Boyce & Bobby Hart* (Varèse Sarabande).
8. Debbie Gibson, *Greatest Hits* (Atlantic).
9. Monkees, *The Monkees Greatest* (Rhino).
10. Hanson, *Middle of Nowhere* (Mercury).

Music From The Motion Picture Soundtrack

Until The End Of The World

A Film By Wim Wenders

LP—The "long-playing" phonograph record; introduced by Columbia Records in 1948.

A significant alteration in the technology for storing and retrieving music, the 12-inch LP played at 33⅓ rpm seemed like wish fulfillment. The music industry had merely honored demands created by the older 78-rpm format. But, of course, the LP transformed music production and reception. Without the LP, would John Coltrane have improvised at such lengths? Would the Beatles have stopped performing live? How did the LP's extended playing time structure the daily activities of increasingly distracted listeners? Then, in 1982, Philips introduced the compact disc. To the extent that this new format was received as the realization or fulfillment of the LP's aspirations, it repeated a proof: recording technology evolves; it's goal directed. Notice, therefore, how teleology is constructed, how it is manufactured.

Readings

Michael Chanan. 1995. *Repeated Takes: A Short History of Recording and Its Effects on Music*. New York: Verso.

Evan Eisenberg. 1987. *Recording Angel: Explorations in Phonography*. New York: McGraw-Hill.

Ted Fox. 1986. *In the Groove*. New York: St. Martin's.

Keith Negus. 1992. *Producing Pop: Culture and Conflict in the Popular Music Industry*. London: Edward Arnold.

Brian Priestley. 1991. *Jazz on Record: A History*. New York: Billboard.

Jed Rasula. 1995. "The Media of Memory: The Seductive Menace of Records in Jazz History." In *Jazz among the Discourses*, ed. Krin Gabbard, pp. 134–62. Durham, N.C.: Duke University Press.

Russell Sanjek and David Sanjek. 1996. *Pennies from Heaven: The American Popular Music Business in the Twentieth Century*. New York: Da Capo.

Interview—George Avakian reflects on the invention of the LP and its effects on recording (June 1994)

I was put in charge of Columbia's popular album department, which meant very little in the 78-rpm days. But when the LP was invented, that became the department that brought in the most money. LPs simply took over the business. That had to be in 1949.

And Columbia entered what was to become a huge software war with RCA over 45- versus 33-rpm formats.

When I finally joined RCA in 1960, one of the questions I asked was "How did you guys come up with 45?" Their propaganda said that it was the best speed for sound; it was the best medium—that is, a 7-inch disk—for the most important money-earning aspect of classical music, namely operatic arias and overtures: compositions that ran about five minutes or so. One of the guys laughed and said, "Oh, we decided we weren't going to follow Columbia. We had to be creators. We simply subtracted 33 from 78 and came up with 45." I could never get anybody else to say whether that was true. But this one guy said, "George, it really is true, but nobody else will admit it." I can see why.

Here we are in 33-rpm albums. The big breakthrough that came in building up sales was the 12-inch popular LP. It was more than just an extension of the old 78-rpm album with eight sides: four, 10-inch disks translated into eight tracks on a 10-inch LP. What made the 12-inch LP really go was, first of all, you had better variety and selection of material. And the price was right.

The first 12-inch pop LPs were priced at $4.95. That was a little high. Jim Conkling was the president of Columbia Records, a man who never got the credit he deserved because the man who replaced him, Goddard Lieberson, got so much publicity. Jim was a brilliant guy who came up with a conception that put across the 12-inch popular LP. He did it in a strange way which, at first, people thought was crazy. He figured how to drop prices by $1.00. In those days, the magic numbers ended in five instead of eight. You know, everybody talks about $3.98. It used to be $3.95. Why, I don't know.

How could we afford to do a $1.00 price drop? Everybody knew what the manufacturing costs were, the union scale for musicians apart from the advances that had to be paid, royalties set up. Well, Jim came up with an idea. If we could get publishers to lower the standard rate of two cents per composition to one-and-a-half cents, they would earn much more money because the company would be able to sell that many more records. By saving the six cents per disk, that would put us in a position of making profit. If we had big hits, we would really make profit. Otherwise, we'd be spinning our wheels, breaking even, trying to establish something.

Jim got practically every publisher to agree except one, who told him and me, when we had our meeting, "Fellows, I'm going to stick to two cents, and you know something? I'll still make much more money than you think, because, even though you won't want to use my stuff you've got to." This was the publisher who had the bulk of Gershwin, Cole Porter, Richard Rogers, Jerome Kern, all the big names—an organization called Music Publishers Holding Corporation. It was owned by Warner Brothers, which was, oddly enough, a company that did musicals in movies on a pioneer basis, but not with any record company ties. That's why, in 1958, when Jim Conkling left Columbia to organize Warner Brothers Records, I went with him. It was a fantastic opportunity to start something new.

We now had a situation where the competition didn't realize that we had these deals. They thought we were crazy; they figured we were losing money. But we weren't. Finally, the word got out, and everybody else went the same way. But we had such a huge head start that it was unbelievable. Also, Jim got the conception of starting our own record club, and that was the first big record club. There was only the Book-of-the-Month Club and a couple of small mail-order operations before that. There again, the volume jumped like crazy.

I'll give you a statistic that is really scary, and it's true. In the middle of 1957, I remember a report that New York University and *Billboard Magazine* were working on every quarter. The companies paid for this service. It was a confidential report which broke down all record sales in the United States, by company and by category. Then it broke down each category within each company. As a result, I saw this report cross my desk. It practically knocked me out of my chair. Columbia's pop LP department, again partly thanks to the record club, was bringing in 26 cents of every dollar spent in the United States for records of all types and, within the company, 82 cents out of every dollar. You can imagine what that did to my insides. I was working like hell. I'd finally managed to get two assistants, who I stole from other departments because the budget didn't call for more people in my department. I realized I can't go on this way, killing myself and getting a raise and a bonus every year. It isn't worth it. That's when I left to go with Jim to form Warner Brothers Records.

How did the LP affect the presentation of popular music?

Already, the concept that I used in making 10-inch LPs—pop LPs—was to think of them as radio programs in which the entire package has a purpose. It's programmed. You start with something which catches the attention of the listener on the outside first track. In fact, I did this deliberately on both sides. I'd try to find a real attention grabber. Then I'd pace the program and end with something that makes the person want to turn the record over. I applied that to everything, including the reissues from the old 78-rpm albums. (That's how the 10-inch LPs really began.) Gradually, I created more and more new product just for that type of recording.

But the 12-inch LP opened up something else again. I realized, now we've got some real space. With jazz musicians, we could give them a chance to stretch out. They weren't limited to a three-minute performance on every recording. The first artist I recorded on LP was Erroll Garner. I deliberately told him, he was one who could do this, "Let's make some recordings where you play approximately six minutes for each track. We'll have six songs on the 12-inch LP instead of the usual twelve." That worked marvelously, and then I continued with Duke Ellington and Buck Clayton, where for the first time there were studio jam sessions which ran as long as, I believe, 27 minutes for one continuous performance. That was one way of creating an LP in a way that didn't exist previously. This went on into other things like recording dance bands on location, which had never been done deliberately. It was always accidental that somebody happened to record, say, the Benny Goodman Orchestra of 1937 off the air.

Interview—Pat Metheny, after releasing *Beyond the Missouri Sky (Short Stories)*, an album of duets with Charlie Haden, addresses the problem of sequencing (January 1997)

That's a very important issue for me always. This one, because it has such a strong mood and because there are so many ballads on it, I thought was going to be hard. It was obviously better to start out, for four or five tunes, with the duo stuff and then work our way into the more elaborate material—let the album sort of grow as it went. We spent a couple of days at an editing place coming up with the right order. It just fell into place.

Also there are other issues when you're putting together a sequence—for example, key relationships, one tune to the next. The way "Cinema Paradiso" ends and the way "Spiritual" starts is the perfect modulation. It goes up a fourth, which is the best place you can go. Probably, nonmusicians don't realize how important it is, but you hear it. Basically, you have the structure of each song. But then there's another sort of larger structure. This is true whether it's a jazz or rock album. If you get five or six songs in a row that are in the same key, no matter if they're in different tempos, different grooves, or done by different bands, it creates a certain sameness that you can't really put your finger on. But if you can work it so that each song is in enough of a different key, then you get these great lifts. It makes the records have a life to them that's really cool.

Has the longer programming time of compact discs changed sequencing?

The big challenge is that you don't get a part one and a part two. It's one part, and that's a drag actually. It was great when you could make two sets out of it. You could have one story and then another story that was a continuation, but with an intermission in between. Now, it's one long story.

muso—A term [chiefly British] used to disparage a musician who overvalues technique.

The chorus to "I Turned Out a Punk" comprises a mandate. It begins, "Better learn to play guitar, with a plink and a plunk." "I was talking about the choices available," says the song's author, Mick Jones (leader of Big Audio Dynamite and former Clash guitarist). "You don't want to end up like some *muso*." The muso, a consummate professional, adheres to basic modernist values: complexity, individuality, virtuosity, and mastery. Says rock critic Simon Reynolds (*Blissed Out* and *The Sex Revolts*), "It's always been a derogatory term, criticizing the likes of Santana or big prog-rock bands obsessed with developing skills—chops. In the punk context, it had a lot to do with the idea that there was more to great rock 'n' roll than actual music." Note: It is redundant to call a bebop musician a muso.

■

Reading

Donald Barthelme. 1981. "The King of Jazz." In *Sixty Stories*. New York: E. P. Dutton.

Interview—More thoughts on "muso" from Simon Reynolds (Spring 1996)

During the punk era, it went so far to the opposite extreme that you'd have whole pieces on and interviews with bands where their music wasn't mentioned at all. They would talk about politics and subversion and all these eso-rhetorical things. They wouldn't actually mention what the music sounded like.

NME *essays on Scritti Politti.*

Yeah. I actually went through a phase where I was trying to shift attention back to the music when I was first writing. I started trying to use the word *muso* as a positive term, as someone who actually was thinking of sound. Not really muso in the sense of technical skills, but someone who was interested in sound in itself. Like Sonic Youth probably couldn't be regarded as virtuosos, except in the sense that they've invented their own form of virtuosity in their own weird tunings. But they're interested in sound. There isn't this whole ideological baggage surrounding them.

This is a major theme with Eno as well.

Yeah, although he can make a whole ideology after the fact. Robert Fripp would probably be regarded as the ultimate muso.

Nudie—Full name, Nudie Cohen (1902–1984). Hollywood rodeo tailor noted for his flamboyant western wear and for designing Elvis Presley's gold lamé tuxedo (1957). Like Chanel, Dior, and Versace—or, for that matter, Lennon, Lydon, and Madonna—Nudie designates a person whose given name became a brand name.

Taken collectively, as a giant wardrobe, Nudie costumes added a category to the set of visual types that signify "American entertainer." They made "country & western" performers legible, distinct from "cowboys" and "hillbillies." Taken singly, Nudie costumes served as *aide-memoires*, helping audiences identify individual performers. For example, an appliqué sewn on the lapel of a jacket might form a sartorial rebus that (as in heraldry) punned on a client's name or persona. Hence, wagon wheels decorated Porter Wagoner's suits. Ferlin Husky got dogs. Gram Parsons—whose suit, like those of many other performers, was created by Manuel Cuevas, Nudie's most gifted protégé—emblematically portrayed the singer's death wish.

■

Ten Record Covers, Ten Great Nudie Suits

Flying Burrito Brothers, *The Gilded Palace of Sin* (Edsel).
Buck Owens, *The Buck Owens Collection (1959–1990)* (Rhino).
Dolly Parton/Linda Ronstadt/Emmylou Harris, *Trio* (Warner Bros.).
Webb Pierce, *King of the Honky-Tonk, From the Original Decca Masters, 1952–1959* (MCA/CMA).
Elvis Presley, *50,000,000 Elvis Fans Can't Be Wrong: Elvis' Gold Records, Volume 2* (RCA).
———, *Walk a Mile in My Shoes: The Essential '70s Masters* (RCA).
Hank Snow, *The Essential Hank Snow* (RCA).
Sly Stone and the Family Stone, *Fresh* (Epic).
Lefty Frizzell, *Life's Like Poetry* (Bear Family).
Hank Williams, *40 Greatest Hits* (Polydor).

Interview—Q&A with clothes designer Manuel Cuevas (July 1997)

You designed the suit Elvis wore at his Vegas debut, right?

For a while, Elvis had been in a rut. Colonel Parker was kind of worried about that. He said, "You know, we want to bring this guy to big audiences, to adult audiences. We just signed a contract. We're going to open the International Hotel in Los Vegas." That was its name before it became the Hilton. "We have to create an image for this man, something that's absolutely different." I thought of the jump suit—turn him into an American rock 'n' roller, but at the same time without forgetting the roots of country, the roots of American clothing—which can be measured between Texas and the Indians, the old with the new. I came up with the grommets and eyelets and little pieces of metal. They were becoming popular at the time. I made him a belt with eagles and bugles. I made him a belt with lion heads and tiger heads—custom belts for this special set of outfits. We were making a white, a black, and a light blue.

Although I had made suits that were one piece, Elvis was unfamiliar with what I had planned. He couldn't understand. I said, "Well, a jump suit is like a dancer's suit."

"What do you mean a dancer?"

I said, "You're a dancer. What are you talking about? You dance. You have your steps. This is going to look good."

He was a little doubtful. But then I made it up, and he came into the shop in north Hollywood. Colonel Parker asked him to go and get the guitar and play it in the dressing room. Elvis fell in love with all the fringe, all the stuff. He just loved it. He said, "This is actually comfortable!"

I remember telling Elvis—I had done his wardrobe in about six or seven movies; we were familiar with each other—I told him, "The cavalry twill that the suits are made of is very heavy. It's like 18–19½ ounces in weight. You're going to sweat a lot."

He said, "Hey, for a million dollars, I don't mind sweating for two hours."

It was a great thing to hear. I said, "You know, cavalry twill really shows your body well. It keeps the form."

I assume that you and Gram Parsons worked together on his suit.

We worked on that—Gram and I—for about two months. I never realized until way past his death that that's what we were talking about. The fire on the cross—that's the way he wanted to die. Although we have been friends forever, Phillip Kaufman and I hadn't really talked about Gram, but Gram had talked to him. Phil had promised Gram that, if he died, he would burn his body.

I was just making the outfit according to all the ideas that we put together: the nude girls, the pills and the marijuana plants, and the California poppies. The fire up the pants. The cross in the back. Although I captured the idea—we developed it into a great form—it wasn't until a few years after his death that I really started thinking about it. "This boy was really telling me how he was going to die."

Was that typical for a musician to bring ideas to you?

I don't believe in making the same clothes for everybody. You have no idea of the difficulty that I went through with the Jacksons and, later on, with the Osmonds trying to be like Elvis Presley, with the same jump suits. It was difficult for me, but I went ahead and made them, tried to make them different. But I knew where that was coming from. They wanted to get into it like everybody else.

I've always entertained myself with odd-looking clothes. I just wanted to put them on somebody else!

Let's say I came into your shop to get something designed. How would you proceed?

First of all, you'd tell me, "We're hitting hard. We're going to be on television. Or we're going to an award thing. What do you think would work for me?"

I'd say, "Why don't you tell me what you like? Show me some pictures of when you were a little kid." I want to see what you were portraying through your life. Believe it or not, the easiest way to a person is through his image. It's because you have your dreams in there.

old school—Relating or belonging to early styles of rap, or to funk and soul.

As constructs—effects of hip-hop culture developing self-reflexive discourse—*old school* and *new school* historicize rap, granting it both a past (the dignity of a classic era, "back in the day") and a future (the promise of a modern age). But as descriptive terms, *old school* and *new school* are far from referentially stable. The line that divides them regularly shifts. Typically, though, *old school* is used to designate any of four times: pre-rap (talk tunes by the likes of Slim Gaillard, Bo Diddley, Iceberg Slim, and Isaac Hayes), proto-rap (that period of gestation whose trimesters are marked by Kool Herc's break-beats, "The Message" by Grandmaster Flash and the Furious Five, and Afrika Bambaataa's Zulu Nation), rap before mass popularization (when Run DMC rocked the mike on stage, video, and LP), or rap before transfiguration (all that came in the wake of Public Enemy).

Readings

Mark Costello and David Foster Wallace. 1990. *Signifying Rappers: Rap and Race in the Urban Present.* New York: Ecco.

S. H. Fernando, Jr. 1994. *The New Beats: Exploring the Music, Culture, and Attitudes of Hip-Hop.* New York: Anchor/Doubleday.

Tricia Rose. 1994. *Black Noise: Rap Music and Black Culture in Contemporary America.* Hanover, N.H.: Wesleyan/University Press of New England.

Adam Sexton, ed. 1995. *Rap on Rap: Straight-Up Talk on Hip-Hop Culture.* New York: Delta.

David Toop. 1991. *Rap Attack 2: African Rap to Global Hip Hop.* 2d ed. New York: Serpent's Tail.

Recordings—These three discs—compiled, produced, and annotated by a hip-hop patriarch—amount to an old-school primer, by any definition

Kurtis Blow Presents The History of Rap, Vol. 1: The Genesis (Rhino).

Kurtis Blow Presents The History of Rap, Vol. 2: The Birth of the Rap Record (Rhino).

Kurtis Blow Presents The History of Rap, Vol. 3: The Golden Age (Rhino).

pop vs. rock—Opposing aesthetics that have conventionally structured American "popular" music.

Here's an anecdote straight out of suburban youth culture. Nathaniel—who at 13 figured he resembled nobody so much as a barely pubescent Kurt Cobain—was being shuttled by one of his parents to a Wednesday afternoon guitar lesson. This week, he had decided to take something of a break and grapple with no items from the Jimi Hendrix Songbook. Instead, he was planning to exchange the 11 bucks crammed in the right pocket of his baggy, beige shorts for instructions on covering the Ramones' "I Wanna Be Sedated." He stared out the window of a Buick wagon and listened to a cassette; it played a tune by Big Audio Dynamite (B.A.D.), the band Mick Jones formed after leaving the Clash.

Older ears—the kind that pay for historical consciousness with stray hairs that sprout around their edges—might be able to contextualize the music Nat heard. The Farfisa organ and pounding bass drums that kicked off the song? They recalled the headlong attack of Elvis Costello's Attractions. The guitar? A Strat—sinewy, raw, and direct. And as for the vocalist, he didn't bellow like Bob Dylan or Joe Strummer; he never snarled like John Lydon (a.k.a. Johnny Rotten). Instead, he intoned. Like Deborah Harry (Blondie's "Rapture") and Tina Weymouth (Tom Tom Club's "Wordy Rappinghood"), this musician was clearly following a trail blazed by hip hop. His song yoked rock's conventional band format to rap's collage aesthetic.

But the kid on the way to his guitar lesson had young ears. He heard little history clinging to the music that filled his family's car. "You know," Nathaniel declared, and it was already evident that he intended to congratulate himself as much as issue a judgment, "this music's pretty cool. But there are people at my school—these guys who think they're punks—they wouldn't listen to it. It's got keyboards." By which Nat and his classmates literally meant sounds associated with traditional keyboard instruments. They had no idea that distinguishing keyboards from other instruments had become tantamount to separating dancer from dance. They only knew that keybs sucked. Or they were for girls. Or pussies. The tautologies—like the stakes—stacked up like chords. The boys liked their music hard. Presumably, it made them feel that way too.

The aesthetic endorsed by Nat's friends is structured by the following opposition:

ROCK	POP
guitars	keyboards
heart	head
passion	detachment
frontier	civilization
straightforward	ironic
faith	skepticism
integrity	compromise
experience	knowledge
rural	urban
masculine	feminine
spontaneity	calculation
genuine	artificial

raw	cooked
rough	polished
America	Europe
straight	gay
vigorous	effete

Both rock and pop hard-liners not only accept this division as "natural"—as an accurate picture of the way music *really* is—they dislike, actually fear, an aesthetic that signifies values they oppose. "There are two crowds," explains Mick Jones. "One's a dance crowd. They need to be shown that guitars can be cool. Then, there's the rock crowd. They need to know not to be afraid of the dance scene."

■

Readings

D. Joseph Carducci. 1990. *Rock and the Pop Narcotic: Testament for the Electric Church*. Chicago: Redoubt.

Robert Christgau. 1991. "Rock Music Is Here to Stay." *Village Voice*, 18 June, 69.

Quem quaeritis—An antiphonal chant of the tenth-century Christian church, reenacting the visit of the three Marys to Christ's tomb on Easter morning. Medieval drama arose from such ceremonial embellishments of the liturgy. [From the Vulgate, "*Quem quaeritis in sepulchro?*" ("Whom do you seek in the sepulchre?"): the question asked by the angel in Matthew's account of the resurrection.]

The *Quem quaeritis* does not mime biblical dialogue. Rather, it articulates spiritual longing as echo, dramatizing the hope of resurrection: *divine comedy*. Centuries later, this echo returns transformed. In 1606, resonating emotional needs that lead to *tragedy*, King Lear quizzes his daughters: "Which of you shall we say doth love us most?" (I, i, 51). Finally, in 1956, longing expressed in the *Quem quaeritis* takes the form of *fairy tale*, one whose subject is physical desire. Bo Diddley sings, "Who do"—make that "Hoodoo"—"you love?"

■

Readings

David Bevington. 1975. *Medieval Drama*. Boston: Houghton Mifflin.

Frederick Buechner. 1977. *Telling the Truth: The Gospel as Tragedy, Comedy, and Fairy Tale*. San Francisco: Harper and Row.

Ann Powers. 1995. "Houses of the Holy." In *Rock She Wrote*, ed. Evelyn McDonnell and Ann Powers, pp. 326–29. New York: Delta.

PHIL SPECTOR

Back to
MONO
(1958-1969)

CD NUMBER ONE

reverb—Echo produced electronically; a device used to simulate echo.

Chicken or egg? Aristotle or Plato? Marx or Hegel? Did the acoustic properties of medieval cathedrals give rise to antiphonal chanting, or were cathedrals erected in order to manufacture the echoes and reverberations that suggest transcendence? Reverb sonically implies the size and shape of imaginary places that hold music. Or rather, it prompts listeners to *fix* sounds in space (exterior or, in the case of psychedelia, interior). Sampling, by contrast, multiplies sonic worlds where music can be transported. It cues listeners to *take* sounds to other places and other times. Thus, by analogy, sampling is to reverb as montage is to *mise en scène* as Sergei Eisenstein is to André Bazin. But beware. As Godard wrote, "Only at peril can one be separated from the other. One might just as well try to separate the rhythm from a melody" (39).

■

Reading

Jean-Luc Godard. 1986. *Godard on Godard*. Trans. and ed. Tom Milne. New York: Da Capo.

Recordings—A case of space: reverberation, echo, and delay

1. Bo Diddley, "Bo Diddley," *The Chess Box* (Chess).
2. Various, *Mystery Train Original Soundtrack Recording* (RCA Victor).
3. The O'Jays, "For the Love of Money," on *Soul Hits of the '70s: Didn't It Blow Your Mind, Vol. 14* (Rhino).
4. Ennio Morricone, *The Ennio Morricone Anthology: A Fistful of Film Music* (RCA).
5. Ry Cooder, *Music by Ry Cooder* (Warner Bros.).
6. Pauline Oliveros, Stuart Dempster, and Panaiotis, *Deep Listening* (New Albion).
7. Ralph Towner, *Solstice* (ECM).
8. Various, *Jenny McCarthy's Surfin' Safari* (I.D.).
9. Sun Ra and His Myth Science Arkestra, "Moon Dance," *Cosmic Tones for Mental Therapy/Art Forms of Dimensions Tomorrow* (Evidence).
10. Phil Spector, *Back to Mono (1958–1969)* (Phil Spector/Abkco).

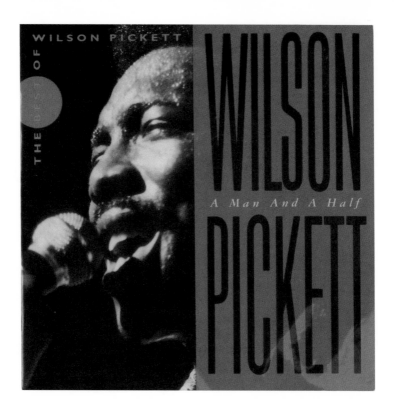

soul music—A commodified, secularized version of an African-American ecstatic tradition (gospel music) that signified the genuine outpouring of passionate feeling.

By the mid-1960s, after Sam Cooke and Ray Charles had delineated its vocabulary and form, soul music was basically a tale of two cities: Memphis and Detroit. Jim Stewart and Estelle Axton (founders of Memphis's Stax/Volt) and Berry Gordy, Jr. (founder of Detroit's Motown) were true beneficiaries of Civil Rights Era America. They understood—or, better, they intuited—that rising black pride and an increasing white fascination with blackness, which took the twin form of envy and remorse, implied not only a change in consciousness, but an emerging market.

Stax/Volt and Motown capitalized on this market. Both companies, using vastly different strategies, delivered musical goods that consumers regarded as authentic: byproducts of passion and conviction, not of calculation and commerce. Stax/Volt followed an agricultural model, producing rough-hewn music that sounded fresh and organic. (It's no accident that Otis Redding, Stax's greatest star, was also the most countrified of all major soul singers.) As a company, it was organized like a cooperative farm (or, perhaps more generously, like an independent film company). By all accounts, Redding, Isaac Hayes, Dave Porter, Booker T. Jones, Steve Cropper, Carla and Rufus Thomas, William Bell, and other laborers understood (1) that they had specific roles to play in the making of musical products but (2) that these roles were open-ended and fluid. On the other hand, Motown followed an industrial model predicated on strict divisions of labor. Patterned after an automobile assembly line (Gordy had once worked at Ford), and thus recalling the Hollywood studio system, it produced quality, reliable, and, every once in awhile, absolutely original products. Motown was a "hit factory," providing the pop audience with pop tunes sung by nonpop voices. It became the most successful black-owned business in U.S. history.

■

Readings

Rob Bowman. 1997. *Soulsville, U.S.A.: The Story of Stax Records*. New York: Schirmer.

Charlie Gillett. 1974. *Making Tracks: Atlantic Records and the Growth of a Multi-Billion-Dollar Industry*. New York: E. P. Dutton.

Roddy Doyle. 1987. *The Commitments*. New York: Vintage.

Gerald Early. 1991. "One Nation under a Groove." *New Republic*, 15–22 July, 30+.

Ian Frazier. 1986. "The Bloomsbury Group Live at the Apollo." In *Dating Your Mom*. New York: Penguin.

Peter Guralnick. 1992. "Soul." In *The Rolling Stone Illustrated History of Rock & Roll*, ed. Anthony DeCurtis and James Henke, pp. 260–65. New York: Random House.

———. 1986. *Sweet Soul Music: Rhythm and Blues and the Southern Dream of Freedom*. New York: Harper and Row.

J. Randy Taraborrelli. 1986. *Motown: Hot Wax, City Cool and Solid Gold*. New York: Dolphin Doubleday.

Daniel Wolff. 1995. *You Send Me: The Life and Times of Sam Cooke*. New York: William Morrow.

Recordings—The seven titles that complete this list are intended to supplement the three box sets that top it.

1. Various, *Beg, Scream & Shout* (Rhino).
2. Various, *Hitsville USA: The Motown Singles Collection (1959–1971)* (Motown).
3. Various, *The Complete Stax/Volt Singles: 1959–1968* (Atlantic).
4. Aretha Franklin, *Queen of Soul: The Atlantic Recordings* (Rhino/Atlantic).
5. Otis Redding, *The Definitive Otis Redding* (Rhino/Atlantic).
6. Ray Charles, *Genius & Soul—The 50th Anniversary Collection* (Rhino).
7. Sam Cooke, *The Man and His Music* (RCA).
8. Al Green, *Anthology* (The Right Stuff).
9. James Carr, *The Essential James Carr* (Razor & Tie).
10. The Impressions, *Definitive Impressions* (Kent/Import).

E v a n   L u r i e

SELLING WATER
BY THE SIDE
OF THE RIVER

tarantella—A lively courtship dance, native to southern Italy and typically in 6/8 time.

During the swing era, the cohabitation of entomology and choreography (insects and dancing) yielded the fast twist-and-twirl of the *jitterbug*; in the rock era, it found full expression as *Beatlemania*. Well before the twentieth century, however, beats and bugs were thoroughly conflated. Legend has it that, from the fifteenth to the seventeenth century, tarantulas (which are technically not insects, but arachnids) set upon the hapless citizens of Taranto (a port city in southeastern Italy) and gave them tarantism, a nervous disorder characterized by an irresistible urge to dance. The cure—the *tarantella*—suggests that dance is a form of socio-homeopathy, a means of culture healing itself. When life gives people ants in their pants, they need to dance.

■

Recordings—"When they play the tarantella . . ."

Al Caiola, "Sicilian Tarantella," *Italian Guitars* (Bainbridge).

Charlie Haden Quartet West, "Tarantella +," *In Angel City* (Verve).

Mario Lanza, "Tarantella," *Double Feature, Vol. I: For the First Time/That Midnight Kiss* (RCA Victor).

The Lounge Lizards, "Tarantella," *Voice of Chunk* (Lagarto).

Evan Lurie, "Tarantella," *Selling Water by the Side of the River* (Island).

Mario Salvi, "Tarantella di Montemarano," *Planet Squeezebox: Accordion Music from Around the World* (Ellipsis Arts).

Turtle Island String Quartet, "Texas Tarantella," *Spider Dreams* (Windham Hill).

Squirrel Nut Zippers, "La Grippe," *The Inevitable Squirrel Nut Zippers* (Mammoth).

ukulele—A small, four-stringed Hawaiian guitar.
[From Hawaiian, *uku*, "flea" + *lele*, "jumping."]

In 1879, a boat loaded with people from the Portuguese island of Madeira arrived in Hawaii. If legend can be trusted, they immediately connected with the already Westernized indigenes through music played on a four-stringed guitar called a *braguinha* (or *machete de braga*). In opening a cultural space where Portuguese and Polynesians could communicate, this instrument functioned as a sort of ambassador. For example, it elicited special affection from King David Kalakaua and Queen Lili'uokalani. Put linguistically, the *braguinha* created a type of musical pidgin language (confirming the widely held notion that music is a universal language). By the turn of the century, this pidgin had transformed into creole; the *braguinha* had become the ukulele, an index of all things Hawaiian.

Reading

Jim Beloff. 1997. *The Ukulele: A Visual History*. San Francisco: Miller Freeman. [Written by the associate publisher of *Billboard Magazine*, this coffee-table book concludes with a list of resources on uke history, players, and manufacturers.]

The Passinge Mesures
WILLIAM BYRD
James Nicolson, *Double Virginal & Organ*

Ti-225

virginal—An oblong, portable harpsichord popular in the sixteenth and seventeenth centuries; its strings run parallel to the keyboard. Though its origin is uncertain, the name undoubtedly reinforced European associations of music with femininity.

Two boxes figure prominently in Vermeer's masterpiece, *The Music Lesson*. One, a beautifully decorated virginal, rests on a table. Though clearly visible, it is silent. Its effects remain forever unregistered: latent. The other box—a camera obscura sitting outside the painting's frame—is invisible, but its effects are manifest: fixed (and certainly manipulated) by the painter. Is Vermeer's work a comment on the superiority of painting to music? A gorgeous boast? Or is it a wish committed to canvas? Perhaps Vermeer longs for a technology as adequate to sound as paint is to image. He wants records. He wants movies.

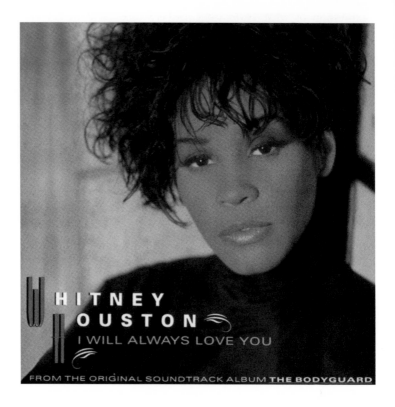

Whitney Houston syndrome—

Common term for melismania, an obsessive compulsive disorder characterized by multiplying the notes sung to every syllable of text; melisma taken to excess.

When the shared values of a culture dissipate—when, as Marx put it, "all that's solid melts into air"—empassioned commitment comes to feel absolutely arbitrary if not positively absurd. WH syndrome—melismania—is both a symptom of and a response to this condition (often labeled "postmodernism"). It seeks to manufacture authenticity—to signify belief in the face of unbelief—through intense virtuosity; in the process, however, it creates rampant "affective inflation" that subverts its own efforts. Earnestness that self-reflexively points to earnestness, the grand gesture calculated to denote artistic sincerity (r&b) or divine majesty (gospel), melismania is a particularly audible

expression of what Lawrence Grossberg calls "sentimental inau-
thenticity." Among Caucasians, it indicates *boltonism*.

■

Readings

Nelson George. 1988. *The Death of Rhythm and Blues*. New York: E. P. Dutton.
Bill Griffith. 1985. *Are We Having Fun Yet?* New York: E. P. Dutton.
Lawrence Grossberg. 1992. *We Gotta Get out of This Place: Popular Conserva-
    tism and Postmodern Culture*. New York: Routledge.

X—Abbreviation for Christ, to Christians the incarnation of God.

When John Lennon declared that the Beatles were more popular than Jesus, what's the chance he really meant—in Bible Code—that they were more popular than Elvis? In both Hebrew and the language of rock 'n' roll, *El* means "God." Lennon, however, couldn't bring himself to say what he meant. Why? It would have been sacrilegious. Remember, it was Lennon who said, "Before Elvis, there was nothing." (And didn't he release a greatest hits album called *Shaved Fish*, and isn't the title "ICHTHUS," Greek for "fish," derived from an acrostic referring to Jesus Christ, Son of God, Savior?)

Young, Neil—To rock music what Helen of Troy is to beauty.

Although Young boasts an immediately recognizable style—he's an innovator much imitated—he seems equally a creation of rock, the incarnation of its spirit. Put less metaphysically, all the codes of rock converge in Young's persona. Or do they emanate—"burn out"—from him? It's hard to tell. Were rock to disappear, Young gives the impression of being capable of reinventing it and, what's more, of wanting to. That's a phrase lifted from Jean-Luc Godard (43). One lifted from Samuel Johnson yields, "A man who's tired of Young, sir, is tired of rock." Which means, Young is hypostatic of the whole of rock's normalized discourse. Anyone who wants to lay it bare has to take him on.

Readings

Roland Barthes. 1974. *S/Z: An Essay*. Trans. Richard Miller. New York: Hill and Wang. [See especially pp. 33–34.]

Simon Frith. 1988. "The Real Thing—Bruce Springsteen." In *Music for Pleasure: Essays in the Sociology of Pop*, pp. 94–101. New York: Routledge. [This essay could be used as a model for analyzing Neil Young.]

Jean-Luc Godard. 1986. *Godard on Godard*. Trans. and ed. Tom Milne. New York: Da Capo.

Barry Hansen. 1992. "Neil Young." In *The Rolling Stone Illustrated History of Rock & Roll*, ed. Anthony DeCurtis and James Henke, pp. 324–31. New York: Random House.

Sylvie Simmons. 1997. "'Instant Feed-Back!'" *Mojo*, July, 76–96.

Recordings—Including Neil Young's work with Buffalo Springfield—but ignoring his stint with Crosby, Stills, and Nash—a Young library should include, in order, the following: *Decade, Rust Never Sleeps, Tonight's the Night, Ragged Glory, After the Gold Rush, Comes a Time, Freedom, Mirror Ball, Zuma,* and *Sleeps with Angels.* All titles are issued by Reprise Records.

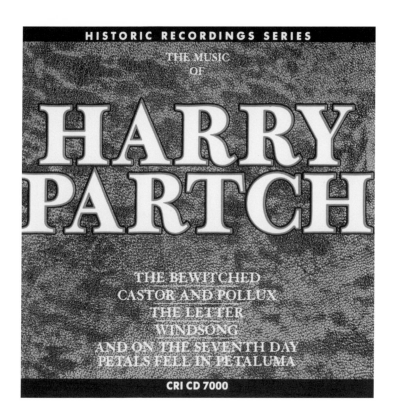

zymo-xyl—A percussion instrument invented by American composer Harry Partch (1901–1974); it consists of two rows of empty liquor and wine bottles stacked upside down, a row of oak blocks graduated in length, two Ford hubcaps, and an aluminum kettle top. [From the Greek *zymo*, denoting fermentation, and *xyl*, denoting wood.]

"The zymo-xyl," says Partch on a record introducing his instruments, "might be called an exercise in hither-and-thither aesthesia" (*The Instruments of Harry Partch*, Columbia). "I suppose that means a chance putting together of elements that came out fortuitously well," speculates Danlee Mitchell, an associate of Partch and a champion of his microtonal music. Dean Drummond—caretaker of the Partch instruments—calls the zymo-xyl "a sort of piccolo of the percussion section. It plays high and brittle as opposed to the more mellow marimbas, like the diamond and the bass marimba." The zymo-xyl was first used in a study piece for *Delusion of the Fury*, titled *And on the Seventh Day*.

■

Readings

Kyle Gann. 1996. "Composing the Lingo: Harry Partch, American Inventor." *Village Voice*, 7 May, 66, 68.

Thomas McGeary. 1991. *The Music of Harry Partch: A Descriptive Catalog.* Brooklyn: Institute for Studies in American Music.

Eugene Paul. N.d. Liner notes to *Harry Partch/Delusion of the Fury: A Ritual of Dream and Delusion* (Columbia).

Partch, Harry. 1991. *Bitter Music: Collected Journals, Essays, Introductions, and Librettos.* Urbana: University of Illinois Press.

———. 1974. *Genesis of a Music: An Account of a Creative Work, Its Roots and Its Fulfillments.* 2d ed. New York: Da Capo.

Question to Danlee Mitchell and Dean Drummond (April 1997)

Did Partch instruct you regarding how he wanted the zymo-xyl played?

DANLEE MITCHELL: What you've got to do with all of his instruments is learn the notation for that specific instrument. That's the problem. Every one has a different notation for reading. His music is what I would call traditional, real-time, nonchance music. It would be the same performance after performance after performance, except for subtle things like dynamics and tempo and whatnot. But it's real-time, Western, conceived music, as opposed to chance music like John Cage's. But each instrument has a different notation, and the zymo-xyl does have some liquor bottles on it. So if there's any instruction I remember, it's "Don't break the liquor bottles!"

DEAN DRUMMOND: I never played the zymo-xyl, so I don't think that I was ever instructed on playing it. Although for someone who plays Partch's other instruments, it's pretty self-explanatory. He always wanted people to play extremely exuberantly and dramatically. He was concerned, not only with the sound they made, but with what they looked like while playing.

volume
two

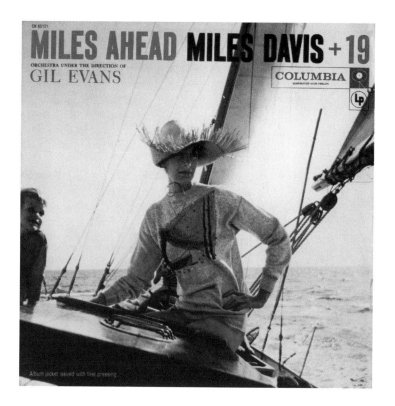

CX 65121

MILES AHEAD MILES DAVIS + 19

ORCHESTRA UNDER THE DIRECTION OF
GIL EVANS

COLUMBIA

Album jacket issued with first pressing

album—A group of musical pieces presented on one or more discs or tapes. [Literally "blank tablet," from the Latin *albus*, "white."]

While records are material objects, "albums" are concepts; they depend on the selection and arrangement of music. Orrin Keepnews, the record producer who worked with Thelonious Monk, Bill Evans, Cannonball Adderley, and Wes Montgomery, says, "I've always held that the first time somebody goes into the studio, he's the concept. You're presenting somebody who hasn't been presented before. So it's a nice idea to get in as many different aspects of his artistry as you possibly can. I do, however, think it is reasonably necessary—not always, but frequently so—that there be some connective thread, some reason why separate performances are put together on the same disc. For the most part, there needs to be a concept. The exceptions to this come about when the artist is enjoying some period of vast popularity, and it becomes possible to just issue the next album by so-and-so: sound the horn and attract crowds of people."

■

Forum (Summer 1994)

Before the advent of rock 'n' roll, it's fair to say that jazz was to pop as Lumière was to Méliès, which is to say, as documentary is to spectacle. Rock 'n' roll is research in the form of spectacle (see Godard on Godard, *181). So here's a question: Did* Sgt. Pepper's Lonely Hearts Club Band *affect jazz production?*

TEO MACERO: It didn't influence me. I always thought we were far ahead of the Beatles. We did experimental things back in the fifties. With Miles Davis, we used to use two or three different microphones, and when we came to the age of eight-tracks and so forth, we had a chance to pick up different sounds. We used to use all kinds of filters and reverb machines to give him the right amount of echo. If the echo didn't please me, we would put it through another monaural machine, play it back at half the speed. We used to do all kinds of experimental things in the studios that nobody was doing. That's why the monaural records—even the records that you hear today—sound so good. They were mixed right then and there, properly.

JOEL DORN: I didn't catch the Beatles at the beginning. I caught them in the middle. At the beginning, they looked like stupid white shit— Frankie Avalon. I really didn't get it. I was at Atlantic Studios once while I was still a disk jockey. The Beatles were still corny to me. But then in that *Rubber Soul* period, King Curtis really turned me on to them. When I saw what was happening, I went berserk. I became like a Beatles junkie. That was really it: Lieber and Stoller, Spector, and the Beatles with George Martin. That was about it. I went from being some guy that wanted to make pop records to a fucking lunatic.

HAL WILLNER: For me, some other things are more influential: records that inspired *Sgt. Pepper*. *Absolutely Free* meant a little more to me, and as an adult, I probably followed the Velvet Underground more and how that stuff came out of Varèse and out of *A Love Supreme* and *Sketches of Spain*. Those are amazing concept records. That came from classical music. Stravinsky and Charles Ives did very conceptual things.

MICHAEL CUSCUNA: It made me take more drugs for a little while. For some reason I was quite taken by the *White Album*, but *Sgt. Pepper's*—the idea of album as a concept—didn't seem to me that revolutionary. *Surrealistic Pillow*, which was the first album that really made me think of rock 'n' roll as not a top-40 situation, it had that effect on me.

the feelies

alternative—Any cultural phenomenon perceived as existing apart from—alongside or opposed to—
the mainstream. Altrock or alternarock refers to a variety
of post-punk popular musics.

Alternative is not a musical genre with identifiable characteristics
(any more than its Other: mainstream, corporate, classic rock).
Rather, it is a catch-all designation for any and all Generation X attempts to manage Baby Boomer hegemony. It is a practice with a history. Like all counterdiscourses before it, alternative inflates the
power of its antagonist and, consequently, situates itself as different, if
not grotesque and besieged. It exists in a steady state of nervousness,
anxious that cooptation is imminent—always already happening.

■

Readings

Jim Collins. 1989. *Uncommon Cultures: Popular Culture and Post-Modernism*. New York: Routledge.

Chuck Eddy. 1997. *The Accidental Evolution of Rock 'n' Roll: A Misguided Tour through Popular Music*. New York: Da Capo.

Richard Terdiman. 1985. *Discourse/CounterDiscourse: The Theory and Practice of Symbolic Resistance in Nineteenth-Century France*. Ithaca, N.Y.: Cornell University Press.

Eric Weisbard with Craig Marks. 1995. *Spin Alternative Record Guide*. New York: Vintage.

Nathaniel Wice and Steven Daly. 1995. *Alt.culture: An A-to-Z Guide to the '90s—Underground, Online, and Over-the-Counter*, New York: Harper-Perennial.

Recordings—Top Ten Altrock Picks (in Alphabetical Order)

Ambitious Lovers, *Greed* (Virgin).

Basehead, *Play With Toys* (Imago).

The Feelies, *Crazy Rhythms* (A&M).

Nirvana, *Nevermind* (DGC).

New Order, *Substance* (Qwest).

Sinéad O'Connor, *I Do Not Want What I Haven't Got* (Ensign/Chrysalis).

Prefab Sprout, *Two Wheels Good* (Epic).

R.E.M., *Murmur* (I.R.S.).

The Replacements, *Let It Be* (Twin/Tone).

The Vulgar Boatmen, *You and Your Sister* (Record Collect).

Interview—From an afternoon spent with the Squirrel Nut Zippers (July 1997)

TOM MAXWELL: After mixing *Hot* [Mammoth], Ken, Chris, and I were listening to so-called alternative stations all the way home—from New Orleans to Chapel Hill. They're so similar in programming as to be astounding, especially when they have the balls to call themselves alternative. What a joke! We said to ourselves, "Well, they'll never play it. But if they did, it might really break. It's so against the grain." The very things that made it difficult for us to break into a national market—our production values, the songs, the instruments, and the different sounds—became our allies. They ended up working for us.

I have hopes and fears about whatever this thing is we're talking about. It's all going to be speculative. The thing that I'm obviously most concerned about is the band, how it goes. That's the priority. One of two things can happen as a result of our newfound success. One, we can strike a blow for diversity. A lot of good bands that don't necessarily bear that much resemblance to us can, perhaps, have an opportunity to be heard. Or, we're going to get a bunch of crap. It's going to be a fad. You're going to be seeing Burger King commercials with a muted trumpet in it, and that's too bad. Maybe both things will happen. What I would prefer to happen is . . .

KATHERINE WHALEN: Both, undoubtedly, will happen. One follows the other.

JIM MATHUS: You can't stay mainstream and underground at the same time.

MAXWELL: I know. But instead of every band coming out, for example, being some sort of nuance or shading of Nirvana, which was essentially a nuance or shading of Led Zeppelin, you might be able to get something else.

MATHUS: You might get sold-out shows at the Louisiana Club to see Al Casey.

MAXWELL: That would also be a beautiful thing. You can apply that observation to something I've been thinking about, which is the illusion of progress, the idea that everything keeps improving. As a musician, I know that's not the case at all. I read Stephen Jay Gould's essays on natural history. A lot of what he talks about in terms of biological evolution has parallels in music and culture. Although you can't draw those lines all the time, I've learned a lot from him about ways of thinking. Evolution is a bush, not a ladder. It's not point A to point B to point C. It's all kinds of things. Like Gould says, the more diversity you have, the better your chance of excellence.

KEN MOSHER: Definitely. You listen to the radio today and that's the problem: It smells stale.

frank morgan

you must believe in spring

bebop chess—An anti-strategy for playing chess that, as a parable, explains bebop; described by alto saxophonist Frank Morgan (February 1989).

I was in one of the prisons in California. I'm trying to think of the grand title they'd put on this one. Oh yeah, the California Rehabilitation Center. There was a senior counselor there who was a rated chess master.

This particular prison was for dope fiends, or for anybody who wanted to say, "I killed my sister 'cause I'm a junkie." They committed people there with a different type of commitment than the prison. You weren't called an "inmate." You were called a "resident." It was a therapeutic community staffed by prison guards, you dig? Guys I used to see in the gun tower at San Quentin, when they opened this place, I looked up and they were counselors with suits and ties on.

They had "dormitories" instead of "cell blocks." They didn't have "cells"; they had "beds."

Anyway, this guy would play sixty simultaneous games. I played every day in prison, played chess and practiced. So I went to play him. And he would go to every board and explain, "I take the white men." (So that gives him the first move automatically.) "And while I'm going to the other boards, I'll expect you to have your move finished by the time I get back to you." And he defined all the rules. He went to everybody's board and gave them that same spiel.

When he got to me, I said, "Stop." I said, "That shit you're going to do—going to those other boards, making those classic moves, those textbook moves. That's not going to work here."

"What do you mean?"

"You're going to have to remember. Every time you get to this board I'm going to say, 'Hi,' and you're going to wait awhile before you make your move, 'cause you're going to have some shit that you're not familiar with. I'm not saying that it's greater than your game, but this is bebop chess. I understand you already have a 35 percent advantage because you have the first move. If you don't make any mistakes, if you make all the classic moves, and then I counter with all of the classic games, the worse you can do is get a draw. But that don't count here. You ain't going to get shit here—but some serious thought."

Every time he would get to my board, I would say, "Hi." I mean, I wasn't equal to him in stature, but I determined within myself, "Ain't no motherfucker in the world going to take me and fifteen other men and fit me into that mold. I'm not going to let it happen. I ain't worth shit as a bebopper if I can't . . ." But I knew, the greatest chess masters in the world, their whole thing is based on the moves that the other masters made. Nothing to do with an illogical move. They don't know how to respond to somebody who can't even play, doesn't play well.

He didn't beat me; I didn't beat him. What happened was, count time stops everything in the penitentiary. When it came time to go back for the noon count, it was just myself and the fellow who had brought me there—a Mexican chess player who was very, very good—was just the two of us and the master that were left. He had beat everybody else already, and he was saying, "We got to go up for count, you know." He looked at my friend's game board, and he said,

"You're going to lose this because I'm going to do this and then do that." And my friend is like, "O.K., I've lost."

I said, "Stop. Don't run that shit when you get here. You know it's not going to work—that standard shit. In other words, the best you're going to get here is a draw."

"No, I'm going to beat you."

I said, "You don't know what the fuck I'm going to do, and you know that. So how can you tell me what you're going to do when you don't know what I'm going to do? Who the fuck do you think you're talking to?"

So he said, "I'm a rated master."

I said, "Have you ever heard me play? I'll bet you don't play chess any better than I play saxophone. I'm just saying that that rated master shit don't mean shit, because this is saxophone. This is life. Chess is nothing but life. It's nothing but mathematics. Music is mathematics." I proved to him that I knew the validity of what bebop is. There is nothing any greater, because it is man at his best, using his fucking brain and his fucking senses, and his heart. Using all your beautiful God-given gifts to produce a product of and about you right now.

He said, "You're going to have to go to count."

I said, "You're our senior counselor. You could put me on the out count. You could pick up the phone and say, 'I have resident Morgan here. Put him on the out count. I have him right here.'"

He has authority to do that, but he wouldn't do it. So finally he agreed to take the draw. Incidentally, he helped to have me excluded from that institution, from that program. He said I was "dangerous."

The prison system is not designed to take you and slap your wrist and send you back out so that you will never do anything wrong in life. It is designed for you to come back and back and back, continue to be cannon fodder.

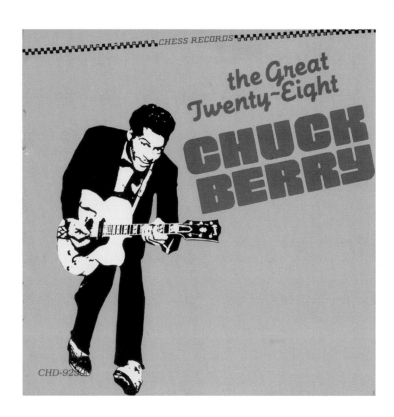

Carol—1. A song of celebration, sung especially at Christmas. 2. A dance craze of the Middle Ages.

Within the realm of rock 'n' roll, "Carol" denotes a song written by Chuck Berry and covered, to great effect, by the Rolling Stones. Its lyric begins, *"Oh, Carol, don't let him steal your heart away. / I'm gonna learn to dance if it takes me all night and day."* This opening couplet introduces a stanza (or verse) that goes:

> *Climb into my machine, so we can cruise on out.*
> *I know a swinging little joint where we can jump and shout.*
> *It's not too far back off the highway, not so long a ride.*
> *You park your car out in the open. You can walk inside.*
> *A little cutie takes your hat, and you can, "Thank her ma'am."*
> *Every time you make the scene, you find the joint is jammed.*

The couplet returns, followed by another stanza (*"If you want to hear some music, like the boys'll play"*). Finally, the couplet is sung twice—first straight, then varied—before the song fades out.

Too bad the dance crowd in twelfth- and thirteenth-century France never got a chance to hear "Carol" sung by Chuck Berry or Mick Jagger! They would have understood. And not just because troubadours and *trouveres* sanctified sex and, thereby, invented "courtly love." For nearly two centuries, the *carole* rated as the principal form of dance at court and popular festivities.

The mother of all dance crazes such as the tarantella, waltz, quadrille, jitterbug, twist, and macarena, the *carole* probably takes its name from the Latin *chorus*, which, in turn, derived from *choreia*, the Greek word for dance. (Saint Vitus' dance, for example, is now labeled Sydenham's chorea.) In an amazing passage from Guillaume de Lorris's thirteenth-century poem, the *Roman de la Rose*, the allegorical Lover is enjoined to *carole*. Very loosely translated, the lines go, *"If she'll dance, we can make it. Come on Queenie* [coronula = "little crown"]. *Let's shake it!"* A little more than a hundred years later (c. 1375), the anonymous author of *Sir Gawain and the Green Knight* associates "caroles newe" with "Krystmasse."

But how did the *carole*, a courtly dance-song, become the "carol," a song that celebrates Christmas? How did it migrate from France to England? The latter question is easy to answer. As John Stevens puts it in the *New Grove Dictionary*, "The English court tradition up to the end of the 14th century was French." Or, to employ the vocabulary of the time, the English and French had regular intercourse. For example, legend has it that, after Henry V defeated the French army at Agincourt (1415), soldiers on the battlefield sang a carol, *Deo gracias Anglia*, to commemorate the English victory. This nicely illustrates a distinguishing characteristic of carols: they can take up virtually any subject. There are political carols, festive or banquet carols, amorous carols, and, of course, religious carols. In fact, chances are that the popularity of the *carole* prompted Franciscans to view the dance-song as a way to further disseminate Christianity. According to Stevens, the Franciscans of England advocated a kind of guerrilla warfare whereby pop songs, emptied of secular content, were given back to God. Or maybe the Church just stamped its imprimatur on what was already happening. Recognizing a good thing, it encouraged carol singing—especially as the processional hymn, which was but wasn't part of the service "proper," and at Christmas, traditionally a time when liturgical conventions were most relaxed. In any event, the "tradition of sacred contrafacta" continues into the present. On her gospel album *Face to Face* (House of Blues), Cissy Houston sings "How Sweet It Is," by Motown's principal writers, Holland, Dozier, Holland. The object of the song's affection becomes Jesus. And in what might be a topper, Willie Neal Johnson and the Gospel Keynotes appropriate Rod Stewart's "Tonight's the Night" and turn it into a Pentecostal hymn!

Until the sixteenth century, carols weren't distinguished by subject matter, but rather by their form, which was fixed. They began with a "burden," a two-line couplet, which alternated with a four-line verse, rhyming *aaab*. Each line contained four stressed syllables (i.e., iambic tetrameter) like so:

I sing a song to my Lady.
Carol, who became my baby.

1. Into my machine, we cruised out.
To a joint, where we'd jump and shout.
Not a long ride, not off the route.
You park your car; you walk inside.

2. A little cutie takes your hat.
Then, the drums go, "Ratta tat tat."
Oh man, you dance like one fine cat!
Deo gratias, Carol looks fine.

And so on, and so on, and scoobie doobie doobie. During its golden age (c. 1350–1550), the carol tended toward, but wasn't limited to, espousing Christian precepts. It was written in a plain style. Often macaronic—meaning it combined English and other languages—the carol also employed stock phrases and traditional imagery. But its essence was the alternation of burden and verse. As time passed, the carol changed. It became increasingly diverse in form but more uniform in subject matter. Many carols—more than five hundred—have survived in manuscript form (e.g., the Fayrfax and Henry VIII MSS).

When Oliver Cromwell seized power in the mid-seventeenth century, the Commonwealth government declared Christmas a day of

Line Dance: Carol History at a Glance

1100–1200	The *carole* sweeps Western Europe
1415	*Deo gracias Anglia* (celebrates Henry V's victory at Agincourt)
1500	Fayrfax manuscript, songbook from the Tudor court
1534	Henry VIII and the British Parliament sever ties with Rome
1644	Christmas declared a day of fasting and penance
1661	*New Carols or the Merry Time of Christmas*
1833	William Sandys, *Christmas Carols Ancient and Modern*
1843	Charles Dickens, *A Christmas Carol*
1871	H. R. Bramley and John Stainer, *Christmas Carols New and Old*
1928	Percy Dearmer, Vaughan Williams, and Martin Shaw, *The Oxford Book of Carols*
1942	Benjamin Britten, *A Ceremony of Carols*
1958	Chuck Berry, "Carol"
1963	Phil Spector, *A Christmas Gift for You*
1965	Elizabeth Poston, *The Penguin Book of Christmas Carols*
1974	*The New Possibility: John Fahey's Guitar Soli Christmas Album*

fasting and penance. Puritan reformers across the pond followed suit. The carol—tainted by connections to Roman Catholicism—was suppressed in favor of the metrical psalm. Not surprisingly, the Restoration (1660) once again allowed the publication of carols. But the art carol was dead, and the popular carol had to rely on oral tradition and transmission by broadsheets.

Thankfully, the British folk revival of the late eighteenth century rekindled interest in the carol (recall, for example, Wordsworth's interest in folk ballads). Old carols were set to newly composed or adopted music, carols in other languages were translated into English, and new carols—or, more typically, Christmas hymns such as Charles Wesley's "Hark, the Herald Angels Sing"—were written. The modern age has brought us several composers—Britten and Vaughan Williams come to mind—skeptical of molding carols to prevailing tastes. Reacting against their Victorian forebears, they have called for a recovery of medieval and folk traditions: a new synthesis. And then there's Chuck Berry's "Carol." His song metaphorically transports us back to the roots of Christmas song and dance.

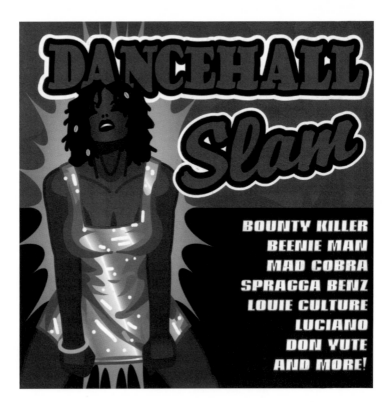

dancehall—Hi-tech reggae characterized by DJs rapping/singing hedonistic lyrics over electronic "riddims." Its emergence in the early 1980s coincided with (1) the death of Bob Marley and (2) the defeat of Michael Manley's socialist People's National Party and the corresponding victory of Edward Seaga's pro-Reagan Jamaican Labour Party.

The term "dancehall" was first applied to Lincoln "Sugar" Minott singing "live" over rhythm-track acetates he had produced at Youth Promotion (his "sound system"). Thus, one may regard dancehall as hip hop's kissing cousin. Formally, both musics exploit the cut 'n' mix aesthetic fostered by electronic culture. Thematically, they signal profound shifts in consciousness: earnestness gives way to cynicism; a concern with roots and culture gives way to an obsession with sex and money. Overly simple perhaps, but that's partly why Otis Redding and Bob Marley wore shirts, while Ice-T and Shabba Ranks bare their pecs.

■

Readings

Steve Barrow. 1997. *Rough Guide to Reggae*. London: Rough Guides.

Dick Hebdige. 1987. *Cut 'n' Mix: Culture, Identity and Caribbean Music*. London: Methuen.

Frank Owen. 1995. "In Praise of Slackness." *Village Voice*, 13 September, 63, 70.

EML—An early analog synthesizer manufactured in Vernon, Connecticut, by Electronic Music Laboratories.

Because the EML was designed to teach schoolchildren about electronic music, its features were basic. "It had to be very simple, and it had to be virtually indestructible," says Allen Ravenstine (formerly of Pere Ubu). Although the EML failed its pedagogical mission—to become a fixture in music classrooms—it managed to alter the landscape of rock 'n' roll when Ravenstine took up the instrument. His 1975 composition, "Terminal Drive" (excerpted on the Ubu box, *Datapanik in the Year Zero*), anticipates the 1990s' confluence of hiphop, dance, and ambient musics known as *electronica*. Ravenstine employed the synthesizer as a machine ("I used the keys as triggers"), not as a keyboard instrument.

Interview—Allen Ravenstine on playing the EML (June 1996)

Somebody saw all the stuff I had and said, "Why don't you get all of it in one box? It's called a synthesizer." At that time, there was a company in Vernon, Connecticut, called Electronic Music Laboratories. They had been contracted by the state government to build a synthesizer that could be used to teach schoolchildren. So it had to have certain properties. It had to be very simple, and it had to be virtually indestructible. It also was designed in such a way that, while it had various elements of a synthesizer in it (oscillators that made sine waves, triangle waves, and square waves; filters, high-pass and low-pass; and an enveloper to change timbre), all of these elements had to be in the box—the same box—but none of them should be connected internally. You had to take patch cords and connect each of these things. So if you wanted to run two oscillators in parallel or in series, you had to connect them that way. And then you had to run them into either the low-pass or the high-pass filter. Via patch cords, you could make the low-pass and the high-pass into a by-pass filter or a kind of reject filter, and then you could run it through an enveloper and do various things. There was a sampler in there, which, in those days, meant something completely different from what it means now. It would take a triangle wave and change it into a stepped triangle. In other words, it would pick segments. You could alter the speed of the sampling and the speed of the wave, obviously by pitch.

One of the synthesizers I bought has a serial number of one hundred and something. Whenever I had a question, I'd talk to the guy who built it. I was the first guy that ever tried to use these things in a rock 'n' roll environment. I never played the keyboard like a keyboard. I can't play a tune on a keyboard. I used the keys as triggers. I had come at this thing strictly from the standpoint of being able to see sound as color; initially, it was a visual thing. I was adding color and atmosphere, adding scenery to the music. I had some sense of the harmonic or the romantic environment for the piece to exist in, and I tried to enhance that.

I was aware that we never get to listen to music in a vacuum. There's the couple arguing next door, or the TV, or the dog outside, or jets coming over. All these things interfere with pure listening. And just as a soundtrack in a movie is often used to enhance the action, I think I was trying create environments in which something could be heard that wouldn't act as a distraction, or something that you wished would go away. It would act more as something that would make the statement more potent. It would enhance the mood with the right environment for the thing to exist in.

Feature Story—Pere Ubu

When conjuring the apocalyptic squall of Pere Ubu, keep this point in mind: The English Bible translates as "apocalypse" words ultimately derived from the Hebrew verb *gala*. Pere Ubu is to rock what Anselm Kiefer is to painting; both represent the big bang at ground zero. Which is one way of saying Pere Ubu sounds exactly like Cleveland in the mid-to-late 1970s. David Thomas, the band's founder and one of rock's great vocalists, explains, "Everything about Pere Ubu is totally devoted to the city that we lived in, which doesn't exist any more. It was totally devoted to a specific period of time, a specific group of people located in a specific location, and a specific culture. We're trapped in that moment. As a band, as an artistic force, we continue to live in what is now a ghost town. It doesn't matter that I live in London. The actual, physical location of Cleveland doesn't exist anymore. There's a place there now—you see on the maps—that says 'Cleveland.' But it's not where we live. We live somewhere else. We live in the true Cleveland. Plato would understand this."

As would Allen Ravenstine. To the incarnations of Pere Ubu documented on the five-disc *Datapanik in the Year Zero* (Geffen), he contributed a startling array of synthesized and concrete noises and distinguished himself as one of rock's greatest "nonmusicians." "The premise behind the band," Ravenstine says, "was that it didn't really make much difference whether or not members knew how to play an instrument, whether or not they were 'good' technically. What was important was their philosophical standpoint. The theory was that, if you put these people together in a room with their instruments, something interesting would come from it."

Basic "do-it-yourself" doctrine? Punk philosophy as article of faith? Hardly. Pere Ubu wasn't (and still isn't) a proto-punk outfit. It is, according to David Thomas, a folk band! "This confuses people," he allows. Maybe Thomas is contemplating the yelped vocals, the synth squall, and the chugging guitar-driven riffs that define Ubu's sound. "But," he adds with emphasis, "true rock is folk music, though not all that masquerades as rock music is folk. Much of it is hierarchical."

Thomas continues, "There are only two kinds of music in the world: hierarchical music, descended from the church, and folk music. They're opposite sorts of things, with opposite intentions and results. In a folk band, people come together with their various intentions, but they share some communal vision. Out of that soup is formed an outside entity that's the band's entity."

"I'm afraid I'm a rambler," says Thomas apologetically. "I can't help it." He knows, however, that abstraction propels Ubu—and grounds it in history, giving it a lineage. "Elvis," Thomas notes, "brought abstraction to the blues and country music, and that was rock music." (And it was good.) Ubu forms part of Elvis's lineage because it employs sound poetically. "We've never been arty people," Thomas declares. "We're pretentious, but we're not arty. Our aspirations are grandiose." He then draws a breath before delivering this manifesto: "We believe that rock music is a true artform. It's the voice of the culture. It's capable of human expression beyond the imagination of any previous generation of artists. The novel and cheesy two-dimensional painting falls by the wayside in comparison with the magnificent potential of rock music. Rock music has at its beck and call not only the usual musical stuff, which we never really cared very much about, harmony and melody and rhythm, but it also has unimaginable power and the ability to direct that power below the level of the conscious mind, directly to the heart and the poetic and visionary elements of each person. It's a serious artform, and it's a dangerous weapon. If people are licensed to drive cars, they should be licensed even more stringently to make rock music. So that's why we're pretentious. We're not arty because we don't fall about sighing deeply over the nonsensical scribblings of Rimbaud and a bunch of French nitwits from the nineteenth century." To which one can only reply, "Goodness, gracious, great balls of fire!"

The Story of Flamenco

HEMISPHERE

flamenco—1. A variety of intense, deep-throated song that developed in southern Spain (Andalusia). 2. The dances and guitar music devised to accompany *cante hondo (jondo)* or flamenco singing.

If gypsies, to cop a phrase Malcolm X coined to explain the Irish, are the niggers of Europe, then flamenco—*el cante* (song), *el baile* (dance) and *el toque* (guitar playing)—is the old-world analog of Delta blues. It resulted when tribes, migrating from homelands in northern India, passed through Egypt (picking up the moniker "gypsy," an alteration of "Egyptian") and, in the late fifteenth century, settled in southern Spain. Reviled and persecuted by the ruling class, these gypsies found respite and release in music. They reshaped the native folk songs of Andalusia according to their own aesthetic, which values rhythm, improvisation, and, above all, *duende* (ineffable soulfulness).

■

Readings

Derek Bailey. 1992. "Flamenco." In *Improvisation: Its Nature and Practice in Music*, pp. 12–18. New York: Da Capo.

Regina Elam. 1995. "Body and Soul: Flamenco Fever." *Village Voice*, 11 July, 33–35.

Isabel Fonseca. 1995. *Bury Me Standing: The Gypsies and Their Journey*. New York: Alfred A. Knopf.

Federico Garcia Lorca. 1961. *The Selected Poems of Federico Garcia Lorca*. New York: New Directions.

Videos

Carlos Saura. 1981. *Blood Wedding*.

———. 1990. *Ay, Carmela*.

———. 1987. *El Amor Brujo (Love, the Magician)*.

groove—A riff that becomes enjoyably redundant.

The riff versus chords opposition (a time versus space dialectic) that structured jazz during the first half of the twentieth century resolved itself in bebop, which required musicians to improvise over complex chord changes at breakneck tempos. In the second half of the century, the opposition structuring rock was grooves versus sonics. Resolution came in the wake of hip hop. Block-rocking beats über alles, drawing together rap, dance, funk, punk, and electronic music.

■

Recordings—Something resembling a dialectic

Riffs: Count Basie, *The Complete Decca Recordings* (Decca).
Chords: Coleman Hawkins, *A Retrospective, 1929–1963* (Bluebird).

Bebop: Various, *The Debut Records Story* (Debut) [includes selections from *Jazz at Massey Hall*, featuring Dizzy Gillespie, Charlie Parker, Bud Powell, Charles Mingus, and Max Roach].

Grooves: James Brown, *Star Time* (Polydor).

Sonics: Jimi Hendrix, *Are You Experienced?* (Experience Hendrix/MCA).

Beats: Public Enemy, *It Takes a Nation of Millions to Hold Us Back* (Def Jam) or DJ Shadow, *Endtroducing . . .* (Mo Wax/FFRR).

Feature Story—Willie Mitchell Recalls (August 1994)

"When I got Al Green," says record producer Willie Mitchell, "everybody else was hot. Stevie Wonder was hot. Marvin Gaye was hot. And I was searching for another sound to get away from all of that. I said, 'OK, I'm going to give him some jazz chords and see how he works with this.' I got him some Charlie Parker records."

In the saga of soul music, if Green plays Jesus meek 'n' mild (and plenty sexy), then the role of John the Baptist goes to Mitchell. He prepared the way for Green by engineering a sound that opened space for the singer's flights. "I tried to get a top on the music that was pleasant," says Mitchell of the sleek Ellingtonian chords that made his and Green's songs models of sophistication. "On the bottom was a thunderous thing," the inimitable Hi rhythm section of Memphis. And well above the fray soared Green. Mitchell had prompted him to stop emulating Otis Redding, to stop singing hard. "You've got to lighten up," he said. "You've got to float." The funny thing is, Green never came down.

harmolodics—A jazz style advanced by Ornette
Coleman and associates. It seeks to move beyond the lead/
rhythm opposition, which has structured all jazz improvisation since Louis Armstrong, by fostering free harmonic
exchange between all members of a group. [Combines
har(mony) + *mo*(vement) + (me)*lodic*.]

Harmolodics signals the deconstruction of jazz improvisation. Working from an insight—that wherever there is an opposition there is a
hierarchy—Ornette Coleman (wielding a white, plastic alto saxophone and fronting a quartet) recommended inverting, then aban-
doning, distinctions between lead and rhythm playing. (For all its
radical import, this doctrine—that everybody and nobody solo all of
the time—was redolent of the dogma that inspired Cubism: dispense

with the figure/ground distinctions that enabled Renaissance perspective.) In place of conventional improvisation, where players work off predetermined chord structures (or key signatures), harmolodics prescribes one's own signature as a means of opening up the tune of a composition. If bebop is physics, harmolodics is pataphysics.

∎

Readings

Francis Davis. 1985. "Ornette's Permanent Revolution." *Atlantic Monthly*, September, 99–102.

Jacques Derrida. 1984. *Signsponge*. Trans. Richard Rand. New York: Columbia University Press.

Gary Giddins. 1985. "The Egg in the Meatloaf" and "Harmolodic Hoedown." In *Rhythm-A-Ning: Jazz Tradition and Innovation in the '80s*. New York: Oxford University Press.

John Litweiler. 1992. *Ornette Coleman: A Harmolodic Life*. New York: William Morrow.

Ben Ratliff. 1997. "A Jazz Radical Collides with Western Tradition." *New York Times*, 6 July, sec. 2, pp. 28, 30.

R. J. Smith and Peter Watrous, eds. 1987. "The Art of the Improvisor: Ornette Coleman." *Village Voice Jazz Special*, June.

Greg Tate. 1992. "Knee Deep in Blood Ulmer" and "Change of the Century: Ornette Coleman." In *Flyboy in the Buttermilk: Essays on Contemporary America*. New York: Simon and Schuster.

Martin Williams. 1983. "Ornette Coleman: Innovation from the Source." In *The Jazz Tradition*, pp. 235–48. Oxford: Oxford University Press.

Recordings—A Harmolodic Top Ten (in Alphabetical Order)

Don Cherry, *Multikulti* (A&M).

Ornette Coleman, *In All Languages* (Harmolodic/Verve).

Jane Cortez & the Firespitters, *Taking the Blues Back Home* (Harmolodic/Verve).

Charlie Haden/Paul Motian, featuring Geri Allen, *Etudes* (Soul Note).

Ronald Shannon Jackson, *Red Warrior* (Axiom).

Pat Metheny/Ornette Coleman, *Song X* (Geffen).

Bern Nix Trio, *Alarms and Excursions* (New World/CounterCurrents).

Old and New Dreams, *Playing* (ECM).

Jamaaladeen Tacuma, *House of Bass: The Best of Jamaaladeen Tacuma* (Gramavision).

James Blood Ulmer, *Odyssey* (Columbia/Legacy).

Interview—Ornette Coleman (at the Ed Blackwell Festival, Atlanta, November 1987)

You've said that you have rapport with Ed Blackwell and Denardo, your son, like no other drummers.

That's true. I've been playing with Blackwell over twenty years. We used to play when I first went to Los Angeles. Blackwell plays the drums as if he's playing a wind instrument. Actually, he sounds more like a talking drum. He's speaking a certain language that I find is very valid in rhythm instruments.

Very seldom in rhythm instruments do you hear rhythm sounding like a language. I think that's a very old tradition, because the drums, in the beginning, used to be like the telephone—to carry the message. For some reason, Blackwell, Billy [Higgins], and Denardo, they have all—as long as they've played with me—they've always played like that. I never really relied upon them to keep time or rhythm for me. In fact, I always prefer musicians that play with me to play independent of myself but with me.

When you first met Blackwell in L.A., I assume you were working on certain musical problems. What were they?

In music you have something called sound, you have speed, you have timbre, you have harmonics, and you have—more or less—the resolutions. In most music, people that play what I call standard music, they only use one dimension, which means the note and the time. Whereas, like say I'm having this conversation with you now. I'm talking, but I'm thinking, feeling, smelling, and moving. Yet I'm concentrating on what you're saying. So that means there's more things going on in the body than just the present thing that the person's got you doing. Like you're interviewing me, although I'm doing more than just talking to you. And the same with you.

To me, human existence exists on a multiple level, not just on a two-dimensional level, not just having to be identified with what you do and what you say. Those things are the results of what people see and hear that you do. But the human beings themselves are living on a multiple level. That's how I have always wanted musicians to play with me: on a multiple level. I don't want them to follow me. I want them to follow themself but to be with me. Denardo and Billy and Blackwell has done that better than anyone I have met.

If music is like a telephone, then you're envisioning it as a network—
a party line.

Yeah, I would think that sound and light is probably the only elements that—regardless of what race you are or what your intellect is or what your handicap—those two things, you can use equally as good as anyone else. I mean, if you decided to go out today and get you an instrument and do whatever it is that you do, no one can tell you how you're going to do it but when you do it. So I think that those elements—light and sound—are beyond democratic. They're into the creative part of life.

When I was in the eighth grade, I did get an instrument—a clarinet.
Let's say that, when I was a few years older, I had gone to New York, and
sought you out for lessons. What would you have told me?

When someone asks me for a lesson, I usually ask them what is it that they want to know—philosophically. In other words, I think that there are lots of people that play music, but, basically, they have other things that are motivating them to play music. So, for instance, if you came to me, [I'd ask,] "Do you want to write? Do you want to improvise? Why do you want to play this instrument? What do you want to do?"

Instead of me giving them lots of beginner's lessons, I could show them the thing they want to do. Then I take them back to the rudiments of what it is to do that: "I want to solo." "I want to read." Whatever it is. Most teachers start a person in the first grade. Then you go to second grade. I never think that way. I think that the best way is to get the information immediately. If you say, "I want to play like you," I say, "Okay, do this." That's what I do.

When you first started playing, what were you after?

Actually, when I was in elementary school, I saw a saxophone. A band came to my school, and I saw this guy get up and play this solo. And I said, "Oh man, what is that? That must be fantastic!" And I asked my mother, "Could I have an instrument?" She said, "Well if you go out and save your money." So I went and got—I made me a shine box. I went out and started shining shoes, and I'd bring whatever I made. About three years later, my mother told me to look under the bed. I looked under the bed, and I took the horn and I played it as good as I played it last night—for the first time. That's the honest-to-gosh truth.

But I didn't know that you had to know music. I thought that everybody just *played* music.

You played the music that was in your head.

Exactly. And that's why I am pro-sound. No one has to learn to spell to talk, right? You see a little kid holding a conversation with an adult. He probably doesn't know the words he's saying, but he knows where to fit them to make what he's thinking logical to what you're saying. Music is the same way. If you desire to play it or write it, then you have to get more information. But the end result is that you play music. Even when you write it, someone's got to play it. So if you can play it and bypass all the rest of the things, you're still doing as great as someone that has spent forty years trying to find out how to do that. I'm really pro—human beings, pro—expression of everything.

Instead of having someone play out of a prescribed key signature, you recommend playing out of one's own signature.

I've written a theory book called *Harmolodics*. I found out that I could translate the clefs into one sound. For instance, if you were behind a closed door and I heard your voice, I would know it was you without seeing your face. But can you imagine if sound is that identifiable—more than your face? That's fantastic, right?

I found out that every person has their own movable C—*do*. When you put your sound or your idea into an arena mixed with other things—if what you're saying has a valid place—it's going to find its position in that total thing, and it's going to make that thing much better. You don't have to worry about being a number one, number two, or number three. Numbers don't have anything to do with placement. Numbers only have something to do with repetition.

That's what I was trying to say when we were talking about sound. I think that every person, whether they play music or don't play music, has a sound—their own sound, that thing that you're talking about. You can't destroy that. It's like energy. Your sound, your voice, means more to everyone that knows you than how you look tomorrow. You might grow a beard or shave your hair. They say, "I can't recognize you." But as soon as you talk, "Oh yeah, it is you!" It's the same thing. If it's that distinctive, then there must be something there. It's amazing that everyone has their own sound. Only actors are the ones that try to cover—when they imitate somebody—but then they're imitating that sound.

When you started playing, you weren't trying to imitate.

After I found out that I was playing music and that I'd have to learn how to read and write music, I started doing that about two years later. Finally, I said, "Oh, that means what I really want to do is to be a composer." But when I was coming up in Texas, there was segregation. There was no schools to go to. I taught myself how to read and how to start writing.

After I left Texas and went to California, I had a hard time getting anyone to play anything that I was writing, so I had to end up playing them myself. And that's how I ended up just being a saxophone player. Originally, I wanted to be a composer. I always tell people, "I think of myself as a composer."

You've gone through a lot of hardships. Still, it's amazing that your original quartet has played together off and on for over thirty years.

Yeah, that's a miracle. Actually, I have another record I made with them in 1976, but I've had such a bad experience with record companies, because I keep my head so much in music and not in business. The reason why I'm playing more now is Denardo's taking care of my business. I feel safer coming out. You know, I'm very inquisitive. It's not that I don't trust human beings. I don't know what they're thinking about. Just because someone says, "I like what you do" or something: They might like it today and tomorrow they might not. I've had that experience with record companies.

I've never had a relationship with a record executive. I always went to the record company by someone that liked my playing. Then they would get fired, and I'd be left with the record company. And then—because they got fired—the record company wouldn't do anything for me. Most of my relationships have been like that—with record companies. I've never had a legitimate business relationship with a company. I've always had a personal relationship with someone in the company. When they left, everything that they were doing had to be changed. And I'd be a part of that system. But Denardo has been really helpful by solving that for me.

Describe your musical and business relationship with Denardo.

Denardo made his first record with me when he was nine. It's called *The Empty Foxhole* [Blue Note], and he played beautifully. Denardo has never once taken on the image of being a drummer. I remember once, we got an interview, and he said, "Dad, these people are writing about me like I'm an adult. Don't they know I'm a kid?" I have never tried to encourage him to get a music image like other musicians have. We get along really well because of that, probably. I made a tour with him and Pat [Metheny] that was unbelievable.

What other projects are in the works?

I've written a theory book. Lots of guys always ask me about harmolodics. They don't know, and some don't believe that I know. The end result of music is you just play it. That's why I haven't been so anxious. But now, lots of people write and say, "I want to find out what you're doing." So I know that this book will enlighten them.

And Denardo, since he's been managing me, I've taken lots of his time from his own drums. But I recorded a piece that he wrote with Don [Cherry] and I about ten years ago.

When again did you go to New Orleans?

In the forties, '47, '49. I stayed down there with Melvin Lastie. I had a really good time in New Orleans, although I had some very tragic times in Baton Rouge. Some guys beat me up and threw my horn away. 'Cause I had a beard, then, and long hair like the Beatles. I didn't want to be bothered with people that were unkind. I thought that if I grew a beard they would leave me alone. Instead of leaving me alone, they thought I was gay or a freak or something. I guess they didn't like my appearance.

And you didn't meet Blackwell in New Orleans.

No, I met Melvin Lastie, a fantastic trumpet player. I met Blackwell in California.

Did he look you up?

We ran into each other from some mutual relationship with other musicians. But from the day I met him, we've always had a good rapport.

So many of the problems you faced have been manifestations of racism.

I think that's true of everybody, black or white or whatever. I never thought about colors or ethnical people. I've always thought about human beings. I remember when David Izenzon came in my house, played for me, and, the next day, he called me and said, "Ornette, I have a great idea. Let's start a David Izenzon/Ornette Coleman Trio." And I'd just met him one day. I said, "If you feel this way, come on over. I'll put you in my band." He stayed with me for a long time. And Scotty LaFaro. I've always thought about human beings. The graveyard has no color.

What are you most excited about now?

I've written lots of music that some people call "classical music." I call it "music that guys read." For the last three years, I've had those people very interested in my writing. Since I think of myself as a composer, I feel really good. I've had lots of guys call me up. I've gotten two or three commissions to write things. I've written lots of movie scores.

I don't really live like a musician myself. I think music is just something that I do, but I'd like to be doing lots of other things.

Such as?

I'd like to cure all kinds of illness. I think that there is something in life . . . No, let me put it better. I think that there are human beings that have never died. Whoever Adam and Eve was, Eve didn't come out of her mother's womb, and she certainly didn't give birth to Adam. Something caused them to exist. I think that that image is still in existence on earth.

All the things that human beings suffer from are how their environment treats them, and how the elements of their planet affects their mind and body—like radiation, cancer, and all. I think those things that are in food are all chemically disastrous when they are placed in the wrong contents where human beings are exposed to it.

I remember once I read a book on mental illness and there was a nurse that had gotten sick. Do you know what she died from? From worrying about the mental patients not being able to get their food. She became a mental patient. I really believe that we as human beings . . . the way we treat others is the only way the world is going to become perfect. If you decide you want to be treated good, and you treat someone else good, or you want to learn something, it's information. It's getting the right, good information.

Your music is beautiful, and you also dress beautifully. Explain your interest in clothes.

It seems to me that in the Western world, culture has something to do with appearance. A person that's out creating good stuff has got to appreciate someone when they take the time to have an appearance that goes with what they're doing. It just makes that person feel that what his work *is* going to be more valid. Who wants to see a guy standing in front, looking like a bum, doing something that bums don't do? This don't make sense.

It's not that I think that everything has to be uniform, but I think that having an appearance that someone can appreciate without you being bourgeois or a snob has got to make a person feel good in your company, especially if you are a nice person. I basically like to have an appearance, first, that is harmless, and, secondly, that is interesting to see. It makes people more comfortable, or it makes people more sensitive about themself in relationship to what it is they want to ask you.

When you write symphonic music, how do you approach it?

Same way as I play. You've got to realize. In the Western world, regardless of what color you are, what title the music is, it's all played by the same notes. When you see Horowitz sit down at the piano, he's still punching C. When you see Willie Nelson get his guitar, he's punching C. Me, I'm punching C. We're all playing the same notes.

It's just someone has labeled us as having a different label to do what you do. I find that labels are the worst thing in the world for artistic expression. It should be like, whatever your name is—you doing what you do—and not labels. It's not nice to put people in categories.

Feature Story—James Blood Ulmer describes his apprenticeship with Ornette Coleman (May 1993)

"See," says guitarist James Blood Ulmer, "I never played harmolodic music till I came to New York, or played any music that was free. When I came to New York, I was thirty-one years old, and I ain't never thought nobody could make no money playing free music. So I always played structured blues, rhythm playing, dance music, or something like that. And I abandoned it! When I came to New York, it was like . . . I just went totally another way. I fell so much in love with the harmolodic idea."

As Ulmer reminisces about those days of woodshedding, he laughs, "Coleman used to drill me, and I used to play for him so much! Like he used to get his horn and say, 'Play B-flat. Play E-flat. Gimme this. Gimme that.'

"I went through about six months of that. I said, 'Listen, I'm going to find out the way to play the guitar where when Coleman asks me to play E-flat or B-flat, I ain't got none.' I went to sleep, and I dreamt the whole tuning—the whole tuning the guitar that totally eliminated scales and chords. I woke up, took my guitar, and tuned the notes to all of the notes that I had dreamed about and started playing it. And it worked!

"I went to show that to Coleman. I sat down and said, 'Alright now, let's play.'

"He said, 'Play B-flat.'

"'I ain't got no B-flat! In fact, all my strings is tuned to one note. I have one note here with six strings tuned to the same sound.' And it got us music!"

Ulmer had successfully extended Coleman's theory and he had discovered his own voice. He clarifies: "Coleman's harmolodic and my harmolodic are totally different except for melody. He writes the symmetrics of harmolodics. I make sure to deal with the diatonics of harmolodics. I'm inside, and he's outside. (It's not inside—outside, but you know what I'm saying.) One is symmetrical; one is tonal. I'm in the key signature, and he's out of the key signature. I make sure to write all my stuff in a tone center, or inside of a tonal drone. By playing from a drone, I can play all twelve notes, instead of eight, and still sound like I'm in key. You can take the whole orchestra and set it inside of that drone—no matter what the notes are."

compact disc maxi-single

importance—A designation indicating significance.

"Importance" is one of the most important words used whenever popular music and musicians become an object of academic study. For example, consider the assertion that takes this form: "_____ is important." Prop it up with modifiers. Make it sound sufficiently provocative. As Simon Frith observes, a study of ideological effects will ensue, and it will follow predictable routes (11–20). More than twenty years ago, Roland Barthes wrote: "Denunciation, demystification (or demythification) has itself become discourse, stock of phrases, catechistic declaration" (166). Perhaps it's time to investigate the importance of "importance." What does it enable us to express? To repress? However predictable the results of such a study—arguments for "importance" allow us to steer a course be-

tween engagement with and aloofness from popular culture—they
might suggest ways to move on.

■

Readings

Roland Barthes. 1977. *Image-Music-Text*. Trans. Stephen Heath. New York:
Hill and Wang.

Jim Collins. 1989. *Uncommon Cultures: Popular Culture and Post-Modernism*.
New York: Routledge.

Simon Frith. 1996. *Performing Rites: On the Value of Popular Music*. Cambridge, Mass.: Harvard University Press.

improvise—To collapse or fold together performance and composition.

"The musician," writes Jacques Derrida in *Signsponge*, "cannot sign [his signature] within the text" (54). Music is not that sort of language; it doesn't provide that sort of space. The musician can, however, stamp his imprimatur upon a work, in the sense of encoding it with an inimitable style. (He can "speak" in his own voice.) Accomplishing that, however, raises a dilemma: What counts as idiomatic is not self-determined but a response to (and an acknowledgment of) an already-given context. What's held in common preordains what can be claimed as personal property. Hence, is a musician's style an act of signing or evidence of being signed? Improvisation is the exploration of plausible answers to this question.

Readings

Derek Bailey. 1992. *Improvisation: Its Nature and Practice in Music*. New York: Da Capo.

Jacques Derrida. 1984. *Signsponge*. Trans. Richard Rand. New York: Columbia University Press. [See pp. 52–56.]

Bill Evans. 1959. Liner notes to *Kind of Blue* (Columbia).

Sasha Frere-Jones. 1996. "Finger Food: The Incredible Improvisations and Interactions of Derek Bailey." *Village Voice*, 8 October, 53.

Marjorie Perloff. 1986. *The Futurist Moment: Avant-Garde, Avant Guerre, and the Language of Rupture*. Chicago: University of Chicago Press. [See pp. 101–2.]

David Sudnow. 1979. *Ways of the Hand: A Meditation between Two Keyboards*. New York: Penguin.

William Zinsser. 1984. *Willie and Dwike: An American Profile*. New York: Harper and Row.

Interview—Sonny Rollins, saxophone colossus (November 1989)

Like all modern jazz, your music emphasizes originality; it can be oblique and difficult. But your attitude towards the audience is different from the classic bebop stance. I regard you as a bridge, a mediation between modern and more popular styles of jazz. Is that a conscious program?

Not really. I like to reach an audience. Of course, everybody does. But I find that when I'm really playing myself, that's when I reach the audience. Trying to do anything else, I realized a long time ago, is counterproductive.

I'm playing mainly improvised, spontaneous music. Everything depends upon what has preceded it directly. If I'm in good musical form, I'm able to utilize my timing—which is very important. I also utilize my sixth senses, because a lot of things I do are intuitive. If I'm in good shape, then I usually find some way to communicate with the audience. If I'm struggling any particular night, then this can all be lost. This is what makes playing so much fun. You want to jump off the roof sometimes. It's not set; it's very problematical. It's so scientific and it's so artistic at the same time.

I just try to be in good shape, and other than that, the way I play—my natural talent, whatever you want to call it—that's what the people react to. It's not a conscious effort to get to people. I don't want to alienate people. No, of course not. But I like to think that it's something in the music beyond my comprehension that the people link with.

Have the founders of bebop been unfairly dismissed as ignoring audience concerns?

It may have been a bad rap, but I think that a lot of guys, as a reaction to the fact that they weren't being appreciated, sort of took it out on the cognoscenti that did go to see them and acted like they didn't like them either. I knew a lot of musicians who used to act like the audience wasn't there. But I think that was just a reaction of the times when guys were starving and they were playing all of this great music and nobody was picking up on it.

Has that changed?

It has changed, not completely. There's still part of that in the whole jazz thing, but I think that it's not the only way to go anymore.

Another tension at the heart of jazz is the one between performance and recording. On the one hand, jazz is unthinkable without recording technology. On the other hand, it opposes the concept of a definitive recording. Are you getting more comfortable with the studio, or do you still feel at odds with it?

I still feel at odds. I really do. And it's strange, because when I look back on my early career, when I first began playing and making records in the late forties, it didn't bother me so much. Of course, I was pretty young at the time, but still I wasn't critical, perhaps because I was usually on somebody else's date. But somewhere along the way I began to become very concerned about wanting to leave a really good recorded legacy, and I was very concerned about all of the notes coming out right. That has persisted up to the present time. I'm not very comfortable in the recording studio.

After playing for so many years, what keeps it fresh for you?

Well one thing is that I try to limit my appearances. I do that by turning down a lot of jobs. We turn down, I would say, about 50 percent of what we're offered. So I'm not out there on the road playing every night. That way I'm primed to play when I do appear. I avoid the habit of playing things that I know will work, playing the same songs, making it into a form. I want to think fresh. So that's one thing I do.

The other thing would be . . . well, when I'm not playing in public, you know, I practice all of the time, and I guess what's keeping it fresh for me is just the gift of music. I really enjoy playing. I can practice by myself and get a lot of kicks out of it, without having to have an audience, without having to have a band. I enjoy playing alone. I've always done that. I used to go out to the beach and play with the ocean, go into the parks or any kind of natural, secluded area.

Your musical influences are either obvious or a matter of public record. Tell me about nonmusical influences.

I have a sense of humor. That gives me a kick in life. I'm a big fan of these guys Bob and Ray. That informs my playing, I think. I used to play a lot of practical jokes when I was in school. They used to call me the Jester. I think my music is more *up* than introspective.

Your musical quotations are often funny. What kind of valence do you place on a citation, say one to "Pop Goes the Weasel"?

It's hard to say. I think about these things. I can put them in the middle of a very involved passage. What am I saying there? Maybe I'm saying that as deep as things are, there's still a light touch to it. But I'm not sure what I'm saying really.

Actually, in the context of a given melody, there's an art to placing quotes that really fit. But when I'm playing, say alone, and I put quotes in—I'm playing a cadenza—then it's very deep. I'm playing stream of consciousness.

I've heard that you're an avid reader. What's caught your attention lately?

Well, I hate to bring in this awful word—because everything I try to do when I get on the stage is antipolitics—but I follow politics. It's the down side of life, but I like to be aware of the down side of life. At the present time, I'm reading a book called *War and Peace in Central America*, and I've got a new book, *The End of Nature*, by this chap McKibben. I'm also into the environment in a big way. So those are things that are diversions for me. But the reason I say I'm antipolitical is because I think music should make people forget about politics—people fighting other people for positions. Music should be the antithesis of all these other things. So I read this stuff. Perhaps I do it so that I can feel more strongly about playing positively.

Music is a highly political scene, though: who gets played, who doesn't. Plus, there was certainly a time in your career when your music was regarded as explicitly political—the time of Freedom Suite, *for instance. Has that changed? Are you less political now?*

It's impossible not to be political in this society. I don't have to try to be political with my music anymore. When I walk on the stage and start playing, I'm political, because to some people it means something immediately. To others it means something else in a political way. I guess that I've changed only in that I don't advertise it as being political, wear it on my sleeve as much as I may have at one time. This is a different time, too.

What remains to be done within the jazz idiom, and, specifically, do you see jazz incorporating the many new rhythms represented by hip hop and world music?

I think that the possibility of incorporating different rhythms within jazz is there. It's always been there. But to be called jazz you have to have a player in the jazz tradition, who is then able to use some of these rhythms within jazz. It's got to be a mix where jazz is dominant. We can't surrender the "jazz sound," whatever that is, to other rhythms. Other than that, it'll be just two different forms of music.

At what point did you begin to concentrate on your sound?

It's such a big, basic part of playing. I don't care how much technique you have. But not just technique. I don't care how many ideas you have. Even if you have some brilliant jazz ideas, it's going to be difficult to get them across unless you have (A) a distinctive sound or

(B) a loud sound. These are musts. You must have either a powerful sound or a sound that's distinctive enough (which can grow out of ideas). A loud sound is something that you have to work on, but it's very important. As a player coming up, I ran into a lot of circumstances where you had to develop a loud sound. There were always guys who had big sounds in those days because a lot of times you had to play without microphones.

These things were impressed upon me coming up in the various sorts of rhythm & blues environments that I took the occasional gig in. Not every great player had a big sound, but most of them did. If they didn't have a big sound like Gene Ammons or somebody, then they had a very distinctive sound. You had to have one of the two to really make it. So I became aware of sound.

So would you say that Lester Young had a distinctive sound and not a big sound?

I might say that, yeah. Lester actually did have a big sound, but his sound was so distinctive that it would be very easy to categorize him as "distinctive sound" rather than as "big sound." But his sound was big enough to do whatever he had to do during the period of the big sound boys: the Websters and the Hawkins and the Don Byases and these guys—Chu Berry.

I can't fail to ask you about your solo on the Rolling Stones' song "Waiting for a Friend." How did that come about? Didn't Mick Jagger hear you at the Bottom Line? Were you well paid?

Yeah, I got my little five-figure check. It was really a case of . . . I was not familiar with their work. So I kind of approached it as sort of a challenge. I really wanted to see if I could do something that fit in with what they were doing. I had no idea that it would be successful or that it would really work.

In some ways it was the perfect pairing because there is a part of your playing that hearkens back to a very hard type of r&b.

My wife liked them. She thought that they were the best rock band around. She kind of convinced me: "Well, listen to them." I'd heard of them, of course. I just wasn't familiar with what they were doing. But, again, it was a challenge. I looked at it, "Let me see if I can . . . I know I can play me, but I want to play something that fits into what this is about." That's how I approached it.

Do you feel that you've found your voice, or do you regard yourself as still looking?

Let me put it this way, I'm not completely satisfied that I've found my sound. I hope that I haven't found my sound yet because I'm still searching for some other things which I hope will develop.

Can those things be expressed in words?

Colors, you know. Different colors. I don't want to be any more specific because I'll give away one of my secrets, what I'm searching for. Some of these young guys will be able to do it before I get to it.

It may be impossible to talk about music without recourse to the language of painting, and vice versa. Given your early interest in illustration, do you regard yourself as painting with sound?

That's possibly true. I used to do a lot of watercolor. I know Phil Woods refers to me as the Salvador Dali of the saxophone. I may be painting, because that was surely my first expressive art. Some of that is carried through in my horn playing.

You overcame a dependence on drugs a long time ago, and it seems to me that the men and women who lived through that experience have a lot to say about the current so-called war on drugs.

I overcame it because I had something else to put my time and energy into, which, in my case, was music. It's very important that people have interests that they can use to circumvent the attraction of drugs, because if not, you just have an empty life and drugs are going to be very appealing. So it's very important to have something that you like to do. There must also be treatment, education. Then it can be beaten.

The problem with drugs is that every culture has their drugs already. So how can we say we're fighting drugs? Every culture uses some kind of drug. It's something which is that much a part of man. I mean, it's kind of silly to think that we can keep people from getting high just by guarding the borders.

Scary and silly.

Yeah, I am for decriminalizing drugs. That's the only way that we'll ever get a handle on this problem. The only way. Even if they arrest all of the people pushing drugs now, there are going to be new drugs that you can make that are much worse. It's just a wrong approach. From my experiences—which were unfortunately . . . I went through a whole lot—this would be my recommendation. People aren't stupid. You know, they listen. It took me a while, but I finally got the message. This is the way to go. It's not the glamorous way.

Do you see the climate for jazz changing within the United States?

I'm not going to bash the States, because we've been playing at some venues that—actually, the music is always good and the people like the music. It's a matter of whether politicians enable people to hear the music. That's really what it's about. The climate is good for jazz now in the States. I think it's as good as it's ever been. The people in the States are behind jazz. It's just up to the politicians to come onboard now.

Can you remember one or two moments that made it worth it all?

Gee, that's a big question. Invariably, I'm going to have to put it in terms of musical nights, because that's the most transcendent thing that ever happens to me. Now it's a matter of which . . . Whenever I'm really on, that's the time. And there have been some times in my life— not a whole, whole lot, but a few, enough to make me keep practicing, hoping that it can happen again.

Jubal—1. In the Old Testament, the inventor of music, "the father of all such as handle the harp and organ." 2. The name of a record label specializing in country music. [From the Hebrew *yabal*, perhaps denoting "productive."]

The story of Cain and his lineage sounds themes that Freud will later theorize in *Civilization and Its Discontents:* uncontrolled desire breeds violence. Cain kills Abel, his brother; he's the archetypical bad seed. But Cain also builds a city, thus demonstrating that desire sublimated is creativity. This motif returns with a vengeance in five generations, when Lamech—who is pure id—kills a man ("just to watch him die"), and then sings what can only be called scripture's first gangsta rap to Adah and Zillah, his two wives. Perhaps their sons take note: Jubal becomes the first journeyman musician; Jabal, the first cowboy; Tubal-cain, the first industrialist (Gen. 4:1–24).

Readings

Walter Brueggemann. 1982. *Genesis: Interpretation: A Bible Commentary for Teaching and Preaching*. Atlanta: John Knox. [See pp. 65–67.]

Sigmund Freud. 1961. *Civilization and Its Discontents*. Trans. James Strachey. New York: W. W. Norton.

Greil Marcus. 1996. "The Murder Mystery," *Mojo*, January, 72–82.

Recordings—However much the brothers Louvin, Everly, Davies, and Gallagher recast the Cain-and-Abel story as public spectacle, they also confirm the pleasures of sublimated violence in their music. In each of the following songs, violence is closer to the surface. The singer or an interlocutor owns up to murderous intent or action. "Blame it on Cain," wrote Elvis Costello.

Black Velvet Flag, "I Shot JFK," *Come Recline with Black Velvet Flag* (Go-Kart).

Johnny Cash, "Folsom Prison Blues" and "Cocaine Blues," *The Essential Johnny Cash, 1955–1983* (Columbia).

T-Model Ford, "I'm Insane," *Pee-Wee Get My Gun* (Fat Possum/Epitaph).

Pat Hare, "I'm Gonna Murder My Baby," on *Blue Flames: A Sun Blues Collection* (Rhino/Sun).

Jimi Hendrix, "Hey Joe," *Are You Experienced?* (Experience Hendrix/MCA).

John Lee Hooker, "Mad Man Blues," *The Best Chess Sides* (MCA/Chess).

Alberta Hunter, "Amtrak Blues," *Amtrak Blues* (Columbia).

Robert Johnson, "32-20 Blues," *The Complete Recordings* (Columbia/Legacy).

The Kingston Trio, "Tom Dooley," on *Troubadours of the Folk Era, Vol. 3* (Rhino).

Furry Lewis, "Furry's Blues," on *Canned Heat Blues: Masters of the Delta Blues* (Bluebird).

L.L. Cool J, "I Shot Ya," *Mr. Smith* (Def Jam).

The Louvin Brothers, "Knoxville Girl," *Tragic Songs of Life* (Capitol).

Bob Marley, "I Shot the Sheriff," *Burnin'* (Tuff Gong).

Ramones, "Psycho Therapy," *Ramones Mania* (Sire).

Jimmy Lee Robinson, "I Shot a Man," on *Chicago Blues Legends, Vol. 17* (Wolf).

The Rolling Stones, "Midnight Rambler," *Let It Bleed* (abkco).

Schooly D, "I Shot da Bitch," *Welcome to America* (Ruffhouse).

Bruce Springsteen, "Nebraska," *Nebraska* (Columbia).

Suicidal Tendencies, "I Shot the Devil," *Suicidal Tendencies* (Frontier).

Talking Heads, "Psycho Killer," *Talking Heads: 77* (Sire).

Neil Young, "Down by the River," *Everybody Knows This Is Nowhere* (Reprise).

Frank Zappa, "My Guitar Wants to Kill Your Mama," *Weasels Ripped My Flesh* (Rykodisc).

krautrock—A term designating a genre of German experimental rock that originated in sixties psychedelia (Faust), culminated in seventies electro-pop (Kraftwerk), and influenced new wave (New Order and PiL), rap (Afrika Bambaataa), and ambient-techno musics (Orb). [From *kraut-eater*, racist slang for a German soldier.]

Minimal and hypnotic, compu-keyboard-driven, Zappaean, psych-industrial, metal-machine prog-rock: To predicate *krautrock*—to assign words to its features—is to fall back on what Roland Barthes called "the normal practice of music criticism," translating sound "into the poorest of linguistic categories: the adjective" (179). But it also exposes the codes that structure pop signification. The antithesis of American roots-rock, *krautrock* was "against nature"—adamantly "inauthentic" and "inorganic." It heralded a return of futurism without fascism, a mobilization of technical resources against the property system.

■

Readings

Roland Barthes. 1977. "The Grain of the Voice." In *Image-Music-Text*, trans. Stephen Heath. New York: Hill and Wang.

Andy Gill. 1997. "We Can Be Heroes," *Mojo*, April, 54–80.

Simon Reynolds. 1995. "Can," "Faust," and "Kraftwerk." In *Spin Alternative Record Guide*, ed. Eric Weisbard, with Craig Marks. New York: Vintage.

Rob Young. 1997. "Inner Space Is the Place," *The Wire*, May, 26–31.

Recordings—These titles give some indication of Krautrock as a genre as well as what happened to that genre once it transmuted.

1. Various, *Space Box: Space, Krautrock and Acid Trips* (Cleopatra).
2. Various, *Unknown Deutschland: The Krautrock Archive, Vol. 1* (Virgin).
3. Can, *Future Days* (Spoon).
4. Faust, *Faust IV* (Carol).
5. Public Image Ltd., *Second Edition* (Warner Bros.).
6. Can, *Soon Over Babaluma* (Spoon).
7. Tortoise, *Millions Now Living Will Never Die* (Thrill Jockey).
8. Kraftwerk, *Trans-Europe Express* (Cleopatra).
9. Tangerine Dream, *Book of Dreams* (Sequel).
10. Trio, *Da Da Da* (Mercury).

Leslie—A loudspeaker system with a rotating treble horn and a bass speaker pointed into a revolving drum, invented by Donald J. Leslie (c. 1940), designed for use with electronic organs.

The overlapping waveforms produced by the Leslie's two speakers—not unlike the effect derived by yelling into an electric fan—generate a sonic moiré pattern (a Doppler effect): the tremulant sound associated with Hammond organs. But other instruments have also been played through Leslie cabinets, substantiating Walter Benjamin's contention that every fundamentally new technology carries beyond its intended goals. The lead guitar part on the Beach Boys' "Pet Sounds" was Leslie enhanced, and the Beatles, writes Ian MacDonald, "at one time or another used it on almost every sound they recorded including vocals" (127). To the psychedelic mind, the Leslie and LSD were homologous; both altered everyday perception.

■

Readings

Ian MacDonald. 1994. *Revolution in the Head: The Beatles' Records and the Sixties*. New York: Henry Holt.

Mark Vail. 1997. *The Hammond Organ—Beauty in the B*. New York: Keyboard Magazine/Miller Freeman.

Recordings

The Band, "Tears of Rage," *Music from Big Pink* (Capitol).

The Beach Boys, "Pet Sounds," *Pet Sounds* (Capitol).

The Beatles, "Tomorrow Never Knows," *Revolver* (Parlophone).

The Vaughan Brothers, "Hillbillies from Outerspace," *Family Style* (Epic/Associated).

Various, *B-3 In'—Organ Jazz* (32 Jazz).

the INDESTRUCTIBLE BEAT of
SOWETO

mbaqanga—A form of popular music, indigenous to South African townships, arising from and incorporating a variety of traditional/rural and rock/urban styles. [From Zulu, literally "cornbread."]

Unintended effects of colonization, *kwela* (pennywhistle street music) and *marabi* (Afro-jazz forged in *sheebeens,* or illegal bars) developed when rural Africans, lured by industry and coerced by apartheid, migrated to the townships. There, Zulu and Sotho music combined with cosmopolitan sounds such as r&b and modern jazz imported from the U.S.A. *Mbaqanga*, beginning in the 1960s, further conventionalized and popularized already hybrid South African musical styles. Its goat-voiced singers and sweet harmonies, its electric guitars and saxophones, and its driving 4/4 rhythms appealed, first, to a large black-urban market, and then (largely through the aegis of Paul Simon's *Graceland*) to the world.

■

Readings

Veit Erlmann. 1996. *Nightsong: Performance, Power, and Practice in South Africa*. Chicago: University of Chicago Press.

Ronnie Graham. 1988. *Da Capo Guide to Contemporary African Music*. New York: Da Capo.

Rob Prince. 1989. "South Africa—Music in the Shadows." In *Rhythms of the World*, ed. Francis Hanly and Tim May, pp. 98–107. London: BBC.

Recordings—It's a start.

Various, *The Indestructible Beat of Soweto* (Shanachie).

Various, *Soweto Never Sleeps* (Shanachie).

Various, *Thunder Before Dawn (The Indestructible Beat of Soweto Vol. 2)* (Earthworks).

Various, *Zulu Jive: Umbaqanga* (Earthworks).

Mekons—1. A socialist surrealist punk band, formed in Leeds, England, 1977. [After the Mekon, a green-headed, evil alien intelligence featured in The Eagle, a 1950s British comic strip.] 2. Poppies. [From Greek μήκων, "poppy."]

"Where the poppy grew/the soil is dead" go the lyrics to "Brutal" (*The Curse of the Mekons*). The song takes the Chinese Opium Wars of the nineteenth century as a metaphor of late capitalism, and thus hints at possibilities latent in the Mekons' name. Still, even cognoscenti may not sense the esoteric depths of this etymological cabal. The word "mekon" conflates dope and shit: Rock 'n' roll is the opiate of the people; it's the fecal matter of pop culture. You see, meconium is the condensed juice of poppies. It is also the greenish-black feces discharged from the bowels of newborn babies.

■

Recordings—The Best of the Mekons

Original Sin (Sin/Twin Tone).
The Mekons Rock 'n' Roll (A&M).
The Curse of the Mekons (Blast First).
I ♥ Mekons (Quarterstick).
The Edge of the World (Quarterstick).

Interview—Mekon Sally Timms weighs in on the perils of recording budgets (November 1995)

There's a limit to how much you should actually spend in making a record. Some people spend millions of dollars, and that's ludicrous. But there's a difference between five grand and ten grand. That can make a big difference. It means that what you make you can make with more of your vision.

Are you ideologically opposed to big budgets?

No. It's a waste of time. There's a limit. If you're recording ten songs, how long can you spend recording those songs? A 24-track studio? You can go to a good 24-track studio, and after a certain point you're not paying for the 24-tracks. You're paying for the location and the staff that it has. You're not paying for anything that determines whether the music stays any good. And there's a limit to how good something can be. The more time you have to spend doing something, often you'll find the crappier it will come out. Some people remix their albums six or seven times, and they probably had it right the first time. It makes music actually blander. I do believe that recording budgets should be capped. Rich pop stars should be taxed. People like me could go around making a hundred albums with what they do with one. How much does a Sting album cost or a Phil Collins album? And it's shit. With a 1 percent tax, think of all the people who could run around making better music. It's so corrupt. But then, I suppose they get the returns.

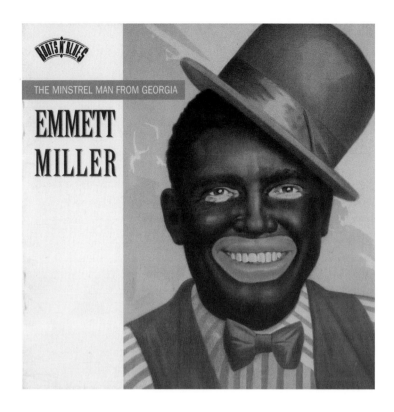

ROOTS N' BLUES

THE MINSTREL MAN FROM GEORGIA

EMMETT
MILLER

nigger—A disparaging term referring to a person of color or, metaphorically, to any socially oppressed person.

Early in *The Commitments*, a novel written by Roddy Doyle and a film directed by Alan Parker, there's a scene that finds Jimmy Rabbitte assembling members of the band he's forming. They convene in a video rental shop, and Jimmy screens a clip of James Brown performing on the *T.A.M.I. Show*. It's a crucial moment. Meaning, heretofore obscured, is uncovered. Jimmy uses the clip to establish a standard for measuring excellence in soul music. Then he declares, "The Irish are the blacks of Europe, lads." The lads are incredulous. Jimmy's equation (black = dispossessed) plays as something of a joke: catachresis or dada minstrelsy. But it's also sufficient to transform a rag-tag band into the Commitments, through an exchange (dispossessed → soul):

- To sing soul, one must be black.
- The Irish are the blacks of Europe; Dubliners are the blacks of Ireland; the Commitments, because they're working-class stiffs from Barrytown, are the blacks of Dublin.
- Therefore, the Commitments have a right—and they've got what it takes—to sing soul.

"At the heart of this film," writes Julian Dibbell, "lies a rather endearing faith in the redeeming and ultimately progressive power of latter-day minstrelsy" (58). Feeling put upon, like you've been shot at and missed, shit at and hit? Jimmy recommends, "Say it once, say it loud, I'm black an' I'm proud." What Dick Hebdige calls "the myth of the Black Man" is democratized in the anthems of soul. A "model of freedom-in-bondage," the Negro, "trapped in a cruel environment of mean streets and tenements," transcends dreary conventions (47–48). Or, as Dylan put it, "When you've got nothing, you've got nothing to lose." Chalk up Jimmy's solution—his heart's cry—to the twin pleasures of identification and projection.

In the novel, Jimmy's more audacious. Without blinking an eye, he calls the Irish "niggers." And Jimmy's mates? "They nearly gasped: it was so true" (9). Common sense says Parker wanted to soften the novel's dialogue for a film audience, though it's possible that Doyle, who collaborated with Parker on the screenplay, suggested the swap. But whatever its origin or motivation, the word "black" compromises Parker's much-vaunted project of forging an authentic world on screen. It's simply not the sort of word the film's diegesis has led us to expect from Jimmy.

He's a character self-satisfied with his oratorical ability, sold on the rhetorical values of shock. Jimmy's language is consistently and casually obscene. Substituting "black" for "nigger," therefore, represents a directorial accommodation of a mass audience. But more significantly, "black" marks the spot where the discourse of liberalism impinges upon and then supercedes the discourse of authenticity. If Jimmy says "nigger," he becomes a problematic hero, and no such character inhabits Parker's simplistic world, though they walk the earth in Quentin Tarantino's films.

The gap, then, between "black" and "nigger," marks a chiasma. It's also the point where history intersects *The Commitments*. According to Dibbell, it was Malcolm X who first said, "The Irish are the blacks of Europe!" (58).

■

Readings

Claude Brown. 1968. "The Language of Soul." *Esquire*, April. Reprinted in *Patterns of Exposition* 7, ed. Randall E. Decker, pp. 230–36. Boston: Little, Brown, 1980.

Julian Dibbell. 1991. "Straight Outta Dublin." *Village Voice*, 20 August, 55–58.

Roddy Doyle. 1987. *The Commitments*. New York: Vintage.

Dick Gregory. 1964. *Nigger: An Autobiography*. New York: Pocket.

Dick Hebdige. 1979. *Subculture: The Meaning of Style*. London: Methuen.

Darius James. 1992. *Negrophobia*. New York: Citadel.

James Naremore. 1995. "Uptown Folk: Blackness and Entertainment in *Cabin in the Sky*." In *Representing Jazz*, ed. Krin Gabbard, pp. 169–92. Durham, N.C.: Duke University Press.

Adam Knee. 1995. "Doubling, Music, and Race in *Cabin in the Sky*." In *Representing Jazz*, ed. Krin Gabbard, pp. 193–204. Durham, N.C.: Duke University Press.

Flannery O'Connor. 1955/1971. "The Artificial Nigger." In *The Complete Stories*, pp. 249–70. New York: Farrar, Straus, and Giroux.

Nick Tosches. 1977/1996. "Cowboys and Niggers." In *Country: The Twisted Roots of Rock 'n' Roll*, pp. 162–217. New York: Da Capo.

Mark Twain. 1993. *The Adventures of Huckleberry Finn*. New York: Modern Library.

Carl Van Vechten. 1926. *Nigger Heaven*. New York: Alfred A. Knopf.

Recordings—Top 10 Nigger Numbers

Ice Cube, "The Nigga Ya Love to Hate," *AmeriKKKa's Most Wanted* (Priority).

John Lennon, "Woman Is the Nigger of the World," *Sometime in New York City* (Capitol/EMI).

Ronald Shannon Jackson, "Slim in Atlanta," *Pulse* (Celluloid).

Curtis Mayfield, "Pusherman," *Superfly* (Curtom).

Richard Pryor, "Supernigger," *Supernigger* (Loose Cannon).

Rudy Ray Moore, "Shine and the Great Titanic," *Greatest Hits* (The Right Stuff).

Sly and the Family Stone, "Don't Call Me Nigger, Whitey," *Stand!* (Epic).

Patti Smith, "Rock 'n' Roll Nigger," *Easter* (Arista).

Swamp Dogg, "Call Me Nigger," *Best of 25 Years of Swamp Dogg . . . Or F*** the Bomb, Stop the Drugs* (Pointblank Classic).

Randy Newman, "Rednecks," *Good Old Boys* (Reprise).

Orpheus—In Greek mythology, the son of Oeagrus (some texts assign paternity to Apollo) and Calliope (a Muse).

After extensive touring with the Argonauts, Orpheus—a musician (vocals, lyre) and poet (oracles) with superhuman talent—marries Eurydice. She dies suddenly. Grief stricken, Orpheus journeys to the land of the dead. He hopes to sing his wife back home—and he nearly succeeds. (Comedy once evoked is averted.) Hades agrees to release Eurydice on the condition that Orpheus not look at her as the two exit the underworld. This interdiction is, of course, violated and the lady vanishes. Orpheus later dies when a band of Thracian women—devotees of Dionysus called the Cicone Youth—rip him to shreds. His head floats to the island of Lesbos; installed in the heavens, his lyre becomes the constellation Lyra.

The tale of Orpheus seems to refer to nothing objective, but to speak of possibly everything. It reads like the archetypal musician's press-kit bio—albeit one inscribed in code. Early in 1988, I asked Bobby McFerrin if the myth applied to his own work. I knew that his first acting role—no dialogue, but improvised vocals—had been the part of Orpheus in a surrealistic film for German television. "The story is interesting," McFerrin replied. "Orpheus was a musician who used his power of singing to enter the nether world, to change the direction of the wind, to stop evil forces. I've often told myself and my audiences, 'Sing for your lives, because it's good for your souls.' Singing invariably helps lift my spirit." This and other comments by the author of "Don't Worry, Be Happy" were combined to create a feature story—an ABC—that I exchanged for my first compact-disc player.

■

Readings

Maurice Blanchot. 1981. *The Gaze of Orpheus, and Other Literary Essays*. Trans. Lydia Davis. Barrytown, N.Y.: Station Hill.

Nick Tosches. 1977/1996. "Orpheus, Gypsies, and Redneck Rock 'n' Roll." In *Country: The Twisted Roots of Rock 'n' Roll*, pp. 4–21. New York: Da Capo.

Recordings—Gluck, Haydn, Monteverdi, Offenbach, and Balanchine have paid specific musical homage, but Orphic themes run throughout popular music, too.

Creedence Clearwater Revival, "Run Through the Jungle," *Cosmo's Factory* (Fantasy).

Charlie Daniels, "The Devil Went Down to Georgia," *Super Hits* (Columbia).

Merle Haggard, "Sing Me Back Home," *The Lonesome Fugitive: The Merle Haggard Anthology (1963–1977)* (Razor & Tie).

Don Henley, "The Boys of Summer," *Building the Perfect Beast* (Geffen).

Lyres, "Buried Alive," *On Fyre* (New Rose).

Mad Professor, "Black Orpheus Dub," on *Red Hot + Rio* (Antilles).

The Rolling Stones, "It's Only Rock 'n' Roll (But I Like It)," *It's Only Rock & Roll* (Rolling Stones).

Underworld, "To Dream of Love," *Second Toughest in the Infants* (Wax Trax!).

Robert Pete Williams, "Talkin' Blues," *Blues Masters, Vol. 1* (Storyville).
Art Pepper, *The Complete Village Vanguard Sessions* (Contemporary).

Videos

Marcel Camus. 1958. *Black Orpheus*.
Jean Cocteau. 1949. *Jean Cocteau's Orpheus* (Orphée).
Peter Hall. 1991. *Orpheus Descending*.
Harry Kupfer. N.d. *Orfeo ed Euridice* [composer: Christoph Gluck].
Steven M. Martin. 1995. *Theremin: An Electronic Odyssey*.
D. A. Pennebaker. 1967. *Don't Look Back*.
Jean-Pierre Ponnelle, N.d. *Claudio Monteverdi: L'Orfeo*.
Richard Schmidt. 1992. *American Orpheus*.

Interview—Record producer and Russian émigré Leo Feigin on censorship (Fall 1987)

The free market's efficiency as a censoring agency is absolutely phenomenal. It can be even more efficient than censorship in the Soviet Union, a totalitarian regime. In Russia, when something is censored, it immediately and automatically becomes a subject of great discussion in the underground. In the West this is not quite so. If you are subject to censorship, you are bound to total obscurity. It's highly possible that nobody will know about you.

Stratosphere Boogie: The Flaming Guitars Of Speedy West & Jimmy Bryant

SPEEDY WEST

pedal steel—An electric guitar mounted on a narrow rectangular table supported by legs. Chords are made by pressing down on the strings with a steel bar and altered by raising or lowering the strings with a system of foot pedals and knee levers.

The pedal steel guitar is a stringed instrument morphing into a keyboard instrument. A brief history: Arabs invent the guitar—a flatbacked lute—and introduce it to Spain (c. 1200). Spanish and Portuguese seamen transport the guitar to Hawaii. There, islanders lay the instrument flat on their laps, fretting it with bone, metal, or the back of a comb. In the 1920s, this style of playing catches on as a Hawaiian-music craze sweeps the U.S.A. By the late 1930s, the steel guitar—electric or acoustic—finds a home in southwestern country music. Finally, Gibson and Fender manufacture electric steel guitars with pedals, and Bud Isaacs, with Webb Pierce, records "Slowly" (1953). The sound of pedal steel becomes the musical correlative of inebriated self-pity, at least within the semiotics of honky-tonk.

∎

Readings

Jean-Charles Costa. 1973. "The Country Guitar: The Mysterious Pedal Steel." *Country Music* 1: 42–44.

Steve Fishell. 1987. "20 Essential Steel Albums." *Guitar Player*, January, 140–46.

Bill C. Malone. 1985. *Country Music, U.S.A.* Rev. ed. Austin: University of Texas Press.

Forrest White. 1994. *Fender: The Inside Story*. San Francisco: GPI.

Recordings—Ten Great Pedal Steel Tracks

Demola Adepoju, "365 Is My Number/The Message," on King Sunny Adé, *Juju Music* (Mango).

B. J. Cole, "Pavane Pour une Enfante Defunte," *Transparent Music* (Hannibal).

Jimmy Day with Ray Price, "Crazy Arms," on *Hillbilly Fever! Vol. 3, Legends of Nashville* (Rhino).

Josh Dubin, "First Song for Kate," on Bobby Previte, *Claude's Late Morning* (Gramavision).

Buddy Emmons, "Silver Bell," *Amazing Steel Guitar: The Buddy Emmons Collection* (Razor & Tie).

John Hughey, "Last Date (Lost Her Love on Our Last Date)," on Conway Twitty, *20 Greatest Hits* (MCA).

Bud Isaacs, "Slowly," on Webb Pierce, *King of the Honky-Tonk: From the Original Decca Masters, 1952–1959* (MCA/CMA).

Sneaky Pete Kleinow, "Christine's Tune," on Flying Burrito Brothers, *The Gilded Palace of Sin* (Edsel).

Ralph Mooney, "I'm a Lonesome Fugitive," on James Burton and Ralph Mooney, *Corn Pickin' and Slick Slidin'* (See-For-Miles).

Speedy West, "Stratosphere Boogie," on Speedy West and Jimmy Bryant, *Stratosphere Boogie: The Flaming Guitars of Speedy West & Jimmy Bryant* (Razor & Tie).

Interview—Excerpted from a talk with composer and drummer Bobby Previte (February 1989)

Two things inspired me to use pedal steel on *Claude's Late Morning*. One was Sunny Adé's music. He plays so little. When you see him in concert, he sits there for half the song, and then he'll play something that'll just blow your mind. Pedal steel is one of those instruments that's been used beautifully in one style of music, but hasn't really come out in other things. It's amazing, the things that it can do. Playing it is a religion. It's got a million pedals, levers, two fret boards, things for your knees.

I also was listening to a lot of world music at the time, a lot of gamelan music—Balinese music, music from Java. I was interested in the notes between the notes. I kept hearing elasticity in the music. You notice a lot of strings on the record. I very rarely asked players to tune up at the recording session. It was a conscious decision. When you get all of those strings together and they're just a little bit out, you get those notes between the notes, those different harmonics. I started to hear that—a lot of the sliding that the pedal steel can do: approximating, approaching a note rather than playing the note. That's what I was really drawn to, the way it can circle around a note but not get there.

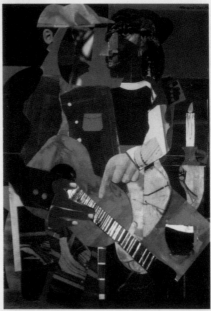

JERRY GRANELLI A SONG I THOUGHT I HEARD BUDDY SING

KENNY GARRETT   JULIAN PRIESTER   BILL FRISELL   ROBBEN FORD   ANTHONY COX   J. GRANELLI

quiz—A staple of music publications; requires readers to access specialized knowledge.

Behind every advertisement, there's a product wanting consumers, calling them. It's inviting participation in a process that Louis Althusser labels "interpellation," whereby people are constructed as "subjects" when they answer the solicitations of ideology. Quizzes work more "phatically" (Roman Jakobson's term). They're messages to the already called and confirmed. They determine and reaffirm established relationships with bodies of knowledge, particular taste patterns, and subcultures. They help maintain the channels of communication that enable consumption.

■

Readings

Louis Althusser. 1971. "Freud and Lacan." In *Lenin and Philosophy and Other Essays*, trans. Ben Brewster. New York: Monthly Review Press.

John Fiske. 1982. *Introduction to Communication Studies*. New York: Methuen. [See pp. 14–15.]

Cultural Studies Quiz—Come in out of the Rain and Hear the Jazz Go Down

For all the musicianly advice that goes, "Let the music speak for itself," jazz shows up a lot in print—probably for two reasons. First, writing often aspires to the condition of music; it aims to transform the inwardness of song into the outwardness of space. And second, well . . . ah, jazz provides late sleepers with writing material.

What follows are twenty-five "print bites" informed by jazz (construed in the broadest possible sense). Their authors' names are listed in the box on page 158. Your job? Well, like Louis Armstrong said, "If you gotta ask, you'll never know."

_____ 1. It may have been the gin; something had him fixed up so that he was playing constantly right up to the place where genius and madness grapple before going their separate ways.

_____ 2. All I know about music is that not many people ever really hear it.

_____ 3. It's actually quite difficult to recognize a musician from the tone. Who can you identify this way? Stan Getz when he plays Latin-American style. Miles Davis from his naked, precise, vibrato-less sound. Armstrong by his meticulous crystallization of New Orleans jazz.

_____ 4. I sat down and played "Blue Moon." When I was through he shook his head. "Naw, man. You're just playing shells. You have to fill in those chords."

_____ 5. Storyville nights, where the old only really universal music of the century had come from, something that brought people closer together and in a better way than Esperanto, UNESCO, or airlines . . .

Match the citations with these names and titles:

A. Chester Himes, *The Real Cool Killers*
B. Julio Cortázar, *Hopscotch*
C. George Washington Cable, *The Grandissimes*
D. Leroi Jones, "The Screamers"
E. James Baldwin, "Sonny's Blues"
F. Ntozake Shange, *Sassafrass, Cypress, and Indigo*
G. Frank Conroy, *Stop Time*
H. Xam Wilson Cartiér, *Be-Bop, Re-Bop*
I. Jean-Paul Sartre, *Nausea*
J. Peter Høeg, *Smilla's Sense of Snow*
K. Michael Ondaatje, *Coming through Slaughter*
L. Donald Barthelme, "The King of Jazz"
M. Aristophanes, *Clouds*
N. Toni Morrison, *Jazz*
O. Roddy Doyle, *The Commitments*
P. Langston Hughes, "The Blues I'm Playing"
Q. Thomas Pynchon, *V.*
R. Charles Mingus, *Beneath the Underdog*
S. Dorothy Baker, *Young Man with a Horn*
T. Thomas Merton, *The Seven Storey Mountain*
U. Thomas McGuane, *Nobody's Angel*
V. Ralph Ellison, *Invisible Man*
W. Josef Skvorecky, *The Bass Saxophone*

_____ 6. I'd like to hear five recordings of Louis Armstrong playing and singing "What Did I Do to Be So Black and Blue"—all at the same time.

_____ 7. "Can you distinguish our great homemade American jazz performers, each from the other?"

"Used to could."

"Then who was that playing?"

"Sounds like Hokie Mokie to me. Those few but perfectly selected notes have the real epiphanic glow."

_____ 8. Ben warmed up. He'd pound his mattress enthusiastically during certain riffs: "Listen! Listen! That phrase says, 'Eat shit, whitey. I own a sports car and I'm going to fuck your woman.'"

_____ 9. The jukebox was giving out with a stomp version of "Big-Legged Woman." Saxophones were pleading; the horns were teasing; the bass was patting; the drums were chatting; the piano was catting, laying and playing the jive, and a husky female voice was shouting. . .

_____ 10. Oceola's background was too well-grounded in Mobile, and Billy Kersands' Minstrels, and the Sanctified churches where religion was a joy, to stare mystically over the top of a grand piano like white folks and imagine that Beethoven had nothing to do with life, or that Schubert's love songs were only sublimations.

_____ 11. That grand wild sound of bop floated from beer parlors; it mixed medleys with every kind of cowboy and boogie-woogie in the American night.

_____ 12. Will rhythm buy the groceries?

_____ 13. When Patrick thought of Ornette Coleman running an elevator in Los Angeles with a room full of scores and his mother sending him food from Texas, he developed grave doubts about the District of Columbia.

_____ 14. He suddenly became aware that the weird, drowsy throb of the African song and dance had been swinging drowsily in his brain for an unknown lapse of time.

_____ 15. You had your Shakespeare and Marx and Freud and Einstein and Jesus Christ and Guy Lombardo but we came up with *jazz*, don't forget it, and all the pop music in the world today is from that primary cause.

_____ 16. For the moment, the jazz is playing; there is no melody, only notes, a myriad of tiny jolts.

_____ 17. Alice Manfred had worked hard to privatize her niece, but she was no match for a City seeping music that begged and challenged each and every day. "Come," it said. "Come and do wrong."

_____ 18. Don't ya know we is all sad ladies because we got the blues, and joyful women because we got our songs?

_____ 19. I suppose I got some five or six hours of fitful sleep, and at about eleven we were all awake, sitting around disheveled and half stupefied, talking and smoking and playing records. The thin, ancient, somewhat elegiac cadences of the long dead Beiderbecke sang in the room.

_____ 20. The usual divisions prevailed: collegians did not dig, and left after an average of 1½ sets. Personnel from other groups, either with a night off or taking a long break from somewhere crosstown or uptown, listened hard, trying to dig. "I am still thinking," they would say if you asked. People at the bar all looked as if they did dig in the sense of understand, approve of, empathize with: but this was probably only because people who prefer to stand at the bar have, universally, an inscrutable look.

_____ 21. Our band was called Red Music, which in fact was a misnomer, since the name had no political connotations: there was a band in Prague that called itself Blue Music and we, living in the Nazi Protectorate of Bohemia and Moravia, had no idea that in jazz blue is not a color, so we called ours Red.

_____ 22. Militant memories: For months, years after his passing Double would appear through my sleep to bump a lesser dream, still bopping with the armed resistance of his dedication to "jazz"—which he said was "two, say three broad crooked jumps off to the side of the mainstream straight and narrow, out to where sound becomes sight, as it should be!"

_____ 23. Thought I knew his blues before, and the hymns at funerals, but what he is playing now is real strange and I listen careful for he's playing something that sounds like both. I cannot make out the tune and then I catch on. He's mixing them up.

_____ 24. —Polyrhythms! Polyrhythms! I ask you! That's not the people's sound. —Those polyrhythms went through Brother Parker's legs and up his ass. —And who did he play to? I'll tell you, middle-class white kids with little beards and berets. In jazz clubs. Jazz clubs! They didn't even clap. They clicked their fingers.

_____ 25. The repeated rhythmic figure, a screamed riff, pushed in its insistence past music. It was hatred and frustration, secrecy and despair. It spurted out of the diphthong culture, and reinforced the black cults of emotion.

Answers: 1S, 2E, 3J, 4G, 5B, 6V, 7L, 8Y, 9A, 10P, 11X, 12M, 13U, 14C, 15R, 16I, 17N, 18F, 19T, 20Q, 21W, 22H, 23K, 24O, 25D.

rockabilly—Archetypical rock 'n' roll. It was invented by Elvis Presley et al., Sam Phillips's Sun Studios, 706 Union Avenue, Memphis, Tennessee, July 5, 1954.

Conventionally understood as musical miscegenation—the intersection of Grand Ole Opry and Beale Street (hillbilly song form plus blues-gospel feeling)—rockabilly was less a marriage than a mutation. It arose from social conditions that characterized the lives of working-class Southerners (so-called "white trash") just as surely as the blues resulted from conditions that prevailed throughout the Delta. It was to country music as bebop was to swing. First, it marked a new attitude: youthful insolence. Second, it signaled a paradigm shift: not harmony and melody, but rhythm and sound—echo from a twangy guitar, slapped bass, pounding piano, or a dixie-fried voice—became the *raison d'être* of popular music.

Readings

Stanley Booth. 1991. *Rythm Oil: A Journey through the Music of the American South*. New York: Vintage.

Colin Escott with Martin Hawkins. 1992. *Good Rockin' Tonight: Sun Records and the Birth of Rock 'n' Roll*. New York: St. Martin's.

William Faulkner. 1990. *As I Lay Dying: The Corrected Text*. New York: Vintage.

Peter Guralnick. 1994. *Last Train to Memphis*. Boston: Back Bay/Little, Brown.

———. 1992. "Rockabilly." In *The Rolling Stone Illustrated History of Rock & Roll*, ed. Anthony DeCurtis and James Henke, pp. 67–72. New York: Random House.

Barry Hannah. 1978/1994. *Airships*. New York: Grove/Atlantic.

John Hartigan. 1997. "Unpopular Culture: The Case of 'White Trash.'" *Cultural Studies* 11: 316–43.

Greil Marcus. 1991. *Dead Elvis: A Chronicle of a Cultural Obsession*. New York: Doubleday.

———. 1990. "Elvis Presliad." In *Mystery Train: Images of America in Rock 'n' Roll Music*, 3d ed., pp. 120–75. New York: Dutton Obelisk.

Flannery O'Connor. 1988. *Collected Works*. New York: Library of America.

David Adler. 1993. *The Life and Cuisine of Elvis Presley*. New York: Crown Trade Paperbacks.

Nick Tosches. 1982. *Hellfire: The Jerry Lee Lewis Story*. New York: Dell.

Carl Perkins with David McGee. 1996. *Go Cat, Go! The Life and Times of Carl Perkins, the King of Rockabilly*. New York: Hyperion.

Recordings

Johnny Cash, *The Sun Years* (Rhino).

Buddy Holly, *The Buddy Holly Collection* (MCA).

Jerry Lee Lewis, *18 Original Sun Greatest Hits* (Rhino).

———, *"Live" at the Star Club, Hamburg* (Rhino).

Ricky Nelson, *The Legendary Masters Series, Vol. 1* (EMI USA).

Carl Perkins, *Original Sun Greatest Hits* (Rhino).

Elvis Presley, *The Sun Sessions CD* (RCA).

Gene Vincent, *The Capitol Collector's Series* (Capitol).

Various, *The Sun Story* (Rhino).

Various, *Rock This Town: Rockabilly Hits, Vol. 1* (Rhino).

Various, *Rock This Town: Rockabilly Hits, Vol. 2* (Rhino).

Videos

Steve Binder. 1968. *Elvis, His 1968 Comeback Special*.

Jim Jarmusch. 1989. *Mystery Train*.

Jim McBride. 1989. *Great Balls of Fire*.

Steve Rash. 1978. *The Buddy Holly Story*.

Alan Raymond and Susan Raymond. 1987. *Elvis '56*.

Richard Thorpe. 1957. *Jailhouse Rock*.

THE **2** TONE COLLECTION

A CHECKERED PAST

ska—Jamaican rhythm and blues. It antedated rocksteady and reggae but has twice been resurrected: first, during Britain's punk era; later, during the "alternative" era. [From Jamaican English *ska-aska-ska-aska*, imitative of the music's driving, offbeat rhythms.]

In 1956, while a white kid in Memphis was retooling "race" and "hillbilly" music, a group of young black men in West Kingston, Jamaica, was initiating similarly momentous changes. Stimulated by a developing record industry (itself an effect of the "sound systems"), they stopped merely covering r&b favorites broadcast from radio stations in New Orleans and Miami; they began to transform these objects of affection by incorporating Rastafarian-derived "ridims" and jazz ideas. In this way, second-hand "rudie blues" became ska. These young black men—trombonists Don Drummond and Rico Rodriguez, tenor saxophonists Tommy McCook and Roland Alphonso, guitarist Ernest Ranglin, and others—formed the Skatalites.

■

Readings

J. D. Considine. 1994. "Wailing Souls: A Reggae Hall of Fame." *Rolling Stone*, February, 41–44.

Stephen Davis. 1979. *Reggae Bloodlines: In Search of the Music and Culture of Jamaica*. Rev. ed. Garden City, N.Y.: Anchor.

Dick Hebdige. 1987. *Cut 'n' Mix: Culture, Identity and Caribbean Music*. London: Methuen.

Max Perlich. 1993. "Clement 'Sir Coxsone' Dodd." *Grand Royal*, Fall/Winter, 5.

Timothy White. 1981. "Jump Up!" *Rolling Stone*, April, 83–86, 88–89.

Recordings—The third and most recent incarnation of ska hasn't yet received an anthology that it deserves.

Various, *A Checkered Past: The 2 Tone Collection* (Chrysalis).

Various, *Roots of Reggae: Ska* (Rhino).

Various, *Respect to Studio One: 33 Dancehall, Reggae and Ska Classics* (Heartbeat).

Interview—Mick Jones, former lead guitarist with the Clash and leader of Big Audio Dynamite (B.A.D.) (May 1995)

Reggae was punk's other chosen music. There weren't enough good punk records, and so DJs used to supplement them with what was happening on the reggae scene. One of the main DJs was Don Letts, who was in the first Big Audio Dynamite. He used to turn everybody on to new records from Jamaica. Also, where we grew up [in Brixton], there was a big West Indian population. There was bluebeat and ska—before reggae. We grew up around that music as well. In the way that the

Stones used to cover the latest r&b hits, when they started, the Clash did "Police and Thieves." It was the latest hit of that summer. That's how we ended up doing it. We weren't trying to *do* reggae. We were trying to do our approximation—where we were coming from. It turned out differently. It wasn't like the Police doing a "wet" reggae thing.

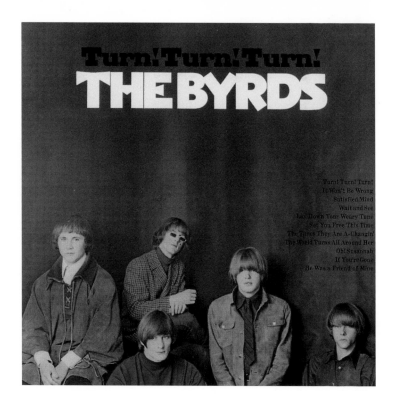

trope—Text or music interpolated into a liturgical chant. [From Greek *tropos*, turn.]

Tropes began when singers embellished the vowel sounds of important words in the liturgy, and as they became more elaborate, additional words were added to aid memorization. This practice had profound consequences. First, from the *Quem quaeritis* tropes, medieval drama developed. Second, tropes anticipated the Protestant Reformation (1517). By amplifying holy texts—in effect by jazzing them up—tropes tended toward glossolalia and plurality. They implied that Scripture was not a closed book but was subject to endless interpretation. At the Council of Trent (1545–63), Church Fathers finally responded to this potential threat to their hegemony. They suppressed all but four tropes and, unwittingly, prompted this modern analogy: If classical music is the Roman Catholic Church, then Louis Armstrong is Martin Luther.

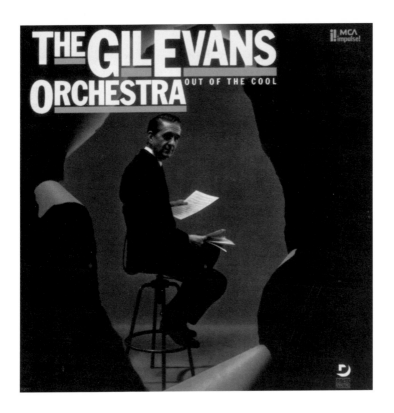

urbane—Adjective denoting self-assurance seasoned with politeness and refinement; cosmopolitan.

Finding a record label debut more impressive than the four titles Impulse! released in 1961 would be a chore. The music—by Ray Charles, Gil Evans, Oliver Nelson, and Jay Jay Johnson/Kai Winding—was superb. And the sleeves—the jackets protecting the albums—were absolutely distinct. One could easily identify an Impulse! recording, with its orange-and-black color motif, by design features alone. "It was a unique physical concept for LP packaging at that time," Creed Taylor recalls. "Maybe classical records had been done that way. But even aside from the graphics, the gatefold made the packages stand out. Also sheet lamination created that glossy look you couldn't get from spray lacquer."

Taylor founded Impulse! Records and guided its launch right down to the logo he designed for the label. When he moved—to Verve,

A&M, and later to start CTI—he continued to emphasize the look of jazz. "I thought that the audience for jazz was, generally, of a higher level of intelligence," says Taylor. "Gil Evans's *Out of the Cool*, if you recall, has a photograph of Gil seated on a stool; he's holding a manuscript. Instead of making him seem like the shadowy artistic type, it was set up to give him a Madison Avenue look, to make people think, 'He's a pretty good looking guy. He's intelligent looking. I thought jazz was down-in-the-basement and seedy.'"

Well, almost. Take the case of Blue Note Records. "Even back in the days of 78s, in all their ads," says executive producer Michael Cuscuna, "it was a Bauhaus, art-deco style that Alfred [Lion, label president] was leaning towards." That visual identity was developed and extended through the work of Reid Miles, a brilliant designer who didn't care for the sound of jazz. Taylor, on the other hand, envisioned a different image and, more significantly, a different audience for jazz. And he and a few other like-minded record producers—such as, George Avakian at Columbia and Norman Granz at Verve—helped shift its connotations. Instead of signifying left-leaning bohemian values (typically associated with the audience for "folk" musics), jazz came to signify urbanity (modernism as subscribed to by the middle class). Nowhere is the new jazz listener pictured more vividly and satirized more hilariously than in *Jailhouse Rock*'s cocktail party, when Vince Everett (Elvis Presley) responds to a woman's question about the musical direction of Dave Brubeck, Paul Desmond, and Lennie Tristano. He declares, "Lady, I don't know what the hell you're talking about."

■

Cover Story—From an interview with producer George Avakian (June 1994)

The cover photo on the first version of Miles Davis's second album, Miles Ahead, *features a white woman and a boy tacking along in a sailboat. They're models of leisure-class urbanity. George Avakian—who produced the album—tells its story.*

I'd already put Miles on the first cover, *'Round about Midnight,* a photograph my brother took. I was tempted to do the same on the second one. I wanted to establish his face. The conception of the *Miles Ahead* cover was arrived at by Neil Fujita, the art director. I told him, "This is the title. I don't know what we're going to do on the cover."

He said, "I have an idea." The next day he comes in with this stock photograph that he'd gotten from a photographer somewhere.

When Miles saw it, he said, "George, how can you put that white bitch on the cover? Get her off there. Put a black girl on there. Put Frances." Frances was his girlfriend. She was a dancer in *West Side Story*, a wonderful girl. Boy did he abuse her. Talk about O. J. Simpson beating up on Nicole.

I said to Miles, "We'll change the cover." In the back of my mind, I'm thinking, "Gee, we can't put a black girl on a sailboat. I hate to lose the concept of the cover." Then I said, "Look, what we should do is have you on the cover again because we really want to establish you as a rising force on Columbia Records. Pick out any photograph of yours that you want." He picked another of Aram's pictures. That was done after I left Columbia. The 50,000 odd covers that we had already manufactured lasted that long.

The way Miles agreed to let the [original] cover stay on until the supply was exhausted was very simple. Miles thinking ahead, thinking of his career. I said, "Miles, if we kill the cover, it'll take many weeks to create a new cover and manufacture it. Meanwhile, we had these covers made in advance. They were easy to make, and it was economical to make them. All we have to do is put pressings into them and ship within forty-eight hours, maybe twenty-four, as the orders come in. You don't want to lose weeks and weeks of an album that is beginning to sell very well.

He said, "No. Keep the fuckers, but then change it." That's what we did.

verity—The condition of being true or real.

In our consumer culture, as expressions of truth, aphorisms (nonfalsifiable formulations of individual tastes and aesthetic judgments) have taken the place of axioms (universally established principles grounded in empiricism). What we're experiencing, notes Robert Ray following Charles Baudelaire and Roland Barthes, is "a later manifestation of dandyism," a phenomenon that appears when people, denied the possibility of political progressivism, fall back on ruse and devious attitudes (126). Taste becomes a self-conscious political gesture, shopping a form of combat, and pessimism and rejection reign.

■

Readings

Roland Barthes. 1977. *Roland Barthes*. Trans. Richard Howard. New York: Hill and Wang. [See p. 106]

Charles Baudelaire. 1964. "The Dandy." In *The Painter of Modern Life, and Other Essays*. Greenwich, Conn.: Phaidon/New York Graphic Society.

Ann Powers. 1993. "Camp Counselors [Pet Shop Boys]." *Village Voice*, 2 November, 73, 89.

Robert B. Ray. 1995. *The Avant-Garde Finds Andy Hardy*. Cambridge, Mass.: Harvard University Press.

Susan Sontag. 1966. "Notes on 'Camp.'" In *Against Interpretation*. New York: Delta.

Andy Warhol. 1975. *The Philosophy of Andy Warhol*. New York: Harvest/HBJ.

Oscar Wilde. 1983. *The Complete Works of Oscar Wilde*. London: Hamlyn.

Pop Truths (After Oscar Wilde)

1.   Small wonder that Michael Jackson sought to buy the bones of the Elephant Man; Jackson was to the reign of Ronald Reagan what John Merrick was to the reign of Queen Victoria.

2.   If Led Zeppelin had realized how awful it was, and if it had been capable of ironizing its awfulness, it could have been U2.

3.   In live performance most bands seek to simulate their recordings—both audio and video. The recordings of the Grateful Dead, however, sought to replicate the band live. That's what made the Dead such an anachronism.

4.   Before kids are granted majority status, they should be required to make one and only one rock 'n' roll record.

5.   Geniuses are a dime a dozen, but an idiot savant is an artistic windfall.

6.   A secularist is one who listens to Sam Cooke and never ever thinks, "God struck that man dead."

7.   Willie Nelson is the Bing Crosby of country music.

8.   MTV tried (but failed) to correct television's most vexing problem: too much time between commercials.

9.   Avant-gardism in rock 'n' roll is always a means of assuaging pop guilt.

10. Elvis Costello's biggest career blunder was not to die in 1982.

11. No record collection is complete without the cover to *Sgt. Pepper's Lonely Hearts Club Band*. The recording itself is optional.

12. Except for Ray Davies, England has produced no singer more hilarious than Morrissey.

13. Rockabilly—a form of guerrilla warfare—proved decisively that the Civil War never ended.

14. In jazz, as in classical music, the avant-garde is less a site of innovation than the academic branch of an artform.

15. Next to Chic, the best rhythm section in popular music probably belonged to the Rolling Stones—or to Fleetwood Mac.

16. Nothing dates faster than lyrics calculated to shock.

17. In "Sonny's Blues," probably the best short story ever written about jazz, James Baldwin labels the housing project a case of architectural satire. He says, "It looks like a parody of the good, clean, faceless life." He also characterizes bebop as musical analog to the housing project. It was opposed to what funkster George Clinton would later call "the vanilla suburbs." Over the received structures of Tin Pan Alley, bebop erected symmetries, smearing coolness, like stucco, over hot-house emotions. Sun Ra and his Arkestra found this strategy way too subtle. Inverting the major tenet of bop—that technique must always serve impeccable taste—they embraced tawdriness. Their experiments with sound and rhythm—cosmic slop wrung from electronic keyboards, early beatboxes, and horns that brayed, squealed, and grunted—gave Arkestra recordings an ethnographic feel or mood. Ra—the point man of pop—peered into the future, spied psychedelia (then Pere Ubu and Public Enemy), and filed a report.

18. Wittiness is the last refuge of a folk musician.

19. The biggest difference between the Mothers of Invention and Parliament-Funkadelic? Frank Zappa never found juvenile humor funny; George Clinton did.

20. When the number of kids allowed to attend rock concerts exceeds the number of kids forced to attend Baptist churches, it's a sure bet that American popular music is in a state of decline. Internalized guilt ensures great music.

21. To become art, jazz didn't have to sell its soul; it only had to forfeit its sense of humor.

22. In the 1950s the best musicians felt guilty about being bad Christians; in the 1960s the best musicians prided themselves in being bad citizens.

23. The Jeff Beck rule: Technical proficiency is inversely proportional to creativity.

24. With the possible exception of Bob Dylan—well, yeah, and there's Beethoven—John Coltrane inspired more boring music than anyone in history.

25. Without the aura of theft, sampling is pointless.

26. Somewhere, Marx suggests something to the effect that all music of great importance occurs, as it were, twice. He forgot to add: the first time in the guise of an "original," the second as hip hop.

27. "Authenticity" is one of the names given products that evoke feelings of guilt brought about when one culture colonizes another culture's property.

28. The postwar avant-garde failed to achieve mass acceptance, not so much because it excluded the audience (what Susan McClary labels "terminal prestige"), but because its most daring experiments were so brilliantly coopted by rock 'n' roll.

29. One of Christianity's great apologists, Amy Grant casts God as desirable by making listeners want to see her—that's Mrs. Grant, not God—naked.

30. For Benny Goodman syncopation seemed to require ebullience; for Artie Shaw it demanded restraint. Or, by way of analogy: Shaw is to Goodman as Fred Astaire is to Gene Kelly—that is, as grace is to virtuosity.

31. How to parade virtuosity without seeming pretentious, that's the problem animating Louis Armstrong's art.

wah-wah pedal—a foot-controlled effects device used to vary the tone of an instrument, most often an electric guitar.

Responding to a trumpet player's request for a device that could electronically simulate a pitch-bending, muted horn, Vox manufactured the wah-wah pedal in 1965. They called the first model the Clyde McCoy, in honor of the trumpet player who had petitioned the company. ("Cry Baby" is the proprietary name for the pedal that the Thomas Organ Company began distributing in the U.S. in 1968.) Nobody could have anticipated how far the effects wrought by the pedal would deviate from the intentions of its creators. Under the boot of Jimi Hendrix, the wah-wah made the electric guitar speak a new language. And when Miles Davis yoked a wah to his trumpet, he perpetrated a musical metalepsis—wah-wah, through an imaginary leap, referred back to plunger-mute and the sound that first elicited the wah-wah.

■

Recordings—A Wah-Wah Top Ten

1. The Jimi Hendrix Experience, "Voodoo Child (Slight Return)," *Electric Ladyland* (MCA).
2. Isaac Hayes "Theme from *Shaft*," *Greatest Hit Singles* (Stax).
3. Sly and the Family Stone, "Sex Machine," *Stand!* (Epic).
4. The Temptations, "Cloud Nine," *The Temptations Anthology* (Motown).
5. Miles Davis, "Black Satin," *On the Corner* (Columbia/Legacy).
6. Stevie Wonder, "Tuesday Heartbreak," *Talking Book* (Tamla).
7. J. J. Cale, "Crazy Mama," *Naturally* (Mercury).
8. The Beatles, "Across the Universe," *Let It Be* (Apple).
9. Morphine, "All Wrong," *Cure for Pain* (Rykodisc).
10. Eddie Harris, "Funkaroma," *Artist's Choice: The Eddie Harris Anthology* (Rhino/Atlantic).

Interview—Record producer Teo Macero runs the hoodoo down (July 1997)

I understand from some people who've gone back into the vault, that they would come up with a tape and compare it with the recording and say, "It doesn't sound like the same tune." Of course it doesn't. Not by the time we used reverb, loops, and all kinds of things that I thought his music should have to make it contemporary. What is it, thirty something years? You listen to *On the Corner*. It sounds like it was done today. It's got a freshness about it—the funk—all the things with the wah-wah pedal. Miles was just learning to use the pedal. I remember—the first day he had it in the studio—it was terrible. I said, "Don't worry about it. We'll wah-wah it in the editing room." And that's what I did. If he made a mistake, I'd take the tapes, and when I did the editing, I'd use the wah-wah pedal and punch it in. Wah-wah them to death. People didn't know that.

If something didn't work, I'd take it out. When I made a record with Miles, I tried to make it as if it were my own. Miles was a great artist. I'd check with him on everything that we were doing. I used to say to Miles, "How do you like that?"

[Imitating Davis's whispered growl] "Yeah, alright!"

And I'd say, "We're going with it—coming out in a month."

After that first album, though, he became very proficient with the wah-wah. He'd do it over long vamps.

After a while, I used to record Miles on two or three microphones so that I could take one program and wah-wah the shit out of it and, at the same time, keep the original program in. It would create a whole different sound. Also, it would go through an amplifier. We'd pick it up direct from the amp. He had a little mike on his bell. We had the natural microphone. Then, I might have had another one nearby. He had a tendency to walk away from the microphones that I used to mark. So we were covered anyway! That's a simple technique, and a lot of producers won't even talk about that. They think it's a phony way of working. But if you go back and listen to it you'll hear. In those days, if you had a solo of the trumpet with a mute, the clipper would automatically reduce the impact of the trumpet. I turned the thing around and made it a monaural and a two-track, so that you get a strong trumpet sound in the middle, the rhythm on the left and the right.

Question for Morphine's Dana Colley (April 1993)

How'd you come up with the sax solo on "All Wrong" [off Cure for Pain*]?*

When I was in high school, I used to play a tenor with a pickup and a Morley power-wah pedal. I played through an amplifier, and, basically, the wah became the instrument. I put it down, though, because I realized that I didn't know what I was doing on the saxophone. I was just playing an effect. But it's always been a sound in the back of my head.

After having done that solo on "All Wrong" as a straight tenor solo, I began to think that it would be great as a wah solo. Essentially, what we did was take the solo that was on tape, put it through another channel, and wah-wahed it in the studio. The effect can be very easily overdone. It probably won't make its way into another song. It found its place, and I'm happy about it.

X—Border radio.

The call letters of every Mexican radio station begin with X, but the designation acquired symbolic resonance when "border blasters" muscled their way onto radio dials. Manifestations of the electronic unconscious, these monsters from the south articulated what North American broadcasting had sought to repress. First, they exposed the politics of radio. In the 1920s, the United States and Canada had colonized the airwaves, divvying up frequencies, shutting out Mexico. In 1930, when Reynosa revved up border station XED, the dispossessed scored a vindictive triumph. Second, border blasters exploited the technology of radio. Their transmitters were enormous (XERA boasted 1 million watts), and their pioneering use of prerecorded "electrical transcriptions" paved the way for postwar programming with records, tapes, and discs. Finally, border radio institutionalized an aesthetic. Through it, the world heard country music: Jimmie Rodgers and the Carter Family.

■

Reading

Gene Fowler and Bill Crawford. 1987. *Border Radio*. Austin: Texas Monthly Press.

Recordings

Dave Alvin, "Border Radio," *King of California* (Hightone).
ZZ Top, "Heard It on the X," *Fandango* (Warner Bros.).
The Blasters, "Border Radio," *The Blasters Collection* (Slash/Warner Bros.).
Wall of Voodoo, "Mexican Radio," *Call of the West* (I.R.S.).
Warren Zevon, "Carmelita," *I'll Sleep When I'm Dead: The Warren Zevon Anthology* (Rhino).

Videos

Allison Anders. 1988. *Border Radio*.
Ken Burns. 1991. *Empire of the Air: The Men Who Made Radio*.
George Lucas. 1973. *American Graffiti*.
Allan Moyle. 1990. *Pump Up the Volume*.

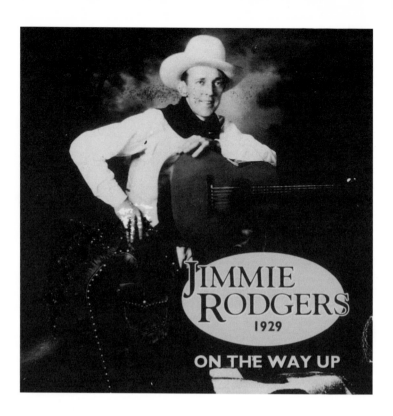

JIMMIE RODGERS 1929

ON THE WAY UP

"Yodeling Cowboy"—A song recorded by Jimmie Rodgers, October 22, 1929, designating a shift in the connotations that would eventually redefine country music as mythically "western," not "hillbilly."

"How many of you can say, '*Oh*'?" asks yodeling cowboy Don Walser. (He admits that he's repeating a lesson picked up from Sourdough Slim.) "How about '*Oh-EE*'—with a falsetto on the '*EE*'?

"Put a '*lay*' in the middle of that—'*Oh-lay-EE.*'

"Put a '*dee*' on the front of it—'*Dee-oh-lay-EE.*'

"Then, put a '*tee*' on the end of that—'*Dee-oh-lay-EE-tee*'—and an '*eye*' in the front—'*Eye-DEE-oh-lay-EE-tee.*'

"You can switch it out to an '*A*'—'*A-DEE-oh-lay-EE-tee.*'

"Use those tones. There's only half a dozen, eight or so. That's the way you yodel." You might also sport a suit designed by Nudie, and saddle up a palomino named Trigger.

■

Recordings—My picks

Eddy Arnold, *The Essential Eddy Arnold* (RCA).

Merle Haggard, *Same Train, A Different Time: Merle Haggard Sings the Great Songs of Jimmie Rodgers* (Koch).

Emmett Miller, *The Minstrel Man from Georgia* (Columbia/Legacy).

Jimmie Rodgers, *The Essential Jimmie Rodgers* (RCA).

Louis Sarno, producer, *Bayaka: The Extraordinary Music of the Babenzélé Pygmies* (Ellipsis Arts).

Sly and the Family Stone, "Spaced Cowboy," *There's a Riot Going On* (Epic).

Don Walser, *Rolling Stone from Texas* (Watermelon).

Slim Whitman, *Greatest Hits* (Curb).

Hank Williams, *40 Greatest Hits* (Polydor).

Various, *Cattle Call: Early Cowboy Music and Its Roots* (Rounder).

Interview—Don Walser's picks (July 1996)

I like "Casting My Lasso" and "Chime Bells" and "Cowpoke." And I like the ones I've written: "Yodel Polka" and "Rolling Stone from Texas." I like the "California Blues" and "All Around the Water Tank," "Waiting for a Train": Jimmie Rodgers type songs. Elton Britt had one called "Cannonball Yodel" that I really enjoyed. Roy Rogers used to do some yodeling, like "Devil's Great Grandson" and some of those kind of things. Eddie Arnold's "Cattle Call" is one of my favorites. He didn't write it. I think the words were written by Fred Rose. And Tex Owens wrote a version of it, but he really just wrote a version of it. The same way with Fred. I got a book here of cowboy songs. There's probably twenty-five or thirty different sets of words for that song.

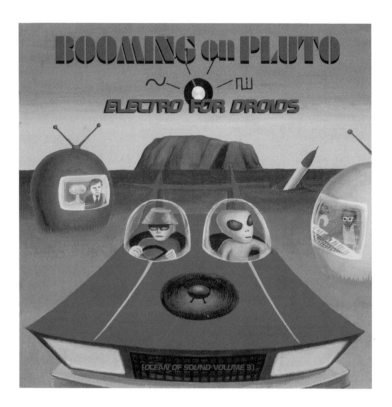

Zulu Nation—Afrika Bambaataa's designation for a transglobal, hip-hop utopia.

"Electro," a dance genre celebrating the interface of human beings and machines, found expression with "Planet Rock"—a 1982 single produced by Arthur Baker and featuring Afrika Bambaataa rapping over 808 beats and a Kraftwerk melody. Zulu Nation, the utopian vision announced by Bam's hit song, had much earlier generic origins. Its evocation, not of a fully developed social program, but of some barely apprehended alternative to ordinary life, recalled the "dream satires" and "fantastic journeys" of literature (not to mention the space mythologies of Sun Ra, St. EOM, and George Clinton). For example, Mikhail Bakhtin's comments on Dostoevsky's "Dream of a Ridiculous Man" apply equally to "Planet Rock" and Zulu Nation: "The life seen in the dream makes ordinary life seem strange, forces one to understand and evaluate ordinary life in a new way (in the light of another glimpsed possibility)" (147).

■

Readings

Mikhail Bakhtin. 1984. *Problems of Dostoevsky's Poetics*. Trans. Caryl Emerson. Minneapolis: University of Minnesota Press. [See pp. 147–53.]

John Corbett. 1994. "Brothers from Another Planet: The Space Madness of Lee 'Scratch' Perry, Sun Ra, and George Clinton." In *Extended Play: Sounding Off from John Cage to Dr. Funkenstein*, pp. 7–24. Durham, N.C.: Duke University Press.

S. H. Fernando, Jr. 1995. "Afrika Bambaataa." In *Spin Alternative Record Guide*, ed. Eric Weisbard with Craig Marks, pp. 27–28. New York: Vintage.

George Lipsitz. 1994. "Diasporic Noise: History, Hip Hop, and the Postcolonial Politics of Sound." In *Dangerous Crossroads: Popular Music, Postmodernism and the Poetics of Place*. London: Verso.

David Toop. 1996. "A to Z of Electro." *Wire*, March, 18–21.

Recordings

Afrika Bambaataa, *12" Mixes* (ZYX).

Funkadelic, *One Nation Under a Groove* (Priority).

Sun Ra and His Intergalactic Solar Arkestra, *Soundtrack to Space Is the Place* (Evidence).

Various, *Booming on Pluto: Electro for Droids* (Virgin/Import).

Various, *Electro Funk, Vols. 1 and 2* (Priority).

volume
three

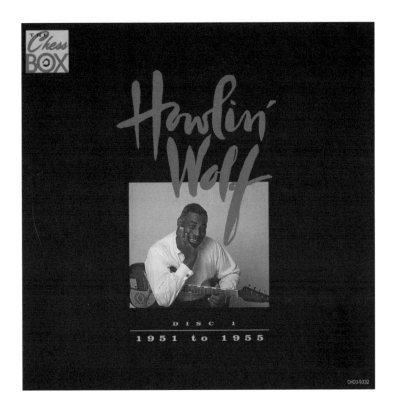

authenticity—In music, the effect of realism;
derived not from adhering to a formal paradigm (as in
film) but through displaying codes of passion (available
only to those *perceived* as dispossessed or worldly wise).

To describe popularization—what semioticians call conventionalization—music writers typically borrow a model derived from
nineteenth-century physical science. The process is characterized as
the cultural equivalent of the second law of thermodynamics: Energy
tends toward a state of equilibrium. "Innovative, unconventional
codes gradually become adopted by the majority," writes John Fiske
(87). In *Introduction to Communication Studies*, Fiske uses this entropy
model to explain the "broad cultural acceptance" of jazz during the
Swing Era. Dick Hebdige, in *Subculture: The Meaning of Style*, a now
classic study of "punk" culture, relies on the same model. What

Simon Frith and Andrew Goodwin call a theory of "progress by attrition" is, perhaps, *the* foundational myth of popular music (ix). It lies at the heart of all distinctions that attempt to delineate a boundary between the authentic and the commercial, in whatever guise that may take: rock vs. pop, black vs. white, modern vs. postmodern, alternative vs. mainstream.

Popularization, though, like its counterpart in physics, is in itself neither negative nor positive, neither good nor bad. It just is—or so the discourse of communication theory would have us believe. If we perceive conventionalization or popularization as a "lowering of quality because it involves appealing to the 'lowest common denominator,'" writes Fiske (following Basil Bernstein), "we should be aware that it [such a judgment] is made from within a particular value-system" (87). All the same, descriptions of conventionalization typically, perhaps always, employ a rhetoric of degeneration. They chart it as a downward course—a semiotic diaspora—and rely on readers decoding such a journey Platonically, as a deviation from the Good. Hence, popularization receives a plot—tragedy—and thereby the very notion of the authentic (pure code) is erected as something opposed to the conventional (popularized code).

As any reader familiar with the literature of deconstruction knows, it would be possible to prove this opposition untenable. The catch is, I lack the patience (and the necessary philosophical orientation) to reenact what has become the most standard sort of reading. Instead, I want to reread (then misread) the rhetoric of degeneration that informs the history of popular music. My first example is a brief tragicomic history of jazz, but it could be read allegorically as the "progress" of rock 'n' roll. Hebdige writes:

> As the music fed into mainstream popular culture during the 20s and
> 30s, it tended to become bowdlerized, drained of surplus eroticism, and
> any hint of anger or recrimination blown along the "hot" lines was delicately refined into inoffensive night club sound. White swing represents the climax of this process: innocuous, generally unobtrusive, possessing a broad appeal, it was a laundered product which contained
> none of the subversive connotations of its original black sources. These
> suppressed meanings were, however, triumphantly reaffirmed in bebop, and by the mid-50s a new, younger white audience began to see

itself reflected darkly in the dangerous, uneven surfaces of contemporary *avant-garde*, despite the fact that the musicians responsible for the New York sound deliberately sought to restrict white identification by producing a jazz which was difficult to listen to and even more difficult to imitate. (46–47)

Hot jazz turns to swing, bop turns cool, eroticism becomes lassitude, black bleaches to white, the dirty gets laundered, and the uneven is worn smooth: the structure of this apocalyptic sequence reproduces itself any number of times in accounts of American popular music since World War II. To pick several examples, it is the story of how rock 'n' roll fans could get, first, Little Richard, then Pat Boone, and finally the Beatles singing "Long Tall Sally." Or how sixties rock could become seventies disco before its fundamental values were reaffirmed by late-seventies punk (only to transform into the rave music of the late eighties). It is also evident in the arc of Elvis Presley's career: from 1956–1958 (hot as Memphis asphalt) to 1959–1967 (bland as unbuttered grits) to 1968 (meaner than a hornet).

This model of conventionalization/popularization feels ontologically stable because it explains the process whereby "authentic" music (a narrowcast code) is translated into "commercial" music (a broadcast code) for the purpose of selling music to a wide audience. And it sounds (politically) correct because it explains what Andrew Ross calls "the everyday, plagiaristic, commerce between white ['commercial'] and black ['authentic'] musics"; it conceptualizes the history of American popular music as a series of unilateral, commercially driven energy exchanges that everywhere bespeak "a racist history of exploitation exclusively weighted to dominant white interests" (68). Like all received models, this one has its attractions.

It also has real failings. As Ross points out, the formula "commercialized music = whitened music" simply will not hold. Since "commercial and contractual relations enter into *all* realms of musical entertainment, or at least wherever music is performed in order to make a living," there can be "no tidy coincidence" between "discourse about color ('whitened' music)" and "discourse about commercialization ('alienated' music)." To subscribe to such an equation "is to imagine a very mechanical process indeed, whereby a music, which is authentically black, constitutes an initial raw material which is then appropriated and reduced in cultural force and meaning by contact with a white industry. Accordingly, music is never 'made,' and only ever exploited, in this process of industrialization" (69–70).

But the biggest failure of the heat-death model of conventionalization/popularization is this: it cannot account for innovation. By picturing the history of popular music as a downward spiral of "progress" by attrition, it fails to explain how so-called authentic music arises. More specifically, it continues to rely on the thinly disguised metaphysical assumption that genius visits select musicians, or (the more contemporary view) that the rock 'n' roll muse does not strike so much as she resides within a "tradition." Serious musicians locate her by searching their "soul" or their "roots." Listeners, on the other hand, find "authenticity" when they tune in to the exotic (Delta blues or world music), the esoteric ("alternative" music), or the canonical ("classic" rock).

We need a better theory. Surprisingly enough, I nominate one that extends the possibilities suggested by the old theory of conventionalization/popularization. It exploits the potential energy of decay (decomposition) and, in providing an account of innovation in rock 'n' roll, suggests a paradigm of invention that could be generalized to other fields. In other words, I want to sketch out a theory that, without denying "degeneration," insists that something is gained through conventionalization. Before initiating that project, however, I want to emphasize the overlap of "authentic" and "commercial" music. Only by unsettling this opposition can we begin to rethink a cultural model of conventionalization predicated on heat-death.

Our experience of twentieth-century popular culture is defined by what Frith calls "the contrast between music-as-expression and music-as-commodity." He writes: "However much we may use and enjoy its products, we retain a sense that the music industry is a bad thing—bad for music, bad for us" (11). For me (a white, male, and, now, middle-aged music consumer), "music-as-expression" has always meant African-American music. It was "authentic," a genuine outpouring of real feeling (quality is a function of proximity to the blues). I have long regarded commercialization as corruption: an "essential human activity" colonized (Frith, 12). I dote over artists such as Aretha Franklin, James Brown, Otis Redding, Chuck Berry, Muddy

Waters, Al Green, Sly and the Family Stone, Junior Kimbrough, and Parliament because, simply put, there "ain't nothing like the real thing, baby"; I love Bob Dylan, the Rolling Stones, the Velvet Underground, Talking Heads, Elvis Costello, the Replacements, Roxy Music, and the Pet Shop Boys because they are—I tell myself—"ironic." But there are two problems with this belief:

1. It is romantic and, ultimately, racist. It updates Rousseau's doctrine of the noble savage as the standard for measuring civilization's descent from its origins.
2. It supposes, as Frith points out, "that music is the starting point of the industrial process—the raw material over which everyone fights—when it is, in fact, the final product" (12).

When I state that white people exploited, and continue to exploit, black people, I'm acknowledging injustice, but I am also articulating a central tenet of the music industry. It literally banks on—makes money off—my belief. The assumption that bad (commercial) things happen to "authentic" music is sufficient to generate the real/fake distinction that has become musical common sense (Frith, 57). It creates a consumer who understands the history of American popular music as a series of authentic moments (innovation) degrading into convention (imitation). For every Jesus, you get twelve disciples.

There is, however, an alternative way of viewing the history of popular music and the process of conventionalization. It involves investigating decomposition as an image sufficient not only for explanation but for innovation. Nathaniel Mackey opened up the possibilities of this image when, in his epistolary novel *Bedouin Hornbook*, he wrote: "There must be some way, I'm convinced, to invest in the ever so slight suggestion of 'compost' I continue to get from the word compose" (78–79). Brian Eno, a recording artist best known for his production work with David Bowie, Talking Heads, and U2, took it further. "I would think you'd have mixed feelings about new artists doing something that really isn't new art," an interviewer commented. Eno replied:

> If you think of culture as a great big garden, it has to have its compost as well. And lots of people are doing things that are . . . not dramatic or radical or not even particularly interesting; they're just digestive pro-

cesses. . . . If you think about music in that way, it makes it much easier to accept that there might be lots of things you might not want to hear again. They happen and they pass and they become the compost for something else to grow from [laughs]. Gardening is such a good lesson for all sorts of things. (Quoted in Tannenbaum, 72)

Eno must have been thinking about composer John Cage when he recommended gardening as an analogy for musical production. After all, during the interview just cited, Cage—an expert on fungi (and founder of the New York Mycological Society)—was seated in the room with Eno.

In *Silence*, Cage wrote: "I have come to the conclusion that much can be learned about music by devoting oneself to the mushroom." Why mushrooms? The secondhand bookshops that stock "'field companions' on fungi" are "in some rare cases next door to shops selling dog-eared sheets of music" (274). Cage's "logic" should alert us. Anything mushrooms can teach us about music results from a fortuitous, arbitrary allegory (an accident of signification). What, then, is the lesson of mushrooms? Simple. All the Baptist ministers I heard pontificating against pop music while I was growing up were right: Rock 'n' roll is a mushroom, a fungus in the garden of culture. ("My records are parasites on the music business," says Eno [quoted in Greenwald, 39].) But given my conception of fungi, the ministers' accusations were not nearly as damaging as they were intended to be. In practice, I responded to ministerial admonitions much as David Arora, author of *Mushrooms Demystified*, responded to parental admonitions to "stay away from mushrooms." They "inspired me to get closer," he writes in the dedication to his work. As Gregory Ulmer notes, the lesson taught by mushrooms—or, more properly, fungi, since a mushroom is the reproductive structure (fruiting body) of a fungus—is *symbiosis*. The kind of fungi hunted and eaten by Cage ("the fleshy, fruity, 'higher' fungi, Boletus, Morels, and the like") are "not parasites, but *saprophytes* (any organism that lives on dead organic matter)." They exist in a "mutually beneficial relationship with their hosts (the green plants and trees which supply the organic 'food')" (Ulmer, "The Object of Post-Criticism," 105). "They are nature's recyclers," writes Arora. In feeding on dead matter, they "reduce complex organic compounds to simpler building blocks, thereby enabling plants to re-use them" (6). The saprophyte—which is to say, rock 'n' roll—feeds off the decay of tradition. It treats culture as compost.

To comprehend what this means, note that "something becomes an object of knowledge . . . only as it . . . is made to disintegrate" (Ulmer, 97). Popularization does to ideas what decay does to organic materials—it turns them into compost so that they can be transformed into something new. What makes Eno especially interesting is that he has turned this process into a compositional methodology. In the liner notes to *Ambient 4/On Land*, he describes his interest in treating "found sound"—"pieces of chain and sticks and stones, . . . recordings of rooks, frogs and insects," and also the "complete body" of his "earlier work"—as a "completely plastic and malleable material": "As a result, some earlier pieces I worked on became digested by later ones, which in turn became digested again. This technique is like composting: converting what would otherwise have been waste into nourishment."

Although it is difficult to hear any relationship between Eno's static soundscapes and, say, the music of Neil Young or Oasis—Beck and the Chemical Brothers are less of a stretch—his method makes explicit the normal functioning of rock 'n' roll. Conventionalization is the compost from which innovation grows. It fosters artistic renewal by generating conditions that allow for aberrant readings or interpretations. To show how this happens, I want to rewrite, in a highly schematic form, Hebdige's history of jazz, which I cited early in this essay. Like him, I begin with "white swing."

Conventionalization. White swing—less a monolithic style of music than a variety of "popular" musics vying for a "cut" of the market—promotes itself as a privileged mode of expression (Collins, 70).

Aberration. On the levels of production and distribution, conventionalization prompts both experimentation and standardization; on the level of consumption, it allows aberrant decodings ("the rule, not the exception, with mass media messages," writes Fiske [81], recalling Umberto Eco). Musical innovators are aberrant readers; Charlie Parker ("Bird") "misinterprets" the basic materials of swing.

Disputation. Boppers (followers of Bird) vs. Moldy Figs (followers of Bunk Johnson—traditional jazz). Conflicts between groups arise over which musics are and are not innovative, legitimate, authentic, original, etc.

Ratification. Bebop, modern jazz, wins the day. A perceived innovation gains legitimacy by soliciting, gaining, or, in some cases, inventing institutional support. It is retroactively interpreted as authentic (and, thus, canonized). This, however, does not mean that other (suppressed) musical forms cease to exist; they've merely lost their position of power.

This process repeats itself when, in an attempt to maintain or increase the size of their audience, music makers conventionalize—that is, aberrantly read—"authentic" sounds. In jazz, this happened when bebop was conventionalized as hard-bop (a style almost as diverse as "white swing"), then aberrantly read by Ornette Coleman. The origins of rock also followed this pattern. In one version of its story, black rhythm & blues (a heteroglot style that had secularized black gospel) was aberrantly read by Little Richard and Elvis Presley, and, following a dispute with what, for lack of a better term, might be called "classic pop" (recall Frank Sinatra's and Mitch Miller's denunciations of the new style), it was institutionalized as rock 'n' roll.

Scene: Tower Records, South Street, Philadelphia. Mr X walks up to the sales counter and presents a clerk with a major credit card and a compact disc—Elvis's *Sun Sessions*.

CLERK: Elvis Presley, huh?

MR. X: Yeah.

CLERK: I don't know, man. If I wanted to hear good Dean Martin, I'd just buy the real thing.

In every case, the rock musician perceived as innovative is the one who has creatively misread a previously recognized innovation. That's what popularization is. Steering a course between repetition (redundancy) and incomprehensibility (entropy), he or she parlays an aberrant or perverse reading of the past into an authorized reading for the present. Elvis Presley's "misreading" of Dean Martin (a conventionalized version of the saloon singer) offers a good example of this.

Marion Keisker, the office manager of Sam Phillips's Sun Records studio in Memphis, remembers that Elvis, during his first audition, relied so heavily on Dean Martin material that she thought "Elvis had decided '. . . if he was going to sound like anybody, it was going to be Dean Martin'" (quoted in Spedding, 129). Picking up on this clue, Chris Spedding argues that many of Elvis's "actions previously dismissed (or considered perverse when they could not be ignored)" can be explained by his admiration for the actor-singer who was, during the mid-1950s, "*the* most bankable of matinee idols." Comparing Martin's big hit of 1955, "Memories Are Made of This," with "the song Elvis always said was *his* favorite cut, 'Don't Be Cruel,' a hit in the summer of the following year," Spedding notes:

> Now, apart from the fact that Elvis borrowed that descending-bass-run-followed-by-guitar-chord ending from Martin's arrangement, other common elements are that sexy, wobbly, almost hiccuping baritone vocal—not yet identifiably "rock" until Elvis made it so—and Martin's novel use of a four-piece gospel-type vocal group which we may now assume inspired Elvis to introduce the Jordanaires on *his* cut, effectively integrating them into a unique blend with his own lead vocal, thus establishing another rock archetype. (129–30)

The joke is, Elvis's music was a poor imitation of Dean Martin's, and that, strangely enough, has something—maybe everything—to do with why his music is so much better than Martin's ("50 million Elvis fans can't be wrong"). Elvis's method, not just the noise Elvis made, is the essence of rock 'n' roll. Overly simple, sure, but consider the history of rock as a series of four revolutionary moments when something new grew out of critical misreadings of available material: musical compost. Elvis and Little Richard (mid-1950s) perversely read rhythm & blues and country & western music; Bob Dylan and the Beatles (mid-1960s) perversely read early rock 'n' roll and American folk music; the Sex Pistols and the Clash (mid-1970s) perversely read art-pop and reggae; Run DMC and the Beastie Boys (mid-1980s) perversely read popular music's basic material object—the record. Hip hop attains critical mass; pop eats itself. Undoubtedly, there's a dialectic at work here. History unfolds. Hegel believed it was energized by Spirit. Marx thought it was driven by economic forces. And the children of Elvis and Little Richard suspect that obsessive love makes the pop world spin. All the great proper names of rock 'n' roll are or were inspired amateurs, no matter how well they could play or sing.

A French professor of mine once informed me that Barthes's *S/Z* was grossly overrated. He said, "If you want to read *good* criticism on Balzac, don't read Roland Barthes." He was, of course, correct, but he had missed the whole point of critical theory. He not only failed to see that what counts as "good" criticism is now up for grabs, but that innovation (or what rhetoricians call invention) means learning how to read aberrantly, how to generate imminently cooptable misreadings. In *S/Z*, Barthes treated Balzac's novella "Sarrasine" as a compost pile, something from which he could fashion another text of his own. Like a rock or jazz musician, he treated his basic materials—and surely you thought of this well before I wrote it—like *shit*. Manure and maneuver are etymologically linked to *manouvrer*, Old French for working with the hands, cultivating.

Classical music and formalism require skills of *rereading*. Typically, they emphasize faithfulness to texts—to established conventions of production through interpretation. In doing so they create continuities with our pasts. Popular music and poststructuralism, on the other hand, reward *misreading*. They require us to maneuver texts into other texts that will feel different and generate authenticity as an effect. Jean-Luc Godard explains this reorientation:

> As a critic, I thought of myself as a film-maker. Today I still think of myself as a critic, and in a sense I am, more than ever before. Instead of writing criticism, I make a film, but the critical dimension is subsumed. I think of myself as an essayist, producing essays in novel form or novels in essay form: only instead of writing, I film them. (171)

There is, of course, no reason to abandon either classical or pop approaches to textual production. Or more prescriptively, there's good reason to keep emphasizing the acquisition of rereading skills: They lead to scholarship. And there's every reason to cultivate strategies of misreading: They lead to creativity. Rock 'n' roll, for example, could function as a tutor text for learning how to misread. Here are several powerful, transferrable lessons it teaches.

1. *Doin' It to Death:* the lesson of *repetition.* Cage wrote: "We know two ways to unfocus attention: symmetry is one of them; the other is the over-all where each small part is a sample of what you find elsewhere" (187). Mechanical reproduction, notes Walter Benjamin in his landmark essay, repudiates the values invested in words such as "art" and "authenticity" (680–81).

   Read: Jacques Derrida, "Dissemination," in *Dissemination.*
   Listen: James Brown, *In the Jungle Groove* (Polydor).

2. *If I Were a Black Man:* the lesson of *simulation.* The "rapp" was a counterfeit coin, worth about half a farthing, that passed as legal tender in Ireland in the eighteenth century, "owing to the scarcity of genuine money" (*OED*). When Malcolm McLaren, the situationist who packaged the Sex Pistols, was sued for "appropriating" others' music to make his own album, *Duck Rock*, he said: "All I can say is that accusations of plagiarism don't bother me. As far as I'm concerned it's all I'm useful for" (quoted in Taylor, 16).

   Read: Robert Smithson, "A Tour of the Monuments of Passaic, New Jersey," in *The Writings of Robert Smithson.*
   Listen: Gang of Four, *Entertainment!* (Infinite Zero/American).

3. *Cut 'n' Mix:* the lesson of *bricolage.* "The process of bricolage involves carefully and precisely ordering, classifying and arranging into structures the *minutiae*, the detritus, of the physical world. It is a 'science of the concrete' (as opposed to our 'civilised' science of the 'abstract')" (Hawkes, 51).

   Read: Gregory Ulmer, "Derrida at the Little Bighorn," in *Teletheory: Grammatology in the Age of Video.*
   Listen: Beastie Boys, *Paul's Boutique* (Capitol).

4. *Bring the Noise:* the lesson of the *parasite.* In French, "parasite" means (a) to inhabit another (as a demon possesses a body), (b) to make noise or static, and (c) to take without giving (Serres, 7). Writes Simon Reynolds: "The power of pop lies not in its meaning but its noise, not in its import but its force" (10).

   Read: Gilles Deleuze and Félix Guattari, "1730: Becoming-Intense, Becoming-Animal, Becoming-Imperceptible . . . ," in *A Thousand Plateaus: Capitalism and Schizophrenia.*
   Listen: Sonic Youth, *Daydream Nation* (Geffen).

■

Works Cited and Suggested Readings

David Arora. 1986. *Mushrooms Demystified: A Comprehensive Guide to the Fleshy Fungi.* 2d ed. Berkeley, Calif.: Ten Speed.

Roland Barthes. 1974. *S/Z.* Trans. Richard Howard. New York: Hill and Wang.

Walter Benjamin. 1985. "The Work of Art in the Age of Mechanical Reproduction." In *Film Theory and Criticism*, ed. Gerald Mast and Marshall Cohen, trans. Harry Zohn. New York: Oxford University Press.

John Cage. 1961. *Silence.* Middletown, Conn.: Wesleyan University Press.

Jim Collins. 1989. *Uncommon Cultures: Popular Culture and Post-Modernism.* New York: Routledge.

Gilles Deleuze and Félix Guattari. 1987. *A Thousand Plateaus: Capitalism and Schizophrenia.* Trans. Brian Massumi. Minneapolis: University of Minnesota Press.

Jacques Derrida. 1981. *Dissemination.* Trans. Barbara Johnson. Chicago: University of Chicago Press.

Brian Eno. 1982. Liner notes to *Ambient 4/On Land* (Editions EG).

John Fiske. 1982. *Introduction to Communication Studies.* New York: Methuen.

Simon Frith. 1988. "Introduction: Everything Counts." In *Music for Pleasure: Essays in the Sociology of Pop.* New York: Routledge.

Simon Frith and Andrew Goodwin, eds. 1990. *On Record: Rock, Pop, and the Written Word.* New York: Pantheon Books.

Jean-Luc Godard. 1986. *Godard on Godard.* Trans. and ed. Tom Milne. New York: Da Capo.

Ted Greenwald. 1991. "The Wayward Art Rocker Rediscovers Songs." *Creem*, February–March 1991, 39–45.

Terence Hawkes. 1977. *Structuralism and Semiotics.* Berkeley: University of California Press.

Dick Hebdige. 1979. *Subculture: The Meaning of Style.* London: Methuen, 1979.

Nathaniel Mackey. 1986. *Bedouin Hornbook.* Lexington: University Press of Kentucky.

Simon Reynolds. 1990. *Blissed Out: The Raptures of Rock.* London: Serpent's Tail.

Andrew Ross. 1989. *No Respect: Intellectuals and Popular Culture.* New York: Routledge.

Michel Serres. 1982. *The Parasite.* Trans. Lawrence R. Schehr. Baltimore: Johns Hopkins University Press.

Robert Smithson. 1979. *The Writings of Robert Smithson*. Ed. Nancy Holt. New York: New York University Press.

Chris Spedding. 1990. "Elvis & Dino." *Musician*, February 1990, 129–30.

Rob Tannenbaum. 1985. "A Meeting of Sound Minds, John Cage + Brian Eno." *Musician*, September 1985, 64–72+.

Paul Taylor. 1988. "The Impresario of Do-It-Yourself." In *Impresario: Malcolm McLaren and the British New Wave*, ed. Paul Taylor, pp. 11–30. Cambridge, Mass.: MIT Press.

Gregory L. Ulmer. 1983. "The Object of Post-Criticism." In *The Anti-Aesthetic: Essays on Postmodern Culture*, ed. Hal Foster. Port Townsend, Wash.: Bay Press.

———. 1989. *Teletheory: Grammatology in the Age of Video*. New York: Routledge.

STAN GETZ
The Girl From Ipanema
THE BOSSA NOVA YEARS
Featuring Antonio Carlos Jobim • Joao Gilberto
Astrud Gilberto • Charlie Byrd • Luiz Bonfa
Laurindo Almeida • The Gary McFarland Orchestra

bossa nova—A form of Brazilian popular song, devised by **Antonio Carlos Jobim**, that combines samba rhythms, cool-jazz harmonies and endearing melodies. In Brazil, it found popularity with João Gilberto's recording, "Chega de Saudade" (1959); in the U.S., with the Stan Getz/Charlie Byrd LP, *Jazz Samba* (1962) and the Getz/ Gilberto hit, "The Girl from Ipanema" (1964). [From Portugese, *bossa*, "trend" + *nova*, "new."]

Formulating an elegant solution to a musical quandary—"How ought we dance to bossa nova?"—Priscilla, a native of Rio, said, "March in place and swivel your hips." Everyone within earshot agreed, "That's Brazilian ideology in a nutshell!" Denied any possibility of effecting social reform through politics, Brazilians in the late 1950s compensated. En masse, they discovered bohemianism—which substitutes aesthetics for politics—and in the mellifluous, casual lilt of the bossa nova embraced a music that evokes *saudade*, the mood accompanying detachment.

■

Recordings—Bossa nova favorites, jingoistic for sure, but then again, the genre was a hybrid of South and North American elements

The Charlie Byrd Trio with Ken Peplowski, *The Bossa Nova Years* (Concord Picante).
Eliane Elias, *Eliane Elias Plays Jobim* (Blue Note).
Stan Getz, *The Girl from Ipanema—The Bossa Nova Years* (Verve).
Coleman Hawkins, *Desafinado* (Impulse!).
Joe Henderson, *Double Rainbow: The Music of Antonio Carlos Jobim* (Verve).
Susannah McCorkle, *Sabia* (Concord).
Gerry Mulligan with Jane Duboc, *Paraiso* (Telarc).
Various, *Antonio Carlos Jobim: The Man from Ipanema* (Verve).
Various, *The Girl from Ipanema: The Antonio Carlos Jobim Songbook* (Verve).
Various, *Red Hot + Rio* (Antilles).

Interview—Q&A with Arto Lindsay (April 1995)

You're the child of missionaries. Did you grow up in boarding school?

We lived in northeast Brazil, in Pernambuco, a town in the interior. I lived at home, but went away for three years, my last three years of high school.

Do you consider yourself an unintended result of that background?

It's hard for me to pin down, because I don't spend that much time thinking about it. I feel that the unexamined situation is worth more than the analyzed situation. It's said that preachers' kids are the wildest, and there's definitely an element of that. Preachers can be very idealistic. Christianity is like any religion—above and beyond daily life. Somehow I turned that into enjoying doing nothing.

That feeling of not belonging to the dominant culture can be incredibly pleasurable or painful.

To me, it was pretty much all pleasure—that aspect of it. I grew up somewhere I wasn't from, and even though, after a while, I was from there, I wasn't really in. I didn't take things at face value. People would think, "Well, this is the way things are. I'd think, "That's the way things are *here*. They're not that way over there, so they must be different over there, in that other place, too. And I wonder what it's like over there."

You became a cultural relativist. As a boy, were you aware of the cultural richness of Brazil, or did that awareness come with adulthood?

I was pretty aware as a teenager how rich culture was here. It's kind of marginal—or has been in this century. Brazilian culture has seen itself as being off to the side. That's one aspect. The other aspect is that, because it is off the beaten path—for historical and economic reasons Portuguese is a minor language in the sense of the number of people who have access to it and its impact on other languages—Brazil is a world unto itself. There's no place like it, really, except the States. It's really like the States. The music there is so many different kinds of music. It's huge down here—and things can develop in isolation. There are all these different points of contact between African and European music, which is basically what makes American music what it is—North and South. It's New World music. There's a lot of good music in North and South America, but basically there's American music, Cuban music, and Brazilian music. Those are the most developed, and they all have a different relation to African music.

brush arbor—A variety of sacred country music, similar to bluegrass, characterized by the collision of string-band delicacy and Pentecostal zeal.

"Bill Monroe did a high, lonesome—some people say a synthetic sound, explains guitarist and singer Jerry Sullivan. "Bluegrass is real precise. Monroe used a mandolin for the drum, and he used the banjo for the piano roll." The brush arbor style, which takes its name from the makeshift shelters Southerners used as places of worship during the Depression, "is more like families sitting down with a guitar, maybe a mandolin, and playing. They followed the Carter Family sound a little bit. It's a mixture between the country sound and bluegrass." When Marty Stuart sent Bob Dylan a copy of Jerry and Tammy Sullivan's brush arbor–inspired album, *At the Feet of God*, he enclosed a note that read, "I hope you enjoy this backwoods, Southern, rock 'n' roll, gospel record."

■

Readings

Dennis Covington. 1995. *Salvation on Sand Mountain: Snake Handling and Redemption in Southern Appalachia.* Reading, Mass.: Addison-Wesley.

Charles Wolfe. 1996. *In Close Harmony: The Story of the Louvin Brothers.* Jackson: University Press of Mississippi.

Recordings—This best-of list represents a variety of country gospel styles

E. C. and Orna Ball, *E. C. Ball with Orna Ball* (Rounder).

The Chestnut Grove Quartet, *The Legendary Chestnut Grove Quartet* (County).

Alison Krauss and the Cox Family, *I Know Who Holds Tomorrow* (Rounder).

Doyle Lawson and Quicksilver, *Rock My Soul* (Sugar Hill).

The Louvin Brothers, *When I Stop Dreaming: The Best of the Louvin Brothers* (Razor & Tie).

Jerry and Tammy Sullivan, *At the Feet of God* (New Haven).

The Whitstein Brothers, *Sweet Harmony* (Rounder).

Stanley Brothers, *The Complete Columbia Stanley Brothers* (Columbia/Legacy).

Various, *Something Got a Hold of Me: A Treasury of Sacred Music* (RCA).

Various, *Southern Journey Vol. 4: Brethren, We Meet Again* (Rounder).

THE ORIGINAL DECCA RECORDINGS

Bing Crosby and Some Jazz Friends

Bing Crosby

DECCA JAZZ

croon—To sing softly—mezzo voce—in low, intimate tones; specifically, a style of singing made popular by male vocalists, 1925–1950.

In the mid-1920s, advances in electronic amplification transformed singing in a manner analogous to cinema's earlier transformation of acting. Just as the movie camera (and, specifically, the discovery of the close-up) eliminated the need for the broad gestures of stage performance, microphones and loudspeakers eliminated the need to project the voice as in classical singing. A wink could be seen on screen, a whisper could be heard on radio, by millions of people. Hence, Bing Crosby is to sound recording what Greta Garbo is to motion pictures. Both are archetypical stars. Above all, they were able to broadcast (amplify and project) intimacy, to communicate emotional directness through mass media.

■

Readings

Michael Chanan. 1995. "Recording Electrified." In *Repeated Takes: A Short History of Recording and Its Effects on Music*. New York: Verso.

Will Friedwald. 1990. *Jazz Singing: America's Great Voices From Bessie Smith to Bebop and Beyond*. New York: Scribner's.

Henry Pleasants. 1974. *The Great American Popular Singers*. New York: Simon and Schuster.

Alec Wilder. 1972. *American Popular Song: The Great Innovators, 1900–1950*. New York: Oxford University Press.

Recordings

Bing Crosby, *The Crooner: The Columbia Years 1928–1934* (Columbia).

Various Artists, *Closer Than a Kiss: Crooner Classics* (Rhino).

Various Artists, *The Crooners* (Columbia/Legacy).

DIDs—Desert Island Discs; a term referring both to prized recordings and to lists (typically of ten titles) that name such recordings.

DIDs grant listmakers pleasure (1) by alleviating the guilt of actually listening to all the music they've hoarded and (2) by encouraging an eschatological revenge fantasy. During an imminent but benevolent apocalypse, the industrial apparatus that produces and sustains music is destroyed without destroying music itself (perhaps with an art-avoidant smart bomb). Consumers are forced to pack up their favorite recordings and abandon a world typified by oppressive abundance and chronic overchoice for an idyllic life spent on an island that bears a suspicious resemblance to Bikini. It's the end of world as we know it, and everybody feels fine.

■

Readings

Nick Hornby. 1995. *High Fidelity*. New York: Riverhead Books.

Greil Marcus, ed. 1991. *Stranded: Rock and Roll for a Desert Island*. New York: Da Capo.

Daisann McLane. 1994. "Tuff Grooves." *Rolling Stone*, February, 42.

Tom Wheeler. 1987. "Essential Guitar Albums: An Introduction." *Guitar Player*, January, 86. [Following Wheeler's introduction are essays—DIDs—on jazz, blues, rock, bass, country, classical, and steel guitar albums.]

Recordings—My DIDs (in alphabetical order; no big boxes)

ROCK

Beastie Boys, *Paul's Boutique* (Capitol).

Clash, *London Calling* (Epic).

Bob Dylan, *Highway 61 Revisited* (Columbia).

Aretha Franklin, *I Never Loved a Man the Way I Love You* (Atlantic).

Al Green, *Call Me* (The Right Stuff).

Pere Ubu, *The Modern Dance*, available on *Datapanik in the Year Zero* (Geffen).

Rolling Stones, *Exile on Main Street* (Columbia).

Sly and the Family Stone, *Greatest Hits* (Epic).

Dusty Springfield, *Dusty in Memphis* (Rhino/Atlantic).

Television, *Marquee Moon* (Elektra).

COUNTRY

Chet Atkins/Les Paul, *Masters of the Guitar—Together* (RCA/Pair).

Ray Charles, *Modern Sounds in Country and Western Music* (Rhino).

The Flying Burrito Brothers, *The Gilded Palace of Sin* (Edsel).

Lefty Frizzell, *Look What Thoughts Will Do* (Columbia/Legacy).

Merle Haggard, *The Lonesome Fugitive: The Merle Haggard Anthology (1963–1977)* (Razor & Tie).

Alison Krauss, *Now That I've Found You: A Collection* (Rounder).

Dolly Parton, *The RCA Years 1967–1986* (RCA).

Hank Williams, *40 Greatest Hits* (Polydor).

Lucinda Williams, *Lucinda Williams* (Rough Trade).

Bob Wills & His Texas Playboys, *Anthology (1935–1973)* (Rhino).

JAZZ

John Coltrane, *A Love Supreme* (Impulse!).

Miles Davis, *Jack Johnson* (Columbia/Legacy).

Duke Ellington, *. . . And His Mother Called Him Bill* (Bluebird).

Charles Mingus, *The Black Saint and the Sinner Lady* (Impulse!).

Thelonious Monk, *The Best of Thelonious Monk: The Blue Note Years* (Blue Note).

Kip Hanrahan et al., *American Clavé* (American Clavé).

Rahsaan Roland Kirk, *Does Your House Have Lions? The Rahsaan Roland Kirk Anthology* (Rhino/Atlantic).

Sonny Rollins, *Silver City* (Milestone).

James Blood Ulmer, *Odyssey* (Columbia/Legacy).

Various, *Masters of Jazz, Vol. 1: Traditional Jazz Classics* (Rhino).

The best of
Doo Wop
Uptempo

doo-wop—An urban folk music popularized in
the 1950s, distinguished by the use of nonsense syllables
(e.g., "doo-wop") repeated to create ornate vocal
harmonies and rhythmic effects.

From one perspective, doo-wop represents the dissemination of a
monster hit: the Orioles' "It's Too Soon to Know" (1948). Another,
more dialectical perspective suggests that it resulted when street-
corner harmonists—part of America's emerging postwar youth culture—established what would become rock 'n' roll's most enduring
strategy. They roughed-up or "misread" songs their parents loved:
spit-polished tunes by the Mills Brothers, the Ink Spots, and the
Ravens. There is, however, a third perspective: Doo-wop signals the
historical moment when rhythm & blues—its effectiveness waning as
it assumed "classical" form—revitalized itself by going for baroque.

Readings

Anthony J. Gribin and Matthew Schiff. 1992. *Doo-Wop: The Forgotten Third of Rock 'n' Roll*. Iola, Wis.: Krause.

Barry Hansen. 1992. "Doo-Wop." In *The Rolling Stone Illustrated History of Rock & Roll*, ed. Anthony DeCurtis and James Henke, pp. 92–101. New York: Random House.

Greil Marcus. 1993. "Is This the Woman Who Invented Rock & Roll? The Deborah Chessler Story." *Rolling Stone*, 24 June, 41–49, 92.

Robert Pruter. 1996. *Doowop: The Chicago Scene*. Urbana: University of Illinois Press.

Recordings

Various, *The Best of Doo Wop Uptempo* and *The Best of Doo Wop Ballads* (both Rhino). Fabulous single-disc surveys.

Various, *The Doo Wop Box* and *The Doo Wop Box II* (both Rhino). Eight discs altogether and, perhaps, more than a mere mortal would want to know about the form.

Various, *A Taste of Doo Wop, Vols. 1–3* (Vee-Jay). Pays special attention to Chicago groups.

electromagnetic tape—A magnetizable
strip of plastic, embedded with particles of iron oxide, used
in recording.

Insofar as pop music is a consequence of tape, its history is a long-running V-E celebration. Tape came to the U.S. as a result of Allied victory in World War II, but its story began in Dresden, during the 1920s. There, Fritz Pfleumer, a chemist working for the tobacco industry, devised a method for suspending metal particles in a ribbon of plastic. This medium, he theorized, could be made to register audio signals. By the mid-1930s, Pfleumer's ideas had been realized; tape recorders—thanks to BASF and Hermann Goering—were ensconced in German radio stations. When U.S. troops invaded Radio Luxembourg, they "liberated" a tape machine and shipped it to the Ampex Corporation; further development was financed by Bing Crosby.

■

Readings

Michael Chanan. 1995. *Repeated Takes: A Short History of Recording and Its Effects on Music*. New York: Verso.

Hans Fantel. 1994. "The Tangled Web of Magnetic Tapes." *Opera News*, August, 37, 42.

Anecdote—From an interview with producer Joel Dorn (July 1994)

The first week I worked at Atlantic, Nesuhi [Ertegun] went to Europe. He left me a note. Eddie Harris was going to have some kind of dental work done. He wanted to come in and record twenty or thirty songs so he'd have albums in case there were problems with his teeth or his embouchure.

He did maybe twenty-one songs in two or three nights. Arif [Mardin] produced it. And there was a young engineer that had just started there named Bruce Tergeson. He was in the first generation of the engineers as artists.

My first job at Atlantic was to listen through all this Eddie Harris shit and pick out the best stuff and make a record. One tune was like a twenty-seven-minute version of "Listen Here." I listened through all the stuff, and I was like, "Oh my God, there's tons of shit here!" Bruce heard "Listen Here," and he said, "This is a hit, if we make it shorter." So more he than me, we edited it down to like seven minutes. Chopped it up. Took a chorus from here and a chorus from there. Whacked it up. It sold like a million singles and a million albums. It was a top-twenty record.

Blues & Roots — Charles Mingus

engineer—In a recording studio, the person tasked with setting up equipment and creating a tape of music produced.

The recording engineer's role is analogous to that of the cinematographer. He aims at conspicuous inaudibility. His passion lies in effacing technique, his art in perpetuating an illusion: namely, that "sound" is captured, not created. Rap and electronica efface conventional distinctions separating musicians and engineers.

■

Reading

Paul Théberge. 1997. *Any Sound You Can Imagine: Making Music/Consuming Technology.* Hanover, N.H.: Wesleyan/University Press of New England.

Interview—From a conversation with engineer Tom Dowd
(August 1995)

At Atlantic, when you were working with Nesuhi Ertegun, would both of you listen to playbacks? Were musicians involved?

Yeah. You see back in the late forties and into the fifties, we were not recording multitrack tapes. That's number one. Your musicians, when they came in to play, were prepared, or they were exquisite readers. An arranger or somebody would put music in front of them, and they would go through it once or twice. They'd make a notation change, an accent change, whatever, and then it's just a matter of, "Are we going to do it two or three times?" "That's a good one. Okay, next!" Boom. Like that. I'm thinking Bud Powell with Dizzy, or Lennie Tristano with Lee Konitz, those kinds of sessions. You didn't find those people hanging out in clubs, playing five and six nights a week for two or three months, dying to record. They didn't have time for that. When they came together to do something, it's, "Hey man, it goes like this!" "Okay, I gotcha."

As an engineer, you just sat there and hoped that you could learn in their one or two rundowns how to capture what it was they were doing and not distort it or screw it up. You were handcuffed! But there was always playback time. In later sessions, when Atlantic started doing things in stereo, normally, when John came in, John Coltrane, he would always be there a good hour before the session, just standing in the corner warming up his instrument and running scales. John Lewis—the same way. He'd be there an hour-and-a-half, two hours early, making sure his piano was clean, wiping the keys and practicing arpeggios.

Coltrane sounds different—I think better—after moving to Atlantic from Prestige.

Bobby Weinstock [owner of Prestige Records] would argue with you! I know because we've talked about it lots of times. But there might be one or two things. I don't know where Bobby was recording Coltrane unless it was at Rudy Van Gelder's.

That's right.

If that's the case, Rudy is a brilliant engineer and a brilliant clinician, but there are some things that he's insistent on—they go with his demeanor—that are alien to some kinds of people who play music. This is not a criticism. But Rudy would not allow—and we're talking the fifties—he wouldn't allow food or coffee or beverages in the studio. He wouldn't allow smoking in the studio. It was like a laboratory condition. That might be an inhibiting factor to some musicians. When they walk into that kind of environment, they develop an attitude. But Rudy would do nothing to hurt a musician or impede making the best possible record. It's like, "Now we've got a chance; we're going to make the perfect record." The perfect record is seldom made in the studio. It's analogous to a laboratory where everybody's looking at everything under a microscope, ogling every damn thing. Live, there's sweat. There's bad odor, bad food, everything else going on. You're hoping, "Man, I hope we get it tonight. I don't want to have to come back again tomorrow."

So did you try to make the studio at Atlantic less clinical?

Our studio started out as an office. We used to roll the furniture up and make it a studio after business hours. When they moved the office out and gave me the space to create a studio, I more or less thought that I was not going to build a technical facility that would get me to the moon. I was going to try and keep within budget to make a facility that was big enough to record eight- and ten-piece bands, where we could do our groups: Joe Turner, LaVern Baker, the Modern Jazz Quartet, and so forth. Working with John [Coltrane], it just worked out very, very well. The room was like a little club room, but we had higher ceilings than most clubs.

Was sound one of the features that attracted you to Miami's Criteria Studio?

There are two or three things that made Criteria worthy. In New York, the little room that we had, I loved it. The next best room for me was a place called Fulton, later known as Coastal Recording. That's where I recorded Tito Puente. I did Bobby Darin, "Mack the Knife," that whole album in that room. There was a beautiful parquet floor, a triple-ceiling that made it like a little chamber hall. The Haydn Society and Angel Records used it for some things. It was that kind of a room. The next big room that I felt comfortable with in New York was the Capitol Studio on 46th Street. Now the Criteria Studio in Miami—the big room—was identical to the Capitol 46th Street Studio. Capturing the artist's performance, without having anything interfere, was the most responsible thing I could do.

Did the coming of stereo and the possibilities of multitracking affect the way you recorded?

If I said it didn't, I'd lie. Saying that I wished it didn't is stating my aspiration. Jazz is a spontaneous thing. It involves collective energy; it's a concerted form of expression. I cringe when you start doing something in the jazz tradition and end up overdubbing. For my money, that's the antithesis of what jazz is about! But it happens, definitely.

But stereo just meant separation, right?

Well, we've abused that term. Historically, records were made "Indian file." You had your principal up front. In back of him, leaning over his shoulder, was the secondary, then, the background—and then, and then, and then. You'd had this in-depth picture. You were looking through the neck of a bottle. We hoped stereo would enable us to set up microphones and get a semicircular picture like a shell in a concert hall, where you see and hear the bass and the tympani in the back left, the violins on the left, and the cellos on the right. You not only get directionalization but depth. What happens with stereo—the way it was most easily adapted—was to take the Indian file, that front-to-back line—and rotate it ninety degrees so it's left to right. There is no depth in stereo recordings today. They add echo but no depth. It's like everybody's standing on a white line painted across the front of the room.

Did you employ different techniques for miking musicians? For example, did you record Elvin Jones's drums differently than, say, Ed Blackwell's?

Oh, good God! Yeah, depending on the kit. Elvin Jones—three, maybe four microphones. I didn't have that many to play with, but Elvin understood that. He'd play to the microphones, and after we made one or two passes, he'd listen. He'd say, "Move this one over there. I'll do this, or I'll do that." Elvin didn't employ a monster, thirty-three-inch bass drum. He had a small bass drum, and because of his speed and the double-flex pedal he was using, he was a little light. I needed a mike somewhere down around the bass drum. If afforded the opportunity, I placed two mikes overhead and one between the high-hat and the snare drum. That covered the whole kit. If I couldn't afford that, then he'd play accordingly.

Blackwell, on the other hand, was a much heavier drummer. I never had to put anything below waist-high on him. Everything came up. If I put a microphone or two about waist-high in front of him and then two more over the back of his shoulder, about six, seven feet up in the air, I caught everything he did.

This goes back to a whole pile of drummers—some jazz, some rock 'n' roll—who abhorred more than one or two microphones. They wanted to play their kit, not have you play it. John Bonham was one. Roger Hawkins, down in Muscle Shoals, was another. Al Jackson, in Memphis, another. Max Roach still another. He didn't want a microphone on every tom-tom and a microphone on every cymbal. "Get that out of here! Put a microphone here and let me hear what it sounds like. I'll adjust my playing, thank you." He'd say, "I can't hit this drum any harder. Move a little closer to this drum and go lower a little bit." Then, he'd listen once or twice, and he'd say, "That's fine. Move it there and don't touch it." From then on, when that artist is playing, they're playing. Their dynamics are adjusted to what they've heard.

The later generation—and they still exist, despite sampling and drum machines—has a microphone on the top and bottom of every tom-tom, a mike in the bass drum, outside the bass drum, by the pedal, under the high-hat, under the snare drum. They have about thirty-seven microphones and gates on the console. You don't know what the hell you're doing. Well, yeah, you know what you're doing. You're manufacturing a sound. And while that's not a criticism, it cannot be compared to an artist playing an instrument. It's like comparing a portrait painter to a sports photographer. They both present pictures. One sweats and hopes the shutter goes at the right speed and the right time. The other one looks at his model and says, "No. Come back tomorrow, and we'll pose again." That's the difference.

Where's Ginger Baker in all of this?

Ginger was a melodic drummer. We joked about it just two years ago at the Hall of Fame thing out in California. My biggest concern, when I did the first Cream album that I was involved with, was protecting Ginger from Jack [Bruce] and Eric [Clapton]. They had two double stacks of Marshalls. I had a big room [Criteria Studio], and was wearing rifle guards to protect my ears, but there's Ginger, sitting in the middle of it. He can't even hear himself playing!

To shift gears a bit, I've never been clear what you did with Dusty Springfield in Memphis and what was added in New York.

When we finished recording Dusty in Memphis, I struck for Miami on another project and Arif [Mardin] and Jerry [Wexler] went back up to New York. Jerry wanted to add some strings and maybe double Dusty's voice in places. I had two or three cuts, and I said, "Jerry, the Memphis horns are coming down to record." I don't know whether it was a Dr. John or a Wilson Pickett record. I said, "I've got an idea for Dusty." He said, "Okay, put them on." I remember sitting in an airplane with a cassette player in my lap and a piece of manuscript in front of me, and I sketched out this part for "Son of a Preacher Man." When the horns showed up in Miami, I said this is what I want to do. They listened to what I sang and to what I played them on the piano, and in a couple of takes, it was done.

With three producers listed on the album credits, it's hard to tell who's doing what. Did you work together?

Oh yeah. We were in each other's face all the time. We shared space, and there was never any ego or animosity. If Jerry was hellbent on a song and I didn't like the song, I'd figure, "Well, he knows something that I don't know, or he's sensitive to something I've got to learn more about." I'd back off and let him do his thing.

Was Springfield easy to work with or was she, as legend has it, a terror?

I had no problems with Dusty, though I, all of a sudden, recognized that she was an exquisite pitch-sensitive musician. Like Mel Tormé or Don Eliot. And she was a devil for "I can do it better" or "I am flat." You say, "That sounds great. Leave it alone." It was later revealed that

Dusty thought I was an egomaniac, an overpowering human being, and I never had words with the woman. Years later, when I was doing Rod Stewart, Dusty came by for a couple of sessions, and she and I are good friends. She has a reputation for being a wicked old witch, but not by me. I can't say anything bad about the woman.

I consider her a goddess.

She was originally, the Springfields were originally, country singers. And as she describes it, she was always accustomed to walking into pre-prepared arrangements. She'd say, "I like that. Make this softer on top—that part." And then she'd sing over the arrangement. We threw her into this impromptu, jazz-type environment. "Here are the chords, guys. Here's the way she's going to sing it. Va-boom-boomp. That's it. Next song." She'd look and say, "What do you mean, that's it?"

Coltrane's also pretty famous about being fastidious, that I-can-do-this-again-better attitude. Was that a case where you'd say, "This is good enough John."

No, Joel [Dorn] and I were talking about that. As I said, John would come in early and know what two or three songs he was going to do. Much in the tradition of a classical musician in a rehearsal room before a concert, he would stand in a corner and run scales and change reeds and mouthpieces—just be warming up and forming his idea for the day. After recording, you'd say, "That was wonderful." He'd say, "No, let me try one more." And that would be it. There was one particular obbligato—something he wanted to try another way—that kind of a thing. He was never an overpowering, demonstrative person. He was never negative.

And Mingus?

Mingus was the worrier. He was overpowering and demonstrative, but he always wanted spontaneity. I remember when we were doing, I think it was *Blues & Roots*. I had devised a means of taping a microphone onto the tail piece of Mingus's bass so he could rotate and turn around. Keeping him still, while he was trying to look at this or that guy, give them a head motion, was tough. I couldn't keep him on microphone; so I managed to fasten the microphone to the instrument. He could roam around, rotate, or do whatever he wanted.

We were doing this one selection. It might have been "Wednesday Night Prayer Meeting." It was something dynamic. Mingus is playing. He looks over and gets the piano player's eye. And he gets the drummer's eye, but he can't get the horn players' attention. He keeps motioning to them. Finally, he picked up the bass while he was playing, and he did a peg-leg across the room, up to where the trombone player stood. It's Jimmy Knepper. He played something, and Mingus pulled the horn away and punched him in the nose and went back to playing. He's like, "I was trying to tell you not to play there, dummy!" It was that kind of expression. Knepper was so deeply entranced in what he was doing. All of a sudden, he's got a fist in his face. That's Mingus.

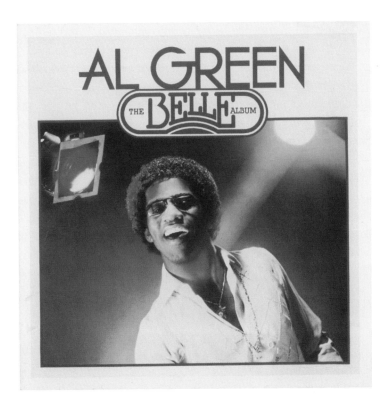

falsetto—The upper register of the male singing voice. [Literally, *"false soprano."*]

Countless male singers rely, not on their "chest voice," but on their "head voice." Falsetto is the norm of popular singing. It's practically ubiquitous. The *OED*, however, defines falsetto as "a forced voice of a range or register above the natural," and the *American Heritage Dictionary* describes the falsettist's voice as marked by "artificially produced tones." What, we might ask, are we hearing when we hear the unnatural but normal sound of falsetto singing? What accounts for its ambiguous cultural status? Singling out several examples, what is "artificial" about the voices of Smokey Robinson, Roy Orbison, Frankie Valli, Barry Gibb, Al Green, Brian Wilson, Aaron Neville, Junior Murvin, Robert Johnson, Papa Wemba, Milton Nascimento, Claude Jeter, Mick Jagger, Morrissey, Jimmy Somerville, and Thom Yorke?

If—as any structuralist with a decent record collection believes—the meaning of falsetto is a social construct, obtained by its relational difference to other voices, then how was this construct constructed? What is its story?

When the Whip Comes Down

We might begin this genealogy of falsetto with the apostle Paul instructing early converts to Christianity. To believers at the First Church of Corinth, he writes, "Let your women keep silent in the churches" (I Corinthians 14:34). Seized upon and installed as a keystone of ecclesiastical dogma, this text—which apparently barred women from making both doctrinal pronouncements and prophetic utterances—provided church fathers with a convenient and authoritative foundation for institutionalized misogyny. It profoundly shaped not just church music, but opera and pop as well. Saint Paul, it turns out, regulates the voice box of Western civilization much as Plato regulates its writing arm. And, by a neat twist of fate or providence, he lends his name to the hometown of a great falsettist—Prince.

Have You Seen Your Mother, Baby, Standing in the Shadow?

Women weren't widely introduced into the choirs of Catholic churches until the nineteenth century. Keeping them silent that long created plenty of problems. More than hard work, it was ultimately impossible. Though absent—or, better, through absence—women's voices were still heard. To drown out this collective and incessant voice of the voiceless, the Church tried two quick fixes. It covered the higher parts of polyphonic masses and motets by employing boys— the Little Anthonies, Frankie Lymons, and Michael Jacksons of the Middle Ages. And it enlisted men capable of singing falsetto. Up to a point, these ersatz female voices did the trick. But they offered no final solution to what Susan McClary calls "the social 'need' for adult males who could sound like women" (181). Boys become men (unless they're Peter Pan), and falsettists lack the volume and dramatic expressiveness needed to complement powerful tenors.

Nutted by Reality

Castration provided a means of bionically engineering an ideal female voice—and of simulating transcendence, signifying the realm of angels. The *castrato* or *evirato* ("emasculated man") was cut off from the desires of the flesh, and though it's uncertain what circumstances occasioned his appearance in fifteenth-century cathedrals, he was not entirely unknown to Christianity. Origen, a celebrated theologian of the third century, had voluntarily undergone castration, as had the Valesii and a few other sects of radical ascetics. Even earlier, in an account recorded in Acts 8:26–39, a eunuch—a minister in the service of Candace, queen of Ethiopia—had converted to Christianity. His ready assimilation into the Church provided a precedent that echoed for centuries in policies governing the treatment of *castrati*. Marjorie Garber writes:

> The legal strictures against castration were ambivalent, to say the least. Although anyone who participated in any way in such an operation was excommunicated, there was no punishment imposed upon the castrate, and the money was good: poor families thus sometimes found the castration of a son financially expedient. (254)

The physical effects of castration were predictable; its aesthetic consequences were not. Surgery couldn't guarantee a good voice, but it determined that the castrated boy would develop neither primary nor secondary sexual characteristics; he would retain the soprano or alto range (i.e., a prepubescent larynx) after his chest and lungs matured. "The castrato embodied paradox," Garber observes. "His body was changed so that his voice would not. One kind of 'performance' was denied him so that success in another could be achieved" (254).

Hard Times Killing Floor Blues

Castrati were known as *voci artificiali*, "artificial voices," to distinguish them from *alti naturali*, "natural alto" and falsetto singers (Slonimsky, 159). By the fifteenth century, they had became a fixture of Church music, used in "ecclesiastical settings from which women were excluded" (Corbett, 66). By the time European opera evolved into a major artform, castrati had achieved star status in Italy and Germany. Enid Rhodes Peschel and Richard E. Peschel estimate that castrati accounted for 70 percent of *all* opera singers in eighteenth-century Italy (quoted in Garber, 254). They emerged, McClary notes, at a time when women singers were making serious bids for fame—and when thousands of women were being executed as witches (50).

More Than a Woman

However perverse and unfortunate, it's not surprising that the lower range of the male voice came to signify certainty and decidability—masculinity—while the upper range came to signify emasculation and, by transference, effeminacy and artifice. Falsettists and castrati were literalizations of a dream image—men, through an operation of subtraction, morphing into women. Or, put less psychoanalytically, they were actors. McClary again observes: "As late as the 1780s, Goethe could still write that by observing female impersonators on the Roman stage, 'we come to understand the female sex so much the better because some one has observed and meditated on their ways'" (181–82).

Sail Away

The European discovery of the Americas and the concomitant institution of slavery complicate an already complex tale. African males—unaware of the gender codes structuring European music—often sang "falsetto." What the upper range of their voices meant within their various cultures deserves more study and a full description (well outside the bounds of my expertise). But what became of African falsetto when it encountered European falsetto affects everything we hear today. It's the story of popular music. In America, the falsetto voice qualified as an instance of homonymy. It was a sound shared by two semiotic systems on soil native to neither. And that's a recipe for accruing meaning, for manufacturing polysemia. More specifically, imagine answers to a couple of questions: In the New World, what overt manifestations of African culture would slave owners freely abide in slaves? And of these traces of another world, how many were also manifestations of European culture?

More Than This

In his epistolary novel *Bedouin Hornbook*, Nathaniel Mackey has his protagonist—who's known as N.—respond to an imaginary essay. Written by another character, the Angel of Dust, it's called "Towards a Theory of the Falsetto in New World African Musics." N. writes:

> What you term "the dislocated African's pursuit of a meta-voice" bears the weight of a gnostic, transformative desire to be done with the world. By this I mean the deliberately forced, deliberately "false" voice we get [as] . . . Al Green creatively hallucinates a "new world," indicts the more insidious falseness of the world as we know it. (Listen, for example, to "Love and Happiness.") What is it in the falsetto that thins and threatens to abolish the voice but the wear of so much reaching for heaven? . . . If you let "word" take the place of "world" in what I said above the bearing this has on your essay should become pretty apparent. . . . I'm suggesting, the falsetto explores a redemptive, unworded realm—a meta-word, if you will—where the implied critique or the momentary eclipse of the word curiously rescues, restores and renews it: new word, new world. (51–52)

N. claims that the black falsetto gives voice to the voiceless: to those *cut off* from native land, words, and heaven. It is, according to Simon Reynolds, one example of "the uproar that occurs when desire is not articulated as a programme of demands, but is vented as pure *demand*, blank and intransitive" (13). Falsetto in the New World informs all sorts of diasporan musics, including blues (Robert Johnson and Buddy Guy), doo-wop and early rock 'n' roll (Frankie Lymon and Little Richard), soul (Sam Cooke and Levi Stubbs), gospel (Claude Jeter and Alex Bradford), reggae (Junior Murvin and the Congos), and samba (Milton Nascimento and Caetano Veloso). It shares familial ties with the moan, shout, and yodel—other bliss sounds that render audible the indescribable (cf. Romans 8:26, where God's Spirit is portrayed as translating the desire behind words of prayer into orgasmic "groanings which cannot be uttered").

Babylon

The title of this section acknowledges the Rasta-reggae conceptualization of America as Babylon, but it actually refers to a song by the

New York Dolls. It intends to evoke—and through evocation to confound—the falsetto as duality in song. In the New World, people speak and sing in tongues. They Babel-on in loops of feedback, as the following case studies demonstrate.

Yodeling Cowboy

As a child in Meridian, Mississippi, and as water carrier on a railroad line, Jimmie Rodgers—the Singing Brakeman—learned the rudiments of music from black laborers. Later, after contracting tuberculosis, the disease that would eventually kill him, Rodgers found manual labor impossible and began a musical career. He performed as a blackface banjo player in minstrel shows, and in 1927, when Ralph Peer gave him the chance, he recorded.

Two years earlier, though, at tryouts held in the Vanderbilt Hotel in Asheville, North Carolina, Peer had passed on Rodgers. Instead, he had recorded Emmett Miller, an entertainer whose shows with the Dan Fitch Minstrels, while perhaps anachronistic, were hardly anomalies.

> [They] started off with the entire cast sitting in a circle, in the classic minstrel tradition, with four blackface end men. A series of skits and music numbers followed. One of them featured female impersonator Johnny Mack, who played "Mammy." Learning that her husband has actually sworn off drinking, she faints; Miller is there to catch her; someone hands him a bottle to give her a swig to revive her; he does, she leaps up to dance, pulls her dress up, and her pants fall off. (Wolfe, 8)

All the while, Miller sings an old black folk song—"Oh Monah"—in a voice prone to leap into a signature yodel that Robert Christgau describes as "breaking upward at will from a squeezed 'normal' voice that sounds as if he compresses his larynx and then routes the vibrations up around through his nose" (52). "People called him Nigger, Nigger Miller," recalled accompanist Turk McBee (quoted in Wolfe, 8). His influence on American music is profound and largely unacknowledged.

Jimmie Rodgers began recording "blue yodels" for Victor in 1928, at about the time Miller, living in New York, began recording in earnest for Okeh Records. But while Miller's star would dim and eventually fade, Rodgers's star rose to unprecedented heights. Miller died a forgotten man—in Macon, Georgia, in 1962 (Tosches, 133). By the time Rodgers died, a little more than six years after making his first record, he had cut 111 sides. He was Victor's biggest-selling artist, the undisputed father of country music (Morthland, 55–57).

Rodgers's blue yodel, according to John Morthland, "was neither the classic Swiss mountain yodel nor the Afro-American falsetto cry common in Jimmie's native Mississippi, but a self-styled cross between the two" (57). A "cross"? Sure. "Self-styled"? Certainly not. Rodgers's style frequently seems an imitation, a simplification, of Miller's. Which is not to declare Rodgers a pretender. (Installing Miller as an original is equally problematic, given his now obscure but equally certain "borrowings.") It's to emphasize a key point about the blue yodel: This device, crucial to distinguishing white country music from black blues, arrives already vexed. To whom should Bob Wills, Hank Williams, and Merle Haggard pay tribute? Is this why Elvis Presley moaned so ethereally when he sang "Mystery Train"?

You Send Me

They're probably coincidental, these three moments from 1928, exhibiting castration anxiety.

1. Louis Armstrong records "West End Blues," a tune featuring a cadenza that will become the most admired in all jazz history. At that time, writes Krin Gabbard, "the jazz trumpet was most flamboyantly representative of sexuality among African American musicians. . . . [It] provided its practitioners with wide latitude for expressing masculinity while avoiding the less mediated assertions of phallic power that were regularly punished by white culture" (140). Theodor Adorno heard Armstrong differently. Recalling a remark made by Virgil Thomson, he likened Armstrong's performances on trumpet "to those of the great castrati of the eighteenth century" (quoted in Gabbard, 138)—which, as Gabbard notes, sounds awfully redolent of a revenge fantasy.

2. William Faulkner finishes writing *The Sound and the Fury*. The novel's first chapter features the internalized dialogue of Benjy, a mentally retarded castrato. He lives beside a golf course and spends his

time chasing stray balls. Luster, who's charged with taking care of Benjy, constantly tells him, "Shut up that moaning."

3. As the talkies come in, Walt Disney directs his first animation with synchronized sound—*Steamboat Willie*. It features the musical antics of Mickey Mouse, now the world's most recognizable falsettist (and, perhaps, castrato). He is, note Howard and Judith Sacks, "the most graphic offspring of blackface minstrels' portrayals of the plantation slave. Black, wide-eyed, childlike, falsetto-voiced, and ever the clown, Mickey Mouse even takes his costuming from the burnt-cork brotherhood: see the oversized white gloves, suspender buttons (minus suspenders), big feet, coy stance" (158).

Ain't That Peculiar?

The operatic use of castrati clearly gave rise to the *bel canto* style favored by Italian-American pop singers (Garber, 255). That style, in turn, helped fashion the rock universe. Dean Martin's croon profoundly affected Elvis Presley, but it also attracted the black gaze of desire. Chuck Berry comes from this tradition (though perhaps by way of Slim Gaillard). And Marvin Gaye readily admitted: "My dream was to become Frank Sinatra. I loved his phrasing, especially when he was very young and pure. . . . I also dug Dean Martin and especially Perry Como" (quoted in Early, 30).

Move on Up

Falsetto singing had its heyday, first with doo-wop and later with soul. In doo-wop, writes Simon Frith, the male voice was broken "into its component parts such that the combination of *all* its sounds, from low to high," articulated an assemblage that defined masculinity (80). In soul, this convention continued, especially at Motown, where Smokey Robinson, Marvin Gaye, Michael Jackson, Levi Stubbs, and Eddie Kendricks made records that appealed to the broadest sort of audience.

Optimists can claim that the crossover appeal of doo-wop and soul signified gains in racial toleration. History—particularly the arc of the Civil Rights Movement—somewhat supports this contention. Theorists will argue, however, that crossover success depended on marketing black voices that were nonthreatening and, ultimately, reassuring to the white audience. Frankie Lymon, Little Willie John, and Michael Jackson are eternal boys. And as for Smokey Robinson and Marvin Gaye? They were, first and foremost, lovers—not fighters fomenting revolution. "In rock convention," notes Frith, "the sexiest male voice is the least bodily" (80).

I Want to Take You Higher

Consider the case of Barry Gibb. After he employed falsetto on "Nights on Broadway," the disco Bee Gees were created as, in effect, his band. Ann Powers writes: "While the brothers' normal singing voices mixed ardor with androgyny, Barry's falsetto was alien, beyond sex. Always a favorite with the girls, the 31-year-old now secured a unique position within teen idol-dom. His features veiled by a full beard and a blow-dried mane, his skin burnt sienna, he projected a masculine power little girls usually reject. . . . Yet Barry's breathiness made him seem soft, the falsetto confirming him as a pure force inhabiting male form, an abstraction of virility" (59). In short, he was a white angel, the inverse of the castrato's abstracted femininity.

Lightnin' Strikes

Jean Baudrillard's concept of the simulacrum can help us theorize the story of the falsetto as a drama in three acts. It begins within the realm of referentiality: that semiotic space where each sign, according to a presumed "natural law of value," refers unequivocally to a status. Here, the falsetto voice—by definition "false" or "counterfeit"—pays honor in the breach to the "genuine" soprano voice. As art, it synthesizes or counterfeits nature, living entirely off of the gap between semblance and reality (Baudrillard, 95). But then there occurs a mutation of the "law of value." Castrati herald a second order of simulacrum, one based on equivalences: "the commercial law of value." As mechanically reproduced objects (the manufactured equivalent of the ideal female voice), they obliterate the concept of "original." With castrati, production usurps the position once granted to being; hermeneutics (interpretation) usurps mimesis (imitation). The third and so-far final phase of the falsetto story coincides with the colonization of the New World. It is based, not on natural or commercial laws, but on "the structural law of value." Here, the falsetto continues to function as a sign—in ways that it always has—but it also functions heuretically (as a means to invention) (83–106).

Everybody's in Showbiz, Everybody's a Star

Nowadays, the falsetto voice is so overdetermined that it simulates nothing so much as simulation itself. What can't it signify? It is, in Ariel Swartley's phrase, "the ultimate equivocation" (235). It has become a code capable of generating polysemy, a magnet attracting the projections of listeners. Not to realize this is to invite confusion, a point Ray Davies persuasively made when he sang: "Girls will be boys and boys will be girls / It's a mixed up muddled up shook up world except for Lola." Why "except for Lola"? It's because s/he understands that new meanings are created by circulating old forms in new contexts.

■

Readings

Roland Barthes. 1974. *S/Z*. Trans. Richard Miller. New York: Hill and Wang. [Includes Honoré de Balzac's 1830 novel *Sarassine*.]

Jean Baudrillard. 1983. *Simulations*. Trans. Paul Foss, Paul Patton, and Philip Beitchman. New York: Semiotext(e).

Robert Christgau. 1996. "Blackface, Whose Voice?" *Village Voice*, 4 June, 52.

John Corbett. 1994. *Extended Play: Sounding Off from John Cage to Dr. Funkenstein*. Durham, N.C.: Duke University Press.

Gerald Early. 1991. "One Nation under a Groove." *New Republic*, 15–22 July, 30–41.

William Faulkner. 1929. *The Sound and the Fury*. New York: Random House.

Simon Frith. 1994. "Brit Beat: High Signs." *Village Voice*, 7 June, 80.

Krin Gabbard. 1996. *Jammin' at the Margins: Jazz and the American Cinema*. Chicago: University of Chicago Press.

Marjorie Garber. 1992. *Vested Interests: Cross-Dressing and Cultural Anxiety*. New York: Routledge.

Nathaniel Mackey. 1986. *Bedouin Hornbook*. Baltimore: Johns Hopkins University Press.

Susan McClary. 1991. *Feminine Endings: Music, Gender, and Sexuality*. Minneapolis: University of Minnesota Press.

John Morthland. 1984. *The Best of Country Music*. Garden City, N.Y.: Doubleday.

Ann Powers. 1997. "Angels as They Are." *Village Voice*, 20 May, 58–59.

Simon Reynolds. 1990. *Blissed Out: The Raptures of Rock*. London: Serpent's Tail.

Howard L. Sacks and Judith Rose Sacks. 1993. *Way up North in Dixie: A Black Family's Claim to the Confederate Anthem*. Washington, D.C.: Smithsonian Institution Press.

Ariel Swartley. 1995. "This Prince Is No Pretender." In *Rock She Wrote*, ed. Evelyn McDonnell and Ann Powers, pp. 233–37. New York: Delta.

Nicholas Slonimsky. 1989. *Lectionary of Music*. New York: Anchor/Doubleday.

Nick Tosches. 1997. "Get Down, Moses." *Oxford American*, no. 16, 128–33.

Charles Wolfe. 1996. Liner notes to *Emmett Miller: The Minstrel Man from Georgia* (Columbia/Legacy).

Recordings—Falsetto A–Z

Little Anthony & The Imperials, "Shimmy, Shimmy, Ko-Ko-Bop," on *The Doo Wop Box, Vol. 4* (Rhino).

The Bee Gees (Barry Gibb), "More Than a Woman," on *Saturday Night Fever: The Original Movie Soundtrack* (Polydor).

Lou Christie, "Lightnin' Strikes," *Enlightnin'ment: The Best of Lou Christie* (Rhino).

The Delfonics, "Didn't I (Blow Your Mind This Time)," on *Soul Hits of the '70s, Didn't It Blow Your Mind, Vol. 1* (Rhino).

Elvis [Presley], "Blue Moon," *The Sun Sessions CD* (RCA).

Franco (Franco & Rochereau), "Omona Wapi," *Omona Wapi* (Shanachie).

Art Garfunkel (Simon & Garfunkel), "Bridge Over Troubled Water," *Bridge Over Troubled Water* (Columbia).

Eddie Holman, "Hey There Lonely Girl," on *Soul Hits of the '70s, Didn't It Blow Your Mind, Vol. 1* (Rhino).

Impressions (Curtis Mayfield), "It's All Right," *The Impressions' Greatest Hits* (MCA).

Skip James, "Hard Times Killing Floor Blues," *The Complete Early Recordings of Skip James, 1930* (Yazoo).

Eddie Kendricks (The Temptations), "Just My Imagination (Running Away With Me)," *Anthology* (Motown).

John Lennon, "#9 Dream," *Shaved Fish* (Parlophone).

David McAlmont, "Yes," *The Sound of McAlmont & Butler* (Gyroscope).

Aaron Neville (Neville Brothers), "Mona Lisa," *Treacherous: A History of the Neville Brothers* (Rhino).

Roy Orbison, "Crying," *For the Lonely: 18 Greatest Hits* (Rhino).

Prince, "Kiss," *Parade* (Paisley Park).

Queen, "Bohemian Rhapsody," *A Night at the Opera* (Hollywood).

Smokey Robinson (& The Miracles), "Ooo Baby Baby," *Anthology* (Motown).

Swan Silvertones (Claude Jeter), "The Lord's Prayer," *Pray for Me & Let's Go to Church Together* (Vee-Jay).

Tiny Tim, "Tiptoe Through the Tulips," on *Legends of Ukulele* (Rhino).

U2, "Lemon," *Zooropa* (Island).

Frankie Valli (The Four Seasons), "Walk Like a Man," *Anthology* (Rhino).

Brian Wilson (The Beach Boys), "Good Vibrations," *Endless Summer* (Capitol).

X (John Doe), "White Girl," *Los Angeles/Wild Gift* (Slash).

Neil Young, "Tonight's the Night," *Tonight's the Night* (Reprise).

The Zombies (Colin Blunstone), "She's Not There," *The Zombies Greatest Hits* (DCC).

MARION WILLIAMS
Through Many Dangers

Classic Performances from 1966 to 1993

gospel—A collective term referring to the impassioned, rhythmically propulsive music of African-American churches.

As jazz explores the sonic possibilities of instruments, gospel explores the capabilities of the human voice. Jubilee singing, popularized by the Golden Gate Quartet (first recorded by Bluebird in 1937), emphasizes tight arrangements and close harmonies; it's a kind of souped-up barbershop for Jesus. Hard gospel—whose avatar was R. H. Harris and the Soul Stirrers—grants male soloists improvisational freedom akin to that historically enjoyed by female singers such as Sister Rosetta Tharpe, Willie Mae Ford Smith, Marion Williams, and Mahalia Jackson. Soul music secularizes this tradition. It appropriates the daring moans, whoops, gasps, stutters, and slurs of gospel soloists, even as contemporary gospel groups—forming a feedback loop—borrow from soul.

■

Readings

Derrick A. Bell. 1996. *Gospel Choirs: Psalms of Survival for an Alien Land Called Home*. New York: Basic.

Michael W. Harris. 1992. *The Rise of Gospel Blues: The Music of Thomas Andrew Dorsey in the Urban Church*. New York: Oxford University Press.

Anthony Heilbut. 1992. *The Gospel Sound: Good News and Bad Times*. Rev. ed. New York: Limelight.

Zora Neale Hurston. 1981. "Characteristics of Negro Expression." In *The Sanctified Church*. Berkeley, Calif.: Turtle Island.

Willa Ward-Royster, as told to Toni Rose. 1997. *How I Got Over: Clara Ward and the World-Famous Ward Singers*. Philadelphia: Temple University Press.

Alan Young. 1997. *Woke Me Up This Morning: Black Gospel Singers and the Gospel Life*. Jackson: University Press of Mississippi.

Recordings—Though curious listeners should realize that gospel has its share of stars and canonical albums—Congress ought to designate Marion Williams's *Through Many Dangers* (Shanachie/Spirit Feel) and *Sam Cooke with the Soul Stirrers* (Specialty) national treasures—they might also take comfort in knowing that gospel is well served by anthologies. Here are ten, in alphabetical order; they're essential to any collection:

American Primitive, Vol. 1, Raw Pre-War Gospel (Revenant).

The Essential Gospel Sampler (Columbia/Legacy).

The Gospel Sound (Columbia/Legacy).

The Great Gospel Women and *The Great Gospel Men* (both Shanachie/Spirit Feel).

The Great 1955 Shrine Concert (Specialty).

Greatest Gospel Gems (Specialty).

Jubilation! Great Gospel Performances, Vols. 1–2 (Rhino).

Precious Lord: Recordings of the Great Gospel Songs of Thomas A. Dorsey (Columbia/Legacy).

Southern Journey, Vol. 6: Don'tcha Know the Road (Rounder).

Wade in the Water: African-American Sacred Music Traditions (Smithsonian/Folkways).

Videos

Bert Stern. 1958. *Jazz on a Summer's Day*. [This documentary concludes with a performance by Mahalia Jackson.]

Judith Davidson Moyers and Bill Moyers, executive prod. 1990. *Amazing Grace with Bill Moyers*.

Robert Mugge. 1984. *Gospel According to Al Green* (Rhapsody).

George Nierenberg. 1983. *Say Amen, Somebody*.

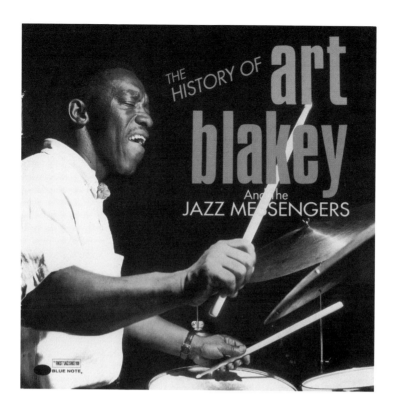

hard bop—Jazz style that conventionalizes the basic materials of bebop by incorporating blues and gospel elements.

Collard greens to bebop's spinach, hard bop combines the melodicism and crisp rhythmic attack of r&b with harmonies and minor modes associated with bebop. It is the sound of modernism: of Blue Note, Prestige, Riverside, and Savoy Records; of Art Blakey, Horace Silver, Lee Morgan, Cannonball and Nat Adderley, Wayne Shorter, and a host of Cold War Era musicians loyal, first, to passion and only secondarily to technique. It lent Miles Davis and John Coltrane a jumping-off place, provided bohemians with a soundtrack for living, and offered mass culture a hip alternative to rock. On television it (and cool jazz) signified fast cars, loose women, hard drugs, shady deals, and weak or addled minds.

■

Reading

David Rosenthal. 1992. *Hard Bop: Jazz and Black Music, 1955–1965*. New
York: Oxford University Press.

Recordings—Two multidisc collections—*Joe Henderson: The
Blue Note Years* and *The History of Art Blakey and the Jazz
Messengers* (both Blue Note)—provide an excellent introduc-
tion to hard bop.

ictus—In a given meter, the accent or stress implied on a beat within a bar. [From the Latin verb, *icere*, "to strike."]

To physicians, "ictus" means a stroke, seizure, or sudden attack. To George Clinton—who "knows" the term in a biblical sense—it refers to the downstroke: "standing on the verge of the Beat." Within the realm of music, then, ictus is the beat one expects, whether or not this expectation is fulfilled in performance. It often constitutes what linguists call a "structuring absence." "The best performers," writes John Cage, "continually anticipate or delay the phrase beginnings and endings." They play around with expectations, "putting more or fewer icti within the measure's limits than are expected. . . . This, not syncopation, is what pleases the hep-cats" (92).

■

Readings

John Cage. 1961. *Silence*. Middletown, Conn.: Wesleyan University Press.

Jason Chervoka and Charles Blass. 1993. "Funken Cyclo-P-Dia." In the liner notes to Parliament, *Tear the Roof Off, 1974–1980* (Casablanca).

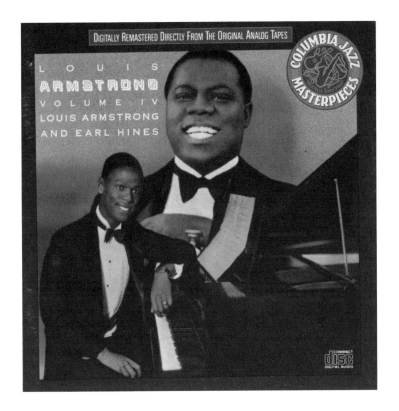

jazz—A musical style and a musical practice, disseminated particularly by **New Orleans musicians** and characterized by improvisation, blues intonations, "nonclassical" timbres, and syncopated rhythms.

Jazz is the art of misreading (standards). A brief history, organized by major styles and proper names, looks like this: Louis Armstrong and Earl "Fatha" Hines (1928) deliberately misinterpret the New Orleans polyphony associated with Buddy Bolden and, more directly, Joe "King" Oliver; they refashion it as a medium for soloists. Their brand of "hot jazz"—once it is conventionalized and labeled "swing"—gains enormous popularity through the efforts of bands as diverse as those led by Benny Goodman and Billy Eckstine. Misinterpreted by Charlie Parker and Dizzy Gillespie (1944), swing transmutes into bebop. Finally, when Ornette Coleman and Miles Davis (1959), in radically different ways, misread "hard bop" (a conventionalized version of bebop), jazz bifurcates and, later, fragments.

■

Readings—Short stories, novels, a guide to jazz fiction, and two books of essays

Richard N. Albert, ed. 1990. *From Blues to Bop: A Collection of Jazz Fiction.* Baton Rouge: Louisiana State University Press.

Vance Bourjaily. 1987. "In and Out of Storyville: Jazz and Fiction." *New York Times Book Review*, 13 December, 1, 44–45.

Marcela Breton, ed. 1990. *Hot and Cool: Jazz Short Stories.* New York: Penguin.

Xam Wilson Cartiér. 1987. *Be-Bop, Re-Bop.* New York: Ballantine.

Julio Cortázar. 1985. "The Pursuer." In *Blow-Up, And Other Stories*, trans. Paul Blackburn, pp. 161–220. New York: Pantheon.

Geoff Dyer. 1991. *But Beautiful: A Book about Jazz.* London: Vintage.

Sascha Feinstein and Yusef Komunyakaa, eds. 1991. *The Jazz Poetry Anthology.* Bloomington: Indiana University Press.

———. 1996. *The Second Set: The Jazz Poetry Anthology, Volume 2.* Bloomington: Indiana University Press.

Krin Gabbard, ed. 1995. *Jazz among the Discourses.* Durham, N.C.: Duke University Press.

———. 1995. *Representing Jazz.* Durham, N.C.: Duke University Press.

John Clellon Holmes. 1953. *The Horn.* New York: Thunder's Mouth.

Art Lange and Nathaniel Mackey, eds. 1993. *Moment's Notice: Jazz in Poetry and Prose.* Minneapolis: Coffee House.

Nathaniel Mackey. 1986. *Bedouin Hornbook.* Baltimore: Johns Hopkins University Press.

William Matthews. 1992. *Selected Poems and Translations 1969–1991.* Boston: Houghton Mifflin.

Michael Ondaatje. 1976. *Coming through Slaughter.* New York: Penguin.

Recordings—101 canonical titles (single or double discs; no boxes); only one album per artist allowed (however ridiculous such a conceit might be)

Cannonball Adderley, *Somethin' Else* (Blue Note).

Toshiko Akiyoshi/Lew Tabackin, *The Toshiko Akiyoshi–Lew Tabackin Big Band* (Novus).

Henry "Red" Allen, *World on a String* (Bluebird).

Albert Ammons/Meade Lux Lewis, *The First Day* (Blue Note).

Louis Armstrong, *Volume IV: Louis Armstrong and Earl Hines* (Columbia).

Art Ensemble of Chicago, *The Third Decade* (ECM).

Albert Ayler, *Spiritual Unity* (ESP).

Count Basie, *The Complete Decca Recordings* (Decca).

Sidney Bechet, *The Legendary Sidney Bechet* (Bluebird).

Bix Beiderbecke, *Volume I: Singin' the Blues* (Columbia).

Art Blakey & the Jazz Messengers, *Mosaic* (Blue Note).

Anthony Braxton, *Creative Orchestra Music 1976* (Bluebird).

Clifford Brown/Max Roach, *Alone Together: The Best of the Mercury Years* (Verve).

Dave Brubeck, *Jazz Collection* (Columbia/Legacy).

Benny Carter and His Orchestra, *Further Definitions* (GRP/Impulse!).

Betty Carter, *The Audience with Betty Carter* (Verve).

Charlie Christian, *The Genius of the Electric Guitar* (Columbia).

Nat King Cole and His Trio, *The Complete After Midnight Sessions* (Capitol).

Ornette Coleman, *In All Languages* (Harmolodic/Verve).

John Coltrane, *A Love Supreme* (Impulse!).

Eddie Condon, *Dixieland All-Stars* (GRP/Decca).

Miles Davis, *Kind of Blue* (Columbia/Legacy).

Johnny Dodds, *Blue Clarinet Stomp* (Bluebird).

Eric Dolphy, *Out to Lunch* (Blue Note).

Jimmy Dorsey and His Orchestra, *Contrasts* (GRP/Decca).

Tommy Dorsey, *Yes, Indeed!* (Bluebird).

Roy Eldridge, *After You've Gone* (GRP/Decca).

Duke Ellington, *The Blanton-Webster Band* (Bluebird).

Bill Evans, *Waltz for Debby* (Riverside/OJC).

The Gil Evans Orchestra, *Out of the Cool* (Impulse!).

Ella Fitzgerald, *Pure Ella* (GRP/Decca).

Errol Garner, *Concert by the Sea* (Columbia).

Stan Getz, *Focus* (Verve).

Dizzy Gillespie, *The Complete RCA Victor Recordings* (Bluebird).

The Jimmy Giuffre 3, *The Jimmy Giuffre 3* (Atlantic).

The Benny Goodman Sextet, *The Benny Goodman Sextet, Featuring Charlie Christian (1939–1941)* (Columbia).

Dexter Gordon, *The Best of Dexter Gordon: The Blue Note Years* (Blue Note).

Charlie Haden/Carla Bley, *The Ballad of the Fallen* (ECM).

Jim Hall, *Concierto* (Epic/Associated/Legacy).

Lionel Hampton, *Hot Mallets: Lionel Hampton's Choice of the Cream of His Small Band Sides, Vol. 1 (1939–40)* (Bluebird).

Herbie Hancock, *Headhunters* (Columbia).

Kip Hanrahan, *Darn It!* (American Clavé).

Coleman Hawkins, *A Retrospective, 1929–1963* (Bluebird).

Fletcher Henderson, *The Fletcher Henderson Story: A Study in Frustration* (Columbia).

Joe Henderson, *The State of the Tenor, Vols. 1 and 2* (Blue Note).

Woody Herman, *The Thundering Herds 1945–1947* (Columbia).

Billie Holiday, *First Issue: The Great American Songbook* (Verve).

Keith Jarrett, *The Köln Concert* (ECM).

James P. Johnson, *The Original James P. Johnson, 1942–1945* (Smithsonian Folkways).

Rahsaan Roland Kirk, *Does Your House Have Lions? The Rahsaan Roland Kirk Anthology* (Rhino/Atlantic).

Steve Lacy, *Evidence* (Prestige).

George Lewis, *Homage to Charles Parker* (Black Saint).

Jimmie Lunceford and His Orchestra, *For Dancers Only* (GRP/Decca).

McKinney's Cotton Pickers, *The Band Don Redman Built (1928–1930)* (Bluebird).

Carmen McRae, *The Great American Songbook* (Atlantic).

Jay McShann Orchestra, *Blues from Kansas City* (GRP/Decca).

Charles Mingus, *The Black Saint and the Sinner Lady* (Impulse!).

The Modern Jazz Quartet, *The Complete Last Concert* (Atlantic).

Thelonious Monk, *Genius of Modern Music, Vol. 1* (Blue Note).

Wes Montgomery, *Far Wes* (Pacific Jazz).

Lee Morgan, *The Best of Lee Morgan* (Blue Note).

Jelly Roll Morton, *Birth of the Hot: The Classic Chicago "Red Hot Peppers" Sessions (1926–27)* (Bluebird).

The Gerry Mulligan Quartet, *What Is There to Say?* (Columbia).

David Murray, *Shakill's Warrior* (DIW/Columbia).

Fats Navarro, *The Complete Blue Note and Capitol Recordings of Fats Navarro and Tadd Dameron* (Blue Note).

Oliver Nelson, *The Blues and the Abstract Truth* (GRP/Impulse!).

James Newton, *The African Flower* (Blue Note).

Herbie Nichols, *The Art of Herbie Nichols* (Blue Note).

Charlie Parker, *Bird: The Complete Original Master Takes, The Savoy Recordings* (Savoy).

Art Pepper, *Winter Moon* (Galaxy).

Bud Powell, *The Best of Bud Powell on Verve* (Verve).

Sun Ra, *The Singles* (Evidence).

Django Reinhardt, *The Best of Django Reinhardt* (Blue Note).

Luckey Roberts/Willie "The Lion" Smith, *Luckey & the Lion* (Good Time).

Shorty Rogers with His Orchestra and the Giants, *Short Stops* (Bluebird).

Sonny Rollins, *Saxophone Colossus* (Prestige).

Jimmy Rushing, *The You and Me That Used to Be* (Bluebird).

George Russell Sextet, *Ezz-thetics* (Riverside/OJC).

Artie Shaw and His Orchestra, *Personal Best* (Bluebird).

Wayne Shorter, *The Best of Wayne Shorter* (Blue Note).

Horace Silver, *The Best of Horace Silver* (Blue Note).

Frank Sinatra with the Red Norvo Quintet, *Live in Australia, 1959* (Blue Note).

Bessie Smith, *The Collection* (Columbia).

Muggsy Spanier, *The "Ragtime Band" Sessions* (Bluebird).

Art Tatum, *The Art Tatum Solo Masterpieces, Vol. 1* (Pablo).

Cecil Taylor, *Looking Ahead!* (Contemporary/OJC).

Jack Teagarden, *That's a Serious Thing* (Bluebird).

Henry Threadgill Sextet, *You Know the Number* (RCA Novus).

Lennie Tristano, *Lennie Tristano/The New Tristano* (Rhino).

McCoy Tyner, *Trident* (Milestone).

James Blood Ulmer, *Odyssey* (Columbia/Legacy).

Sarah Vaughan, *The Roulette Years, Vols. 1 and 2* (Roulette).

Thomas "Fats" Waller, *The Joint Is Jumpin'* (Bluebird).

Dinah Washington, *First Issue—The Dinah Washington Story (The Original Recordings)* (Mercury).

Ben Webster, *The Big Tenor: The Complete Ben Webster on EmArcy* (EmArcy).

Randy Weston, *The Spirits of Our Ancestors* (Antilles).

Lee Wiley, *As Time Goes By* (Bluebird).

Hal Willner, *Amarcord Nino Rota* (Hannibal).

World Saxophone Quartet, *Revue* (Black Saint).

Lester Young, *The Complete Aladdin Recordings of Lester Young* (Blue Note).

John Zorn, *The Big Gundown* (Elektra Nonesuch/Icon).

Videos

Jean Bach. 1995. *A Great Day in Harlem.*

Gary Giddins and Kendrick Simmons. 1987. *Celebrating Bird: The Triumph of Charlie Parker.*

———. 1989. *Satchmo.*

Robert Herridge, prod. 1990. *The Sound of Jazz.*

Vincente Minnelli. 1943. *Cabin in the Sky.*

Robert Mugge. 1986. *Saxophone Colossus.*

Martin Scorsese. 1977. *New York, New York.*

Bert Stern. 1958. *Jazz on a Summer's Day.*

Jack Webb. 1955. *Pete Kelly's Blues.*

Charlotte Zwerin. 1988. *Thelonious Monk: Straight No Chaser.*

kick—*n.* A sensation of pleasure, often sudden. *v.* To cast off an addiction.

Within jazz mythology, drugs corroborate an ideology of control: playing one's body as if it were a horn. Within the realm of rock, the reverse obtains. Drugs underwrite an ideology of freedom; they promise loss of control—the bliss of one's body played as if it were a horn.

■

Readings

Matthew Collin. 1997. *Altered State: The Story of Ecstasy Culture and Acid House*. London: Serpent's Tail.

Holly George-Warren. 1995. "Into the Abyss." In *Rock She Wrote*, ed. Evelyn McDonnell and Ann Powers, pp. 158–67. New York: Delta.

Milton Mezzrow with Bernard Wolfe. 1946. *Really the Blues*. New York: Citadel.

Anita O'Day with George Eells. 1981. *High Times, Hard Times*. New York: Berkley.

Art Pepper and Laurie Pepper. 1994. *Straight Life: The Story of Art Pepper*. Rev. ed. New York: Da Capo.

Charles Perry, Parke Puterbaugh, and James Henke. 1997. *I Want to Take You Higher: The Psychedelic Era, 1965–1969*. San Francisco: Chronicle.

Avital Ronell. 1992. *Crack Wars: Literature Addiction Mania*. Lincoln: University of Nebraska Press.

Recordings—Thirteen discs of junkie business (in alphabetical order); their pleasures derive from the aural equivalent of voyeurism

Chet Baker, *Chet Baker Sings and Plays from the Film "Let's Get Lost"* (RCA Novus).

Derek and the Dominoes, *Layla and Other Assorted Love Songs* (Polydor).

Rocky Erickson, *You're Gonna Miss Me: The Best of Rocky Erickson* (Restless).

Marianne Faithfull, *Broken English* (Island).

Happy Mondays, *Pills 'n' Thrills and Bellyaches* (Elektra).

Billie Holiday, *Lady in Satin* (Columbia).

Fats Navarro, *The Complete Blue Note and Capitol Recordings of Fats Navarro and Tadd Dameron* (Blue Note).

New York Dolls, *New York Dolls* (Mercury).

Charlie Parker, *The Legendary Dial Masters, Vols. 1 and 2* (Stash).

Art Pepper Quintet, *Smack Up* (Contemporary).

Pink Floyd, *The Piper at the Gates of Dawn* (Capitol).

Rolling Stones, *Exile on Main Street* (Rolling Stones).

Sly and the Family Stone, *There's a Riot Going On* (Epic).

Videos

Jack Arnold. 1958. *High School Confidential*.

Danny Boyle. 1995. *Trainspotting*.

David Cronenberg. 1991. *Naked Lunch*.

Sidney J. Furie. 1972. *Lady Sings the Blues*.

Louis Gasnier. 1939. *Reefer Madness*.

Russ Meyer. 1970. *Beyond the Valley of the Dolls*.

Gordon Parks. 1972. *Superfly*.

Otto Preminger. 1955. *Man with the Golden Arm*.

Gus Van Sant. 1989. *Drugstore Cowboy*.

Bruce Weber. 1988. *Let's Get Lost*.

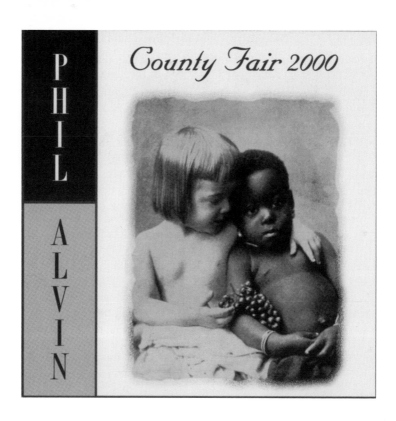

County Fair 2000

PHIL ALVIN

Leno, Jay—American comedian and, since 1992, host of *The Tonight Show*.

In 1992, I asked myself, "If late-night television indexes the Zeitgeist, then what is the Leno/Marsalis pairing saying about, or saying to, America?" The following essay responded to that question. It drew substance from Richard Chase's The American Novel and Its Tradition, *Leslie Fiedler's* Love and Death in the American Novel, *and the book of Job. And while it's no longer timely—Marsalis left* The Tonight Show *some time ago—it is still pertinent.*

■

When NBC tagged Branford Marsalis for Doc Severinsen's old slot on *The Tonight Show*, nobody on my block gasped. Loud hosannas didn't peal across the horizon. Nonetheless, even melancholic jazz fans must have been happy. After all, falling asleep to the wail of a tenor sax is part of our paradigm of felicity. Branford's got chops like a pit bull. Plus a righteous aesthetic. His concentrated intensity beats the lilt of Kenny G, Tom Scott, David Sanborn, George Howard, et al. Post-bop trumps pose-modern any day.

But he was such an obvious choice! Huck and Jim, Ishmael and Queequeg, Natty Bumppo and Chingachgook, the Lone Ranger and Tonto, Daniel Boone and Mingo: shouldn't we have spotted Jay Leno and Branford Marsalis a mile away? They're an American odd couple for the ages. Working together in Los Angeles—too busy entertaining the masses to take time off to burn and pillage—they can't help but erase our collective memory of that city's recent riots as they play out a talk-show version of the myth of perfect fraternal equality between persons of different races. Still, Jack Benny and Rochester they ain't; Branford won't play Stepin Fetchit. Nevertheless, he can't help but play the role of loyal retainer and reverse the image of jazzman-as-cultural-subversive. He's already a billboard for hard work and clean living.

I'm nervous—and ambivalent. Good guys, positive role models black or white, *never* finish last. Bill Cosby proves that. They end up becoming agents of hegemony, which in this country means they instruct us (by design or default, it doesn't matter) how to shrug at or laugh off chronic injustice. That lesson learned, we can all concentrate on important matters: making money, gaining power, gettin' laid.

Certainly, Branford's hip to this. He knows that he's being positioned as a golden child: the long-lost heir to the throne of good-will ambassador Louis Armstrong (his immediate antecedent). Though he's not as sullen or polemical as his brother Wynton, he is just as smart and cynical. But can he manage his persona? Does he control his image? That's the problem. Like an impudent but affable class clown, Branford rules by charisma; on the flip side of this equation, he's also controlled by the desires of others. He's doomed to curry favor. A first-born son (in a family of six boys), he has undoubtedly pleased Mom and Dad. Now, he's ready to make us proud of him too.

So here's a bedtime prayer for Branford.

Dear God, help this jazzman confound our expectations. Not by playing more brilliantly than we could ever have imagined or by giving us lotsa laffs. And especially not by burning out sacrificially like St. Charlie Parker. Instead, help Branford do the right thing and fight the power. We know, Lord, that this request sounds pretty vague and transcendent, so here's a suggestion. Motivate Branford to bag *The Tonight Show*—turn the mutha out. Then, use a little of your highly publicized influence and get executive producer Helen Gorman Kushnick to pass the baton to Ornette Coleman. 'Cause you've got to admit, America may want Branford, but it needs Coleman. Nothing like him has ever been televised because there is, in fact, nobody like him. You know that. He should have landed the gig in the first place. What's the problem? Was his file misplaced? Floppy disk get corrupted? If so, you might consider this handy chart. It contrasts the résumés of these two saxophonists. Maybe it can help you make a decision that suggests at least a modicum of omniscience.

BRANFORD MARSALIS	**ORNETTE COLEMAN**
1. Popularizer	1. Iconoclast
2. Born August 1960	2. Recorded *Free Jazz* (Atlantic) December 1960
3. Studied saxophone with Florence Bowser and Alvin Batiste; attended Berklee School of Music, Boston	3. Bought a saxophone with money earned from shining shoes; claims immediate fluency on the instrument
4. Toured with Sting	4. Gigged with Yoko Ono
5. Current band—an octet—plays bebop	5. Current band—Prime Time— plays funk
6. Daddy's a musician; easily confused with siblings	6. He's dada; may be an extraterrestrial
7. Articulate, witty, and ironic	7. Recondite and gnomic; ever the ingénue
8. Figures prominently in Spike Lee's film *School Daze*	8. Figures prominently in Thomas Pynchon's novel *V.*
9. Wealthy	9. Needs a steady job with large salary

10. Educated by Catholics	10. Invented harmolodics—a music theory, philosophy, and religion
11. Excellent sight reader	11. Unconcerned by impedimenta such as chords, keys, and conventional tonality
12. Willing, anxious, and able to mug for the camera	12. Exudes a certain Brechtian unease before a camera
13. New to the West Coast	13. Worked as elevator operator, stock clerk, and porter while living in L.A.

minstrel cycle—A structuralist theory of identity formation that emphasizes the reciprocity of social roles.

White eyes watching objectified and sexualized black bodies: Eric Lott, adapting a concept developed by Laura Mulvey, dubs this phenomenon the "pale gaze" and argues that it is motivated by the lure of transgressive sex—the bliss promised by miscegenation (36). Plausible? If so, then white boys' obsession with black music—the "crossover" phenomenon (cooptation at the level of consumption)—displaces sexual desire, rechanneling it into consumption. But there's a problem with this theory, and it has nothing to do with its psychoanalytic orientation. The *minstrel model* of cultural appropriation expresses white interests alone, even if only to castigate and, ultimately, atone for those interests. Like all models of cooptation, it ignores, discounts, or represses the possibility of reciprocity. White fantasies and desires don't just prey upon black fantasies and desires, they also feed them. They're reciprocal, forming a feedback loop. Or, as Simon Frith puts it, "white youth becomes an object of black pleasure exactly to the degree that the recurring fantasy of being black is coded into white style, white anxiety, white posture." In fact, this circulation of mutually defining desire—a *minstrel cycle*—is sufficient to create and sustain racial difference. Its operations make race seem like one of the raw materials from which culture is produced, rather than one byproduct of a complex social machine.

■

Readings

Robert Christgau. 1996. "Blackface, Whose Voice?" *Village Voice*, 4 June, 52.

Simon Frith. 1991. "Brit Beat." *Village Voice*, 3 September, 78.

Margo Jefferson. 1994. "Seducified by a Minstrel Show." *New York Times*, 22 May, sec. 2:1, pp. 40+.

George Lipsitz. 1994. "'The Shortest Way Through': Strategic Anti-essentialism in Popular Music." In *Dangerous Crossroads: Popular Music, Postmodernism and the Poetics of Place*. London: Verso.

Eric Lott. 1993. *Love and Theft: Blackface Minstrelsy and the American Working Class*. New York: Oxford University Press.

Laura Mulvey. 1989. *Visual and Other Pleasures*. Bloomington: Indiana University Press.

Michael Rogin. 1992. "Blackface, White Noise: The Jewish Jazz Singer Finds His Voice." *Critical Inquiry* 18: 417–53.

Robert C. Toll. 1974. *Blacking Up: The Minstrel Show in Nineteenth Century America*. New York: Oxford University Press.

Nick Tosches. 1997. "Get Down, Moses." *Oxford American*, no. 16: 128–33.

HONKY-TONK MERRY-GO-ROUND

Nashville sound—A post–World War II musical style developed in Nashville, Tennessee, when pop production (studio craft) was applied to country songs (e.g., Acuff-Rose material) in order to create records for a mass (postpubescent) audience.

Like every musical genre developed within capitalism, the Nashville or countrypolitan sound addressed the general problem: how to make money. More specifically, it arose when two companies—in the wake of rock 'n' roll—enlisted producers to refashion country & western as pop music for adults. Steve Sholes, A&R director at RCA Victor, hired Chet Atkins; Paul Cohen, of Decca, hired Owen Bradley. As a consequence of their labors, Nashville became an institution, and its records (Patsy Cline's are a case in point) bore the marks of conspicuous production. They sounded *made*, not *found*.

■

Readings

Donald Barthelme. 1981. "How I Write My Songs." In *Sixty Stories*. New York: E. P. Dutton.

Mary A. Bufwack and Robert K. Oermann. 1993. *Finding Her Voice: The Saga of Women in Country Music*. New York: Crown.

Nicholas Dawidoff. 1997. *In the Country of Country: People and Places in American Music*. New York: Pantheon.

Paul Hemphill. 1970. *The Nashville Sound: Bright Lights and Country Music*. New York: Simon and Schuster.

Paul Kingsbury, ed. 1994. *Country: The Music and the Musicians, from the Beginnings to the '90s*. 2d ed. New York: Country Music Foundation/ Abbeville.

Bill C. Malone. 1985. *Country Music, U.S.A.* Rev. ed. Austin: University of Texas Press.

Barry McCloud et al. 1995. *Definitive Country: The Ultimate Encyclopedia of Country Music and Its Performers*. New York: Perigee.

John Morthland. 1984. *The Best of Country Music*. Garden City, N.Y.: Doubleday.

Cecilia Tichi. 1994. *High Lonesome: The American Culture of Country Music*. Chapel Hill: University of North Carolina Press.

Cecilia Tichi, ed. 1995. *Readin' Country Music: Steel Guitars, Opry Stars and Honky Tonk Bars*. Durham, N.C.: Duke University Press.

Nick Tosches. 1977/1996. *Country: The Twisted Roots of Rock 'n' Roll*. New York: Da Capo.

obbligato—An accompaniment that is either an integral or an incidental part of a musical piece.

"Obbligato" is a Janus word: a contranym or an antilogy (so is "cover"), which means that it is its own antonym. In one sense of the word, obbligato is an accompanying part, an independent melody absolutely necessary to a piece of music. It is not to be omitted. In the other sense of the word, obbligato refers to an embellishment—a nonessential, supplemental part. It's framing material. Through an etymological pun, obbligato suggests nothing less than "A cat's got to do what a cat's got to do."

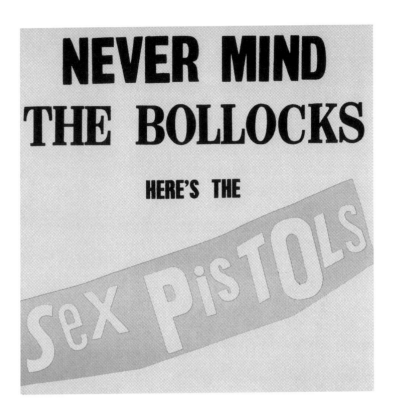

punk—A rock style deriving from an ideology of amateurism: a **DIY** ("do-it-yourself") aesthetic that subordinates consumption to production.

Because rock 'n' roll is, in concept, an egalitarian artform, it routinely wrestles with a recurring dilemma: how to address the gap that separates fans from stars. Punk—which is less a definable style than a set of dreams—denies, bridges, or effaces this gap. In sweet dreams (generative myths), the star is a fan: a working-class stiff or art-school misfit kissed by luck. In nightmares (destructive myths), the fan kills a star. The Clash emblematized the former dream; Mark Chapman literalized the latter. Iconoclasts, they transformed aesthetic principle into radical agenda. As did Kurt Cobain. Like Ian Curtis before him, he played out both punk dreams. The ardent fan who loathed professionalism, Cobain also murdered a rock star—the closest one he could find.

■

Readings

Adrian Boot and Chris Salewicz. 1996. *Punk: The Illustrated History of a Music Revolution*. New York: Penguin Studio.

Caroline Coon. 1995. "The Sex Pistols." In *Rock She Wrote*, ed. Evelyn McDonnell and Ann Powers, pp. 93–104. New York: Delta.

Simon Frith and Howard Horne. 1987. *Art into Pop*. New York: Methuen.

Stuart Hall and Tony Jefferson, eds. 1975. *Resistance through Rituals: Youth Subcultures in Post-War Britain*. London: Hutchinson/Centre for Contemporary Cultural Studies, University of Birmingham.

Dick Hebdige. 1979. *Subculture: The Meaning of Style*. London: Methuen.

Clinton Heylin. 1993. *From the Velvets to the Voidoids: A Pre-Punk History for a Post-Punk World*. New York: Penguin.

John Lydon with Keith Zimmerman and Kent Zimmerman. 1994. *Rotten: No Irish, No Blacks, No Dogs*. New York: Picador.

Greil Marcus. 1989. *Lipstick Traces: A Secret History of the Twentieth Century*. Cambridge, Mass.: Harvard University Press.

———. 1993. *Ranters and Crowd Pleasers: Punk in Pop Music, 1977–92*. New York: Anchor.

Legs McNeil and Gillian McCain. 1996. *Please Kill Me: The Uncensored Oral History of Punk*. New York: Grove.

Lisa Robinson. 1995. "The New Velvet Underground." In *Rock She Wrote*, ed. Evelyn McDonnell and Ann Powers, pp. 89–92. New York: Delta.

Jon Savage. 1992. *England's Dreaming: Anarchy, Sex Pistols, Punk Rock, and Beyond*. New York: St. Martin's.

Neil Tennant. 1992. "Hated It!" *Details*, July, 52.

Recordings—90 minutes of sonic insolence

SIDE I

01)	Patti Smith, "Gloria," *Horses* (Arista).	5:56
02)	The Modern Lovers, "Roadrunner," *The Modern Lovers* (Rhino/Beserkley).	4:05
03)	Pere Ubu, "The Modern Dance," *Datapanik in the Year Zero* (DGC).	3:30
04)	Ramones, "Beat on the Brat," *All the Stuff (And More), Vol. 1* (Sire/Warner Bros.).	2:33
05)	Talking Heads, "Pulled Up," *Talking Heads: 77* (Sire).	4:29
06)	Richard Hell & the Voidoids, "Love Comes in Spurts," *Blank Generation* (Sire/Warner Bros.).	2:04

07) Television, "Marquee Moon," *Marquee Moon* (Elektra).   10:40
08) The Sex Pistols, "God Save the Queen," *Never Mind the Bollocks Here's the Sex Pistols* (Warner Bros.).   3:20
09) The Buzzcocks, "Ever Fallen in Love?" *Singles Going Steady* (A&M/I.R.S.).   2:41
10) Blondie, "Hanging On the Telephone," *Parallel Lines* (Chrysalis).   2:24
11) The Slits, "Instant Hit," *Cut* (Island).   2:43
12) The English Beat, "Click Click," *I Just Can't Stop It* (I.R.S.).   1:28

Total playing time 45:53

SIDE II

01) The Feelies, "The Boy With the Perpetual Nervousness," *Crazy Rhythms* (A&M).   5:09
02) Young Marble Giants, "Credit in the Straight World," *Colossal Youth* (Rough Trade).   2:30
03) Gang of Four, "Capital (It Fails Us Now)," *Solid Gold & Another Day/Another Dollar* (Infinite Zero/American).   4:05
04) X-Ray Spex, "Oh Bondage Up Yours," *Germfree Adolescents* (Carol).   2:48
05) The Raincoats, "Fairytale in the Supermarket," *The Raincoats* (DGC).   2:59
06) The Jam, "In the City," *Greatest Hits* (Polydor).   2:18
07) The Clash, "White Man in Hammersmith Palais," *The Clash* (Epic).   3:59
08) The Undertones, "Teenage Kicks," *Undertones* (Rykodisc).   2:26
09) Wire, "Feeling Called Love," *On Returning (1977–1979)* (Restless Retro).   1:22
10) Pylon, "Cool," *Hits* (DB).   3:19
11) The dB's, "Black and White," *Stands for Decibels* (I.R.S.).   3:07
12) X, "Los Angeles," *Los Angeles/Wild Gift* (Slash).   2:25
13) The Mekons, "Memphis, Egypt," *The Mekons Rock 'n' Roll* (A&M).   3:36
14) The Replacements, "Unsatisfied," *Let It Be* (Twin/Tone).   4:02

Total playing time 44:05

Videos

Wolfgang Büld. 1992. *Punk in London.*
Jack Hazan. 1980. *The Clash: Rude Boy.*
Don Letts. 1978. *The Punk Rock Movie.*
Penelope Spheeris. 1981. *The Decline of Western Civilization.*
Julian Temple. 1979. *The Great Rock and Roll Swindle.*

Qiana—Proprietary name for a silk-like nylon manufactured by Du Pont in 1968; the original, avenging, godfather of disco fabrics.

Qiana—its name picked from a list of 6,500 computer-generated words, its intent to replicate the aesthetics of silk and the performance of nylon—was a "luxury fiber" developed by Du Pont Laboratories. It was first woven into cloth by cottage industry workers in France, Italy, and Switzerland—in May 1968. One more time, that's May 1968: a moment in history when striking students and laborers brought the entire French economy to a standstill. Textile workers were simply too busy trying to topple the government to dye and finish Qiana. The new material thus found its way to Parisian couturiers through a more circuitous route than most fabrics. First, it was sent to textile plants in Switzerland and Italy; then, to Paris for fabrication. By that time the streets were cleared, and de Gaulle was back in power. In

July, more than a hundred garments of Qiana walked out of couture houses and down the runways of high fashion, headed toward spinning machines in Chattanooga and a mass market. Many showed up in discos. "Qiana is comfortable to wear," said Du Point executive James Rumsey, "because it has high covering power with porosity so heat and perspiration are dissipated. Fabrics of Qiana wick moisture like silk." Small wonder, then, that Tony Manero (John Travolta) wore Qiana shirts whenever he hit the dance floor at the 2001 Odyssey Discotheque. The fabric made dandyism affordable, democratizing manufactured unreality. Qiana materialized disco—consistently derided as synthetic music for plastic people—as flannel materialized grunge.

■

Readings

Richard Dyer. 1990. "In Defense of Disco." In *On Record: Rock, Pop, and the Written Word*, ed. Simon Frith and Andrew Goodwin, pp. 410–18. New York: Pantheon.

Editors of American Fabrics and Fashions Magazine. 1980. *Encyclopedia of Textiles*. 3d ed. Englewood Cliffs, N.J.: Prentice Hall.

Anthony Haden-Guest. 1997. *The Last Party: Studio 54, Disco, and the Culture of the Night*. New York: Morrow.

Angela McRobbie, ed. 1988. *Zoot Suits and Second-Hand Dresses: An Anthology of Fashion and Music*. Boston: Unwin Hyman.

Ann Powers. 1997. "Angels as They Are." *Village Voice*, 30 May, 58–59.

James S. Rumsey. 1969. "The Introduction of Qiana Nylon and Its Potential Importance to the Textile Industry." Speech to the American Association for Textile Technology, November 11, Hagley Museum and Library, Wilmington, Delaware.

Recordings—90 minutes of disco, music as smooth as Qiana

SIDE I

01)	Donna Summer, "On the Radio," *On the Radio: Greatest Hits, Vols. I and II* (Casablanca).	5:52
02)	Harold Melvin & the Blue Notes, "The Love I Lost," *The Best of Harold Melvin & the Blue Notes* (Legacy/Epic Associated).	6:25
03)	Barry White, "You're the First, The Last, My Everything," *All-Time Greatest Hits* (Mercury).	3:23

04) Boz Scaggs, "Lowdown," *Silk Degrees* (Columbia).   5:15

05) Marvin Gaye, "I Want You," *The Master, 1961–1984* (Motown).   4:34

06) The Emotions, "The Best of My Love," *Best of My Love: The Best of the Emotions* (Columbia/Legacy).   3:41

07) Chic, "Soup for One," *Dance, Dance, Dance: The Best of Chic* (Atlantic).   3:07

08) Kool & the Gang, "Celebration," *Celebration: The Best of Kool & the Gang, 1979–1987* (Mercury).   3:40

09) Abba, "Dancing Queen," *Gold: Greatest Hits* (Polydor).   3:48

11) Bee Gees, "How Deep Is Your Love," *Saturday Night Fever: The Original Movie Soundtrack* (Polydor).   4:00

Total playing time 43:45

SIDE II

01) Bee Gees, "Stayin' Alive," *Saturday Night Fever: The Original Movie Soundtrack* (Polydor).   4:40

01) Cheryl Lynn, "Got to Be Real," *Got To Be Real: The Best of Cheryl Lynn* (Columbia/Legacy).   3:48

02) Sister Sledge, "We Are Family (Sure Is Pure Remix)," on *Club Mix 95: Non-Stop Play of Remixed Dance Hits* (Cold Front).   4:02

03) Gloria Gaynor, "Never Can Say Goodbye," on *Soul Hits of the '70s: Didn't It Blow Your Mind! Vol. 14* (Rhino).   2:59

04) Heatwave, "Boogie Nights," *Serious R&B and Soul: Legacy's Rhythm & Soul Series Sampler* (Legacy).   5:02

05) Village People, "Macho Man," *Best of the Village People* (Polygram).   3:25

06) Carl Douglas, "Kung Fu Fighting," *The Best of Carl Douglas: Kung Fu Fighting* (Hot Productions).   3:18

07) Wild Cherry, "Play That Funky Music," *Wild Cherry* (Epic).   4:56

08) Alicia Bridges, "I Love the Nightlife," on *Pure Disco* (Polydor).   3:06

09) K.C. & the Sunshine Band, "That's the Way (I Like It)," on *Pure Disco* (Polydor).   3:02

10) Lipps, Inc., "Funkytown," on *Pure Disco* (Polydor).   3:55

11) Donna Summer, "I Feel Love," *On the Radio: Greatest Hits, Vols. I and II* (Casablanca).   3:20

Total playing time 45:33

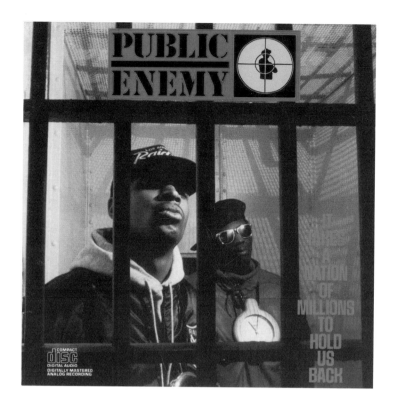

rhapsody—A composition marked by emotional intensity and free, irregular form, often improvised. [From Greek *rhaptein* ("to stitch together") and *oide* ("song").]

In Homer's Greece, a rhapsody was an epic poem—or a part of one suitable for recitation at one time—woven from what were, in effect, sound bites (speech formulas). Much later, through a false etymology that linked "rhapsody" with "rapture," the meaning of the word conflated to include any "effusive outpouring of sentiment" (Rogers, 247). Both senses of the word are expressed in Allen Ginsberg's description of his poetry: "A lot of these forms developed out of an extreme rhapsodic wail I once heard in a madhouse" (quoted in Parkinson, 29). Nowadays, when people see the word "rhapsody," they undoubtedly associate it with rap, a music that lays rhymed lyrics over a bed of stitched-together, sampled beats and breaks.

Readings

Viv Edwards and Thomas J. Sienkewicz. 1990. *Oral Cultures Past and Present: Rappin' and Homer*. Oxford: Basil Blackwell.

Walter J. Ong. 1982. *Orality and Literacy: The Technologizing of the Word*. New York: Methuen.

Thomas Parkinson, ed. 1961. *A Casebook on the Beat*. New York: Thomas Y. Crowell.

Pat Rogers. 1972. "Shaftesbury and the Aesthetics of Rhapsody." *British Journal of Aesthetics* 12: 244–57.

shivaree—1. A satiric serenade, traditionally
performed in front of the houses of newlyweds, with pans,
cauldrons, kettles, etc. [American alteration of *charivari*,
French for "hubbub," from Late Latin *caribaria*, "head-
ache."] 2. In music, a deliberately noisy performance or
composition.

Though its practice is less observed than the noisemaking rituals that
accompany New Year's Eve celebrations, the shivaree provides both
anthropological precedent and impetus for the music of, among others, Spike Jones, Harry Partch, Sun Ra, John Cage, Yoko Ono, Tom
Waits, Einstürzende Neubauten, Last Exit, and Merzbow. Without it,
no cowbell kicks off the Stones' "Honky Tonk Women," no squeals
punctuate Public Enemy's "Don't Believe the Hype." Like the din that

once saluted solar and lunar eclipses (unwanted celestial unions), shivarees saluted unconventional terrestrial unions: second or third marriages or the marriage of couples with significantly differing ages. *Le Charivari*—a satirical newspaper founded by Charles Philipon in 1832—holds the distinction of being the first newspaper to employ lithography and to reproduce images. Without it, no zines.

■

Readings

Jacques Attali. 1988. *Noise: The Political Economy of Music*. Trans. Brian Massumi. Minneapolis: University of Minnesota Press.

Lester Bangs. 1987. *Psychotic Reactions and Carburetor Dung*. Ed. Greil Marcus. New York: Alfred A. Knopf.

John Cage. 1961. *Silence*. Middletown, Conn.: Wesleyan University Press.

Chuck Eddy. 1997. "ObLiGaToRy NOISE!! InTeRlUdE." In *The Accidental Evolution of Rock 'n' Roll: A Misguided Tour through Popular Music*, pp. 243–47. New York: Da Capo.

Deborah Frost. 1995. "White Noise: How Heavy Metal Rules." In *Rock She Wrote*, ed. Evelyn McDonnell and Ann Powers, pp. 127–38. New York: Delta.

Theodore Gracyk. 1996. *Rhythm and Noise: An Aesthetics of Rock*. Durham, N.C.: Duke University Press.

Douglas Kahn and Gregory Whitehead, eds. 1994. *Wireless Imagination: Sound, Radio, and the Avant Garde*. Cambridge, Mass.: MIT Press.

Claude Lévi-Strauss. 1969. "Divertissement on a Folk Theme." In *The Raw and the Cooked: Introduction to a Science of Mythology, Vol. 1*, trans. John and Doreen Weightman, pp. 285–99. Chicago: University of Chicago Press.

Jon Pareles. 1993. "It's Got a Beat and You Can Surrender to It." *New York Times*, 28 March, sec. 4, p. 2.

William Paulson. 1988. *The Noise of Culture: Literary Texts in a World of Information*. Ithaca, N.Y.: Cornell University Press.

Simon Reynolds. 1990. *Blissed Out: The Raptures of Rock*. London: Serpent's Tail.

Mary Russo and Daniel Warner. 1987–88. "Rough Music, Futurism, and Postpunk Industrial Noise Bands." *Discourse* 10, no. 1: 55–76.

Luigi Russolo. 1986. "The Art of Noise" In *Futurism and Futurisms*, ed. Pontus Hulten, New York: Abbeville.

Michel Serres. 1982. *The Parasite*. Trans. Lawrence R. Schehr. Baltimore: Johns Hopkins University Press.

R. J. Smith. 1992. "Dixie Fried: Jim Dickinson's Memphis Productions." *Village Voice Rock & Roll Quarterly*, Summer, 16–23.

Richard Terdiman. 1985. *Discourse/CounterDiscourse: The Theory and Practice of Symbolic Resistance in Nineteenth-Century France*. Ithaca, N.Y.: Cornell University Press.

DOWN HOME STYLE
BROTHER JACK MCDUFF

soul jazz—A music style, associated with organ combos, popularizing hard bop.

Recorded during the Civil Rights Era, soul jazz signified what Rahsaan Roland Kirk dubbed "blacknuss" (as the jazz avant-garde had signified "art"). It was structured by metaphors of Southern food: fried chicken, barbeque ribs, corn bread, mash potatoes, and collard greens. Nowadays—with or without the quotation marks of ironic consumption—soul jazz signifies a negotiation. It's heard as a formal response to the churchified music of Ray Charles (soul), understood as a market response to the success of Berry Gordy (Motown). It was an attempt to win back the mass audience that jazz once claimed during the swing era, while at the same time appeasing St. Coltrane (art). At its best, soul jazz generates the "soul effect" so beloved by postmodern hipsters and remixologists (whose electronics transform it into "acid jazz") by sounding like African-American musicians accommodating cultural conventions that dictate what it means to sound authentically black.

trainspotter—I. An enthusiast, usually an adolescent male, devoted to observing and identifying trains. [Chiefly British.] 2. One who ardently amasses minutiae, shards of data, about a culturally devalued subject or field, such as dance music: *"Techno-trainspotters can listen to a track; work out that it's got a Roland 909 drum on it"* (Simon Reynolds).

Recognition, notes Theodor Adorno in "On Popular Music" (1941), enables one to transform experience (e.g., hearing a tune) into object, making it proprietable. Trainspotting—dilettantism elevated to the level of a surrogate profession (a parody of scientific endeavor)—thus creates effects of possession: illusions of mastery and ownership. It is a response to the problem of feeling disenfranchised: alienated from the products and services of mass culture; drowned by consumer goods.

Readings

Theodor Adorno with George Simpson. 1941. "On Popular Music." *Studies in Philosophy and Social Science* 9: 17–48.

Julio Cortázar. 1966. *Hopscotch*. Trans. Gregory Rabassa. New York: Pantheon. [See pp. 40–75.]

Peter De Vries. 1990. "Jam Today." In *Hot and Cool Jazz Short Stories*, ed. Marcela Breton. New York: Plume/Penguin.

Pete Frame. 1993. *The Complete Rock Family Trees*. New York: Omnibus.

Gordon Legge. 1989. *The Shoe*. Edinburgh: Polygon.

Dave Marsh and James Bernard. 1994. *The New Book of Rock Lists*. New York: Fireside.

Harvey Pekar and R. Crumb. 1996. *American Splendor Presents Bob & Harv's Comics*. New York: Four Walls Eight Windows.

Rosamond Wolff Purcell and Stephen Jay Gould. 1992. *Finders, Keepers: Eight Collectors*. New York: W. W. Norton.

Lewis Shiner. 1993. *Glimpses*. New York: Avon.

Stephen W. Smith. 1939. "Hot Collecting." In *Jazzmen*, ed. Frederic Ramsey, Jr., and Charles Edward Smith. New York: Harcourt Brace.

Nic Van Oudtshoorn. 1992. *The Elvis Spotters Guide*. Harrogate: Take That.

original recordings by
GUILLAUME APOLLINAIRE
JEAN COCTEAU
MARCEL DUCHAMP
LUIGI GRANDI
RICHARD HUELSENBECK
MARCEL JANCO
WYNDHAM LEWIS
FILIPPO TOMMASO MARINETTI
ANTONIO RUSSOLO
KURT SCHWITTERS
TRISTAN TZARA

Ursonate—A "Sonata in Primeval Sounds"
assembled, performed, and recorded—both as concrete
poem and grammophonplatte—by Kurt Schwitters
(1887–1948). It was inspired by the sound poetry of
Dadaist Raoul Hausmann.

Instead of committing himself to one medium, Kurt Schwitters championed a method, *Merz* or "assemblage." An "ur" principle, "*Merz* had manifestations in painting, typography, theater, poetry, music and architecture," says John Elderfield, chief curator at MOMA. For example, "the *Merzbau* [environments or 'dream grottos' that Schwitters designed for *The Cabinet of Dr. Caligari* and built in his home in Hannover] are, in part, a kind of 'primitive' architecture, while the *Ursonate* suggests a 'primitive' soundform from which the sonata might have come." Its patterned phonemes evoke nothing so much as

Babel: the original wall of sound, a *Gesamtkunstwerk* or "total work of art" anticipating multimedia.

■

Readings

Timothy O. Benson. 1987. "Mysticism, Materialism, and the Machine in Berlin Dada." *Art Journal*, Spring, 46–53.

John Elderfield. 1985. *Kurt Schwitters*. London: Thames and Hudson.

Greil Marcus. 1989. *Lipstick Traces: A Secret History of the Twentieth Century*. Cambridge, Mass.: Harvard University Press.

Marjorie Perloff. 1986. *The Futurist Moment: Avant-Garde, Avant Guerre, and the Language of Rupture*. Chicago: University of Chicago Press.

Kurt Schwitters. 1993. *Poems, Performance Pieces, Proses, Plays, Poetics: PPPPPP*. Ed. and trans. Jerome Rothenberg and Pierre Joris. Philadelphia: Temple University Press.

Recordings

Marcel Duchamp, *The Creative Act* (Sub Rosa, Belgium).

Raoul Hausmann, *Poèmes phonetiques complétes* (S Press Tapes, West Germany). [Greil Marcus mentions this title in a note to *Lipstick Traces*; otherwise, I know nothing about it.]

Kurt Schwitters, *Ursonate (1922–32)* (Wergo).

Cecil Taylor, *Chinampas* (Leo).

Various, *Futurism & Dada Reviewed* (Sub Rosa, Belgium).

Interview—Q&A with John Elderfield (July 1996)

On the one hand, Schwitters seems like a radical artist. The Ursonate anticipates sound poetry. But on the other hand, he structures his experiment by relying on the most conventional sort of form. Is that seeming inconsistency typical of his artistic outlook?

It is. He was both radical and conservative at the same time. His art was, to many people, outrageous. But I think he also thought of himself as someone who had sources in the past. It was something he was criticized for. Raoul Hausmann, who also did sound poetry, was critical of Schwitters because of that sonata form. So one could say that, judged from the point of view of sound poetry of the 1920s, Schwitters' use of the sonata form was regressive. The "ur" bit at the beginning—i.e., meaning "primeval" or "source"—suggests that he thought of himself as doing a kind of "primitive" form which preexisted the sonata. It's a kind of regression which then circles back to the present.

Much of what you're saying about Schwitters recalls Rousseau's comments on the origin of language in music. Was Schwitters drawing from an identifiable philosophical tradition?

Out of the German versions of that. Before he became his own kind of Dadaist, he was really an expressionist painter and poet. His early poems come out of German mysticism. What becomes difficult is determining at what point they start to become parodies of it. Or whether in fact they're parodies of it all along. But even parodies acknowledge that they're treating something serious. Otherwise, why parody it?

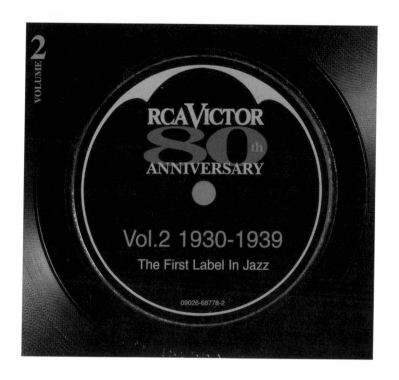

"venerable Frog"—Moniker bestowed on Hugues Panassié, the eminence behind *le jazz hot*, by British poet and jazz critic Philip Larkin.

Hugues Panassié wasn't a musician. He was a pundit turned record producer (and, later, something of a pariah) who helped transform a primitivist aesthetic into an institution. In *The Real Jazz* (1942), the irascible French critic asserted, "Despite all that has been said by the 'intellectualists' on the subject, be-bop music is NOT jazz. This is no mere opinion. This is fact." To Panassié, the music of Charlie Parker, Dizzy Gillespie, Bud Powell, and their modernist successors signaled a perverse rejection or, at very least, a tragic loss of basic jazz verities. Grandstanding solos replaced collective improvisation. Virtuosity replaced feeling. Art (concern for the elements of music) replaced entertainment (concern for the audience that came for the music). Worst of all, bands stopped swinging. They spit, sputtered, and flashed like ribbons of burning magnesium. Where inspired amateurs once prowled stages—stalking their prey with horns that ripped, snorted, slurred, and brayed—ardent professionals, whose sunglasses masked bloodshot eyes, now planted their feet on bandstands and blew plumes of obfuscation. Fans nodded inscrutably. Others vigorously shook their heads, incredulous at what they were hearing. What had become of the sounds they loved? Tackling that question requires backtracking several years.

In 1932, the first book of jazz criticism appeared. Titled *Aux Frontières du Jazz*, it was written by Robert Goffin, a Belgian attorney and an expert on the poet Guillaume Apollinaire. Goffin announced that jazz was sonic surrealism and, thus, an artform worthy of study. Just two years later, Goffin's insights were overshadowed by another work whose pronouncements were delivered—and received by some readers—as holy writ: Panassié's *Le Jazz Hot* (translated into English, as *Hot Jazz*, in 1936). The protagonist of Josef Skvorecky's novel *The Bass Saxophone* likens it to the "Book of Mormon written in the language of angels." Or think of it this way: If Louis Armstrong was the Jesus of jazz, then Panassié was St. Paul. His work of codification formulated a doctrine of musical primitivism (heard then as antifascist, now as racist). "The natural bad taste of the Negro," Panassié declared, is preferable to "an excess of culture."

Panassié, in more theoretical terms, wanted to stipulate the use of the word "jazz." Instead of signifying a variety of syncopated dance musics, as it had for years, "jazz" should henceforth refer exclusively to "hot" music. To further spread his gospel, Panassié joined forces with Charles Delaunay—author of the first reference guide to recorded jazz—and founded *Jazz Hot*, a magazine. He also organized, in 1938, four recording sessions for RCA Victor; their aim was to create museum-quality reproductions of primeval hot jazz. On hand were Sidney Bechet, Tommy Ladnier, James P. Johnson, Mezz Mezzrow, and Al Casey. Eddie Condon wasn't invited. He quipped, "I don't see why we need a Frenchman to come over here and tell us how to play American music. I wouldn't think of going to France and telling him how to jump on a grape." Chalk up the *bon mot* to sibling rivalry. In the company of Bobby Hackett, Jess Stacy, Pee Wee Russell, and Bud Freeman, Condon was cutting hot sides for Milt Gabler's Commodore Records. Soon after, in 1940, Columbia Records authorized George

Avakian to compile four "albums" of historic jazz. Called *Hot Jazz Classics*, they were the first reissues. The so-called New Orleans revival, with its attendant craze for authentic jazz, had effectively begun. It died decisively, not at the hand of modernists with a serious jones for smack and bebop, but when rock 'n' roll coopted the hormones and disposable incomes of American youth.

So understand three points: (1) While musicians had been playing hot for years, and while the metaphorics of heat had long structured jazz, "hot," as a distinct category with meaning, came into being when Panassié and like-minded critics articulated widely held but rarely uttered assumptions about what constitutes authenticity. By trying to determine what would and would not count as genuine jazz, they validated primitivism and unwittingly summoned its other: the "progressive" sounds of bebop. (2) The New Orleans revival (1938–1949)—a misnomer that enables critics to read back "hot" as the sole defining feature of early jazz—gave jazz a history (and a canon) by excising from the past much music previously considered "jazz." (3) Like it or not, we are all heirs of Panassié. As a perceptive outsider, he zeroed in on and then exaggerated the tension that continues to motivate American music: primitivism vs. progressivism.

■

Readings

Whitney Balliett. 1986. "Panassié, Delaunay et Cie." In *American Musicians*, pp. 3–11. New York: Oxford University Press.

Bernard Gendron. 1989–90. "Jamming at Le Boeuf: Jazz and the Paris Avant-Garde." *Discourse* 12, no. 1: 3–27.

———. 1995. "'Moldy Figgs' and Modernists: Jazz at War (1942–1946)." In *Jazz among the Discourses*, ed. Krin Gabbard, pp. 31–56. Durham, N.C.: Duke University Press.

Philip Larkin. 1985. *All What Jazz: A Record Diary*. New York: Farrar, Straus, and Giroux.

John McDonough. 1997. "He Crowned the Kings of Jazz." *Wall Street Journal*, 3 June, A20 [an essay on George Avakian].

Hugues Panassié. 1942. *The Real Jazz*. New York: Smith and Currell.

Frederic Ramsey, Jr., and Charles Edward Smith, eds. 1939. *Jazzmen*. New York: Harcourt Brace.

Josef Skvorecky. 1977. *The Bass Saxophone: Two Novellas*. New York: Washington Square.

Recordings—Ten sets that burn

1. *Masters of Jazz, Vol. 1: Traditional Jazz Classics* (Rhino). More than a history lesson, it's a hot primer; America's gift to the swing-challenged world.

2. *RCA Victor 80th Anniversary—Vol. 1, 1917–1929* (BMG/RCA Victor). By being the first label to record hot jazz, RCA showed (as when they later signed Elvis) that they understood their market: Planet Earth.

3. *The Commodore Recordings* (Commodore). Nobody could stoke a jam session better than Milt Gabler, the record producer who midwifed this thoughtfully assembled introduction to blowing hot (Eddie Condon) and cool (Lester Young).

4. *Black Legends of Jazz* (GRP/Decca). However dumb its title—Quick now, name five white legends of jazz—this limited edition set is a smartly programmed guide to prewar jazz.

5. *Hot Jazz on Blue Note* (Blue Note). Inspired by 1938's Spirituals to Swing concert, Alfred Lion started a record label. His first intention: capture hot jazz on vinyl. Monk and bop came later.

6. *Riverside History of Classic Jazz* (Riverside). Because of his contributions to modern jazz (producing Thelonious Monk, Wes Montgomery, Bill Evans, and Cannonball Adderley), it's easy to underrate Orrin Keepnews's role as archivist. Before their transfer to disc, these sides were on stone tablets.

7. *The Real Kansas City* (Columbia/Legacy). The disc we get thanks to Robert Altman's film; the music arrives courtesy of musicians—Benny Moten, Jay McShann, Count Basie et al.—suckled by Tom Pendergast's political machine.

8. *RCA Victor 80th Anniversary—Vol. 2, 1930–1939* (BMG/RCA Victor). The 78-rpm record was to popular music what the sonnet was to poetry: a form that rewarded compressed ideas. This anthology includes a taste of the Panassié sessions.

9. *Jazz the World Forgot, Vols. 1–2* (Yazoo). An exercise in urban archeology, this marvelous set concentrates on territory bands—local favorites and one-hit wonders—of the 1920s.

10. *The Good Time Jazz Story* (Good Time Jazz). The late 1930s craze for "authentic" New Orleans music quickened the bones of patriarchs (Kid Ory, Bunk Johnson, George Lewis, and others featured here), and it stimulated the creation of Dixieland bands (led by Lu Watters, Turk Murphy, and Bob Scobey).

Patti Smith Horses

watusi—A popular dance, developed in the early 1960s, characterized by slightly pidgeon-toed, side-to-side steps on the balls of the feet.

"Do the watusi like my little Lucy" goes a line from Chris Kenner's "Land of 1000 Dances," and while the dancer's name probably makes no archeological allusion (to the Lucy unearthed by Donald Johanson), the name of the dance is unmistakably African. In 1962, as Belgium turned Rwanda (formerly Ruanda) over to Tutsi (Watusi) leaders, Kal Mann, a staff writer at Philadelphia's Cameo-Parkway Records, wrote "The Wah-Watusi." ("I read the word in a magazine article and liked the sound of it," said Mann.) He delivered the song over to the Orlons, a modified girl group named after a Du Pont product. They choreographed and then performed this idea (about an idea) of Africa on TV's *American Bandstand*.

■

Recordings—"The Wah-Watusi" (in fact, the entire Cameo-Parkway catalog) is tied up in litigation, but let's face it, "Land of a Thousand Dances" is a better song.

Chris Kenner, "Land of 1000 Dances," *I Like It Like That—Golden Classics* (Collectibles).

Cannibal & the Headhunters, "Land of a Thousand Dances," *Land of a Thousand Dances* (Dominion).

Wilson Pickett, "Land of 1000 Dances," *A Man and a Half* (Rhino/Atlantic).

Patti Smith, "Land," *Horses* (Arista).

Mud Boy & the Neutrons, "Land of 1000 Shotguns [Part 2]," *They Walk Among Us* (Koch).

Interview—Steve Caldwell, the Orlons' sole male singer, explains the logic behind his choreography for the "Wah-Watusi" (December 1995)

The dance was something that I'd seen on television. It was a jump-up-and-down thing. Actually, it was more from watching *Tarzan* and safari movies set in Africa. The Watusi were one of the tribes focused on, because they were a dancing tribe. So that's how I was aware of that type of dance.

Now, the Orlons, we had to do a dance that allowed us—all three of us—to be around one microphone with the lead singer on the other microphone. In that day you only used two mikes. So the dance had to be something that we could do together close, as a group with a lead singer.

X—A variable.

For all its variety, popular music during the past twenty years has shared a common methodology. Substituting adaptation for interpretation, it works like so: (1) Let X (and any other variable) stand for a multitrack recording. (2) Assume, as Simon Frith notes, that X is never "finished" (it can always serve as the starting point for new versions) and never "integrated" (coherence of parts is always a temporary condition). (3) Experiment with X by capitalizing on Daniel S. Milo's observation that all experimentation involves at least one of the following procedures: "*adding* to X an element Y which is foreign to it; *removing* from X an element X1 that usually helps constitute it; and *changing the scale:* to observe and analyze X on a scale against which it isn't usually measured" (cited in Ray 1995, 74).

Readings

Jorge Luis Borges. 1956/1962. "Pierre Menard, Author of the Quixote." In *Labyrinths: Selected Stories and Other Writings*, ed. Donald A. Yates and James E. Irby, pp. 36–44. New York: Grove Weidenfeld.

André Breton. 1924/1972. *Manifestoes of Surrealism*. Trans. Richard Seaver and Helen R. Lane. Ann Arbor: University of Michigan Press.

Mark Dery. 1990. "Public Enemy Confrontation." *Keyboard*, September, 81–96.

Simon Frith. 1996. "Technology and Authority." In *Performing Rites: On the Value of Popular Music*. Cambridge, Mass.: Harvard University Press.

Kyle Gann. 1990. "Sampling: Plundering for Art." *Village Voice*, 1 May, 102.

Andrew Goodwin. 1990. "Sample and Hold: Pop Music in the Digital Age of Reproduction." In *On Record: Rock, Pop, and the Written Word*, ed. Simon Frith and Andrew Goodwin, pp. 258–73. New York: Pantheon.

Tim Page, ed. 1984. *The Glenn Gould Reader*. New York: Vintage.

Tom Phillips. 1997. *Humument: A Treated Victorian Novel*. Rev. ed. London: Thames and Hudson.

Robert B. Ray. 1995. *The Avant-Garde Finds Andy Hardy*. Cambridge, Mass.: Harvard University Press.

———. 1991. "Tracking." In *Present Tense: Rock & Roll and Culture*, ed. Anthony DeCurtis, pp. 135–48. Durham, N.C.: Duke University Press.

Hillel Schwartz. 1996. *The Culture of the Copy: Striking Likenesses, Unreasonable Facsimiles*. Cambridge: Zone/MIT Press.

Bonnie Sparling. 1988. "Decoder Process." In *Instant Theory: Making Thinking Popular*, special issue of *Visible Language* 22: 449–54.

Gertrude Stein. 1993. *A Stein Reader*. Evanston, Ill.: Northwestern University Press.

Brian Wallis. 1987. *Blasted Allegories: An Anthology of Writings by Contemporary Artists*. Cambridge: MIT Press.

William Warriner. 1975. "A Guide to Tape Editing: How to Falsify Evidence and Other Diversions," *High Fidelity*, August, 48–53.

William Carlos Williams. 1963. *Paterson*. New York: New Directions.

John Zorn. 1987. Liner notes to *Spillane/Two-Lane Highway/Forbidden Fruit* (Elektra/Nonesuch).

Question to the Beastie Boys (March 1994)

One of the most profound shifts in music that occurs with the advent of rock 'n' roll is an emphasis on sonics. What are some sounds that shaped you?

ADROCK: "Tippy Toes," the Meters' song. An 808 kick-drum.

MIKE D: That's one of the most important sounds. Actually, on this album [*Ill Communication*], we learned that the sound of a djimbe [an African drum] is close to the 808 kick-drum on a more acoustic, traditional level.

ADROCK: Those log drums—those hollowed-out tree trunks?—that's the shit.

MIKE D: Actually, I know another sound: "Naa-na-naa-na-naat."

ADROCK: From *Juice*, "Catch a Groove." That sound? It's hip hop—just one horn line.

MCA: Something that you find out about music from sampling—and working with loops—is that it's not like you can just write out that piece of music and give it to anyone, and they can make something that has the same feeling off of that. It's about much more the minute detail, than twelve pitches or quarter notes or eighth notes. It's like one-millionth notes and overtones. It's the feeling, just the feeling that's in the sound.

MIKE D: Mario rolls the tape a lot and, then, we just go to where the feel is on the tape. There might be a lot of mistakes and stuff, but you go to get the feeling.

Yardbird—1. Nickname of saxophonist Charlie
Parker (1920–1955), patriarch of bebop. 2. A member of
the Yardbirds, a seminal British blues-rock band, best
known for its guitarists—Eric Clapton, Jeff Beck, and Jimmy
Page—and its "dirty" proto-garage/punk sound.

Jazz has two gods: Louis Armstrong and Charlie Parker—Apollo and
Dionysus. Armstrong's nickname—"Pops"—refers to his stature. (In
VooDoo ritual music, says Ishmael Reed, the "papa" or "King" told
people when to stop playing.) Parker's nickname refers to his prodi-
gious appetite. Once, after a car he was in struck a chicken (maybe *the*
chicken) crossing the road, Parker made the driver slam on the
brakes. The saxophonist bolted from the car, retrieved the dead
"yardbird" and, that night, had it prepared for dinner. By metaphoric
transfer—a nomasic joke—Parker then became "Yardbird," "Yard," or

simply "Bird." Which is fitting. "Yardbird" is also an untrained military recruit and a convict: someone unbroken or untamed. The British quintet, whose original moniker was Most Blueswailing Yardbirds, undoubtedly banked on these connotations. Like the Dionysian bop god, they fostered an outlaw aesthetic that seemed explosive and undisciplined.

■

Recordings—Anyone seeking an understanding of American music could start by pondering the chicken. Around it broods (sorry) any number of issues: sex, race, class, and rhythm. Here's a 22-piece bucket of bird songs.

Louis Armstrong, "Struttin' With Some Barbecue," *Portrait of the Artist as a Young Man* (Columbia/Legacy).

The Beastie Boys, "Finger Lickin' Good," *Check Your Head* (Capitol).

Art Blakey & the Jazz Messengers, "Chicken an' Dumplins," *At the Jazz Corner of the World* (Blue Note).

Carla Bley, Andy Sheppard/Steve Swallow, "Chicken," *Songs With Legs* (ECM).

Cab Calloway, "Chicken Ain't Nothin' But a Bird," *Are You Hep to the Jive? 22 Sensational Tracks* (Legacy).

Slim Gaillard, "Chicken Rhythm," *Laughing in Rhythm: The Best of the Verve Years* (Verve).

Louis Jordan, "Ain't Nobody Here But Us Chickens," *The Best of Louis Jordan* (MCA).

Bobby McFerrin, "Chicken," *Bobby McFerrin* (Elektra Musician).

The Meters, "Chicken Strut," *Funkify Your Life: The Meters Anthology* (Rhino).

Amos Milburn, "Chicken-Shack Boogie," on *The R&B Box: 30 Years of Rhythm & Blues* (Rhino).

Charles Mingus, "Eat That Chicken," *Oh Yeah* (Rhino/Atlantic).

Charlie Parker, *Yardbird Suite: The Ultimate Charlie Parker Collection* (Rhino).

Maceo Parker, "Chicken," *Mo' Roots* (Verve).

Lee "Scratch" Perry, "Chicken Scratch—Lee Perry," *Respect to Studio One* (Heartbeat).

Southern Culture on the Skids, "Eight Piece Box," *Peckin' Party* (Feed Bag).

The Jon Spencer Blues Explosion with Rufus Thomas, "Chicken Dog," *Now I Got Worry* (Matador/Capitol).

Super Chikan, "Super Chikan Strut," *Blues Come Home to Roost* (Rooster).

Joe Turner, "The Chicken and the Hawk (Up, Up and Away)," *Big, Bad & Blue: The Big Joe Turner Anthology* (Rhino/Atlantic).

Rufus Thomas, "Do the Funky Chicken," *The Best of Rufus Thomas: Do the Funky Somethin'* (Rhino).

The Trashmen, "Surfin' Bird," *Jenny McCarthy's Surfin' Safari* (I.D.).

Link Wray, "Run Chicken Run," *Rumble! The Best of Link Wray* (Rhino).

The Yardbirds, *Greatest Hits, Vol. 1 (1964–1966)* (Rhino).

Videos

Michelangelo Antonioni. 1966. *Blow Up*.

Clint Eastwood. 1988. *Bird*.

Gary Giddins and Kendrick Simmons. 1987. *Celebrating Bird: The Triumph of Charlie Parker*.

Grand Royal,
man's
best friend

zine—A self-published underground magazine;
a fanzine.

In the nineteenth century, as a direct result of French newspapers generating revenue, and thus space, through advertising, the feuilleton arose. Richard Terdiman notes that it provided the middle class with a forum to practice its characteristic behavior: what Gustave Flaubert, in his *Dictionnaire de idées reçues*, labeled "tonner contre"—"to thunder against." Zines are the feuilletons of the latter part of the twentieth century, a consequence of efficient and affordable photocopiers and computers. Their makers still fulminate—rail against anything they deem objectionable—but more characteristically they publish billetsdoux: lovingly annotated catalogs detailing the often hidden riches and pleasures of consumer culture.

Readings

R. Seth Friedman, ed. 1997. *The "Factsheet Five" Zine Reader: Dispatches from the Edge of the Zine Revolution.* New York: Crown.

Abe Peck. 1985. *Uncovering the '60s: The Life and Times of the Underground Press.* New York: Pantheon.

Chip Rowe. 1997. *The Book of Zines: Readings from the Fringe.* New York: Henry Holt.

Richard Terdiman. 1985. *Discourse/CounterDiscourse: The Theory and Practice of Symbolic Resistance in Nineteenth-Century France.* Ithaca, N.Y.: Cornell University Press.

V. Vale, ed. 1996 *Zines! Vol. 1.* San Francisco: V/Search.

———. 1996. *Zines! Vol. 2.* San Francisco: V/Search.

Appendix: CD Covers

Volume I

Volume 2

Volume 3

Page 250: Leno, Jay—Phil Alvin, *County Fair 2000* (Hightone).

Page 254: minstrel cycle—Beastie Boys, *Check Your Head* (Capitol/Grand Royal).

Page 256: Nashville sound—Patsy Cline, *Honky Tonk Merry Go Round*, Disc 1 in *The Patsy Cline Collection* (MCA)

Page 258: obbligato—Billie Holiday, *The Quintessential Billie Holiday, Volume 8 (1939–1940)* (Columbia).

Page 259: punk—The Sex Pistols, *Never Mind the Bollocks Here's the Sex Pistols* (Warner Bros.).

Page 262: Qiana—Various, *Saturday Night Fever, The Original Movie Sound Track* (PolyGram).

Page 265: rhapsody—Public Enemy, *It Takes a Nation of Millions to Hold Us Back* (Def Jam/Columbia).

Page 267: shivaree—Spike Jones, *Spiked! The Music of Spike Jones* (Catalyst).

Page 270: soul jazz—Brother Jack McDuff, *Down Home Style* (Blue Note).

Page 272: trainspotter—Herbert Distel, *Die Reise* (hat ART).

Page 274: Ursonate—Various, *Futurism & Dada Reviewed* (Sub Rosa).

Page 277: "venerable Frog"—Various, *RCA Victor 80th Anniversary, Vol. 2, 1930–1939* (RCA Victor).

Page 281: watusi—Patti Smith, *Horses* (Arista)

Page 283: X [variable]—Various, *Macro Dub Infection, Volume One* (Caroline).

Page 286: Yardbird—Charlie Parker, *Yardbird Suite: The Ultimate Charlie Parker Collection* (Rhino).

Page 289: zine—Various, *Grand Royal, Man's Best Friend* (Grand Royal).